THE OLDHAM COLLEGE

SOMETHING'S COMING, SOMETHING GOOD

SOMETHING'S COMING, SOMETHING GOOD
WEST SIDE STORY
AND THE AMERICAN IMAGINATION
MISHA BERSON

APPLAUSE
THEATRE & CINEMA BOOKS

An Imprint of Hal Leonard Corporation

OLDHAM COLLEGE

Published in 2011 by Applause Theatre & Cinema Books
An Imprint of Hal Leonard Corporation
7777 West Bluemound Road
Milwaukee, WI 53213

Trade Book Division Editorial Offices
33 Plymouth St., Montclair, NJ 07042

Printed in the United States of America

Book design by Leslie Goldman

Library of Congress Cataloging-in-Publication Data
Berson, Misha.
Something's coming, something good:
West Side story and the American imagination / Misha Berson.
p. cm.
Includes bibliographical references and index.
ISBN 978-1-55783-766-0 (pbk.)
1. Bernstein, Leonard, 1918-1990. West Side story. I. Title.
ML410.B566B57 2011
792.6'42–dc22
2011009104

ISBN 978-1-5578-3766-0

www.applausepub.com

This book is dedicated to my parents,
Minnie and Jacob Berson, and my uncle, Louis Berson,
who passed along their love of Broadway musicals to me,
and to my much-missed friend and soul brother Richard Spector,
who was a Jet all the way to his last dying day.

CONTENTS

ACKNOWLEDGMENTS

This book could not have been completed without the aid, comfort, encouragement, and direct assistance of many friends, relations, and colleagues. My gratitude goes out to them all. For special thanks, I must single out: Michael Messina, who as an editor at Applause loved my idea, and Jim O'Quinn, who recommended me to him. Marybeth Keating and John Cerullo at Hal Leonard, who made it all happen. My agent Carol Mann, who did the deal, and Stephen Wadsworth for suggesting her.

Thanks also to Elizabeth Rhodes for her scrupulous proofreading, and to my *Seattle Times* colleagues Melissa Davis, Lynn Jacobson, and Carole Carmichael, for their understanding and forbearance. Leonard Pitt for the spark, and David Armstrong and Bill Berry for encouragement and the inspiring *West Side Story* at 5th Avenue Theatre. Mary and Doug Bayley, for generously lending me their country home as a writing retreat, and Andrew Himes and Alix Wilbur for stays at their haven. My dear friend Don Shewey, for his unstinting support and suggestions.

Stephen Sondheim, Arthur Laurents, Jamie Bernstein, Martin Charnin, Lin-Manuel Miranda, Peter Boal, and Geoffrey Block, for kindly sharing their *West Side Story* reflections and experiences. Marty Jacobs of the Museum of the City New York, Drew Cohen of Music Theatre International, and Marie Carter of the Bernstein Office, Inc. for their help.

I'd also like to thank Amanda Vaill, Keith Garebian, Nigel Simeone, and the folks behind wssonstage.com, along with all the other writers and researchers whose works were such valuable resources.

Last but most of all, gratitude goes to my wonderful daughter Sarah Stein, and to my husband Paul Schiavo—for his musical expertise, his intellect, and the love, partnership, and belief in me that I value beyond measure.

Winter Garden

PLAYBILL

a weekly magazine for theatregoers

WEST SIDE STORY

Playbill cover for the original Broadway production. Courtesy of Playbill®

PREFACE

*"With a click, with a shock, Phone will jingle,
door will knock, Open the latch . . ."*

—*Something's Coming*

(LYRICS BY STEPHEN SONDHEIM, MUSIC BY LEONARD BERNSTEIN)

My cousin Rochelle's bedroom, with its nubby orange bedspread, shelf of dolls, and shag carpeting, had a double life.

It was a child's lair, but also Jets turf—a rough block of Manhattan's gritty Hell's Kitchen, on a quiet middle-class street in Detroit. A swatch of urban territory the both of us would fight hard to hold on to, even die for, as street brothers united womb to tomb, sperm to worm. Whatever a sperm was.

I'd be Riff, if I was lucky. Rochelle would be Tony, if she wasn't. And instead of bounding up chain-link fences and chasing around graffiti-adorned streets, we'd leap off Rochelle's bed, singing, "When you're a Jet / You're a Jet all the way!" at the top of our young lungs.

We were little Jewish girls, eight or nine years old. Neither of us had ever been to New York City, or witnessed a "rumble," or sat on a tenement fire escape with a paramour. But the world evoked by the Broadway musical *West Side Story* was thrillingly immediate to us during those Sunday-afternoon let's-pretend sessions. In our ravenous imaginations, we belonged to the league of Jets and Sharks as much as Riff and (Sharks leader) Bernardo did.

And if a recruiter had appeared at Rochelle's window like some Peter Pan in blue jeans and high-tops, and invited us to join the musical gang? We'd enlist in a heartbeat, Daddy-o.

We were not alone. And we're not the only ones who never outgrew our fascination with the show. *West Side Story* inflamed many a baby boomer imagination after its 1957 debut on Broadway. And its popularity grew exponentially in the 1960s, after the hugely popular movie version came out. Today, the show and movie can still enthrall kids with surging hormones—even adolescents who are much worldlier (and more cynical) than we were at the same age.

Why does this well-worn Broadway tuner, which is so much a product of late 1950s America, still have its mojo? Why can an earful of "The Jet Song" or the anthem "Tonight," or other gems from the Leonard Bernstein–Stephen Sondheim score, still transport us to some mystical urban never-never land of young love, young death, and balletic gangbangers?

I still am awed by the process of cultural osmosis that pumped *West Side Story* into my prepubescent consciousness. The power of television offers a partial explanation. *The Ed Sullivan Show,* that Sunday-night TV variety program watched religiously by entire American families in the 1950s and 1960s, regularly featured live numbers from new Broadway hits—including a now-grainy but still crackling version of "Cool" and the heart-throbbing "Tonight" duet, performed by first-run cast members of *West Side Story* under director Jerome Robbins's watchful eye.

Then there was the potency of the show's initial cast album—not just Bernstein's glorious music pressed into that chart-busting vinyl LP, but also the $33^{1}/_{3}$ rpm disc's talismanic cardboard cover.

It is a black-and-white photograph of a young woman in a summery cotton dress, her long, dark hair streaming behind her and a ravishing smile on her beautiful face, running down a Manhattan street lined with grimy apartment houses. Chasing close after her is a handsome boy her age, clad in jeans and his own winning smile. He is clearly besotted with her.

Shot by theatrical photographer Leo Friedman on a street in Hell's Kitchen, it is a quintessential image of young romantic rapture—infatuation, pursuit, impending doom. It's the portrait of a slum Eden with a radiant Adam and Eve, just before the fall.

The musical's juxtaposition of violence and innocent romance, dreamy sexuality and hateful ethnic prejudice, is perhaps the greatest seduction of *West Side Story.* Love, death, and the whole damn thing—who can beat it?

But this landmark show was compelling in more ways—some obvious, others still revealing themselves. Nearly every facet of the piece brought something fresh and vitalizing to the American musical stage—from the subject matter, to the score, to the athletic-balletic dance numbers.

West Side Story and its illustrious creators—librettist Arthur Laurents, composer Leonard Bernstein, choreographer-director Jerome Robbins, lyricist Stephen Sondheim—have been written about and analyzed and recounted in every history of twentieth-century Broadway musical theater, and in many other studies, biographies, and works of scholarly criticism. This is the first full-length book, for a general readership, to survey *West Side Story* from a variety of angles, in a kaleidoscopic appreciation. And it will also suggest the ways, both obvious and subtle, this concentrated act of imagination has seized and inspired the national imagination.

I hope the book will be a revealing guide for those who see the show, for those who wish to study it for pleasure or inspiration, and for actors, directors, and designers working on productions of it.

As a theater critic raised on Broadway musicals, I have seen *West Side Story* many times, in many arenas, starting with the national touring of the original production that came to Detroit in 1959. (My dance teacher insisted our parents take us—thank you, Harriet Berg!) I've viewed the Hollywood film repeatedly, and the songs are in my musical marrow.

Yet I'm still somewhat mystified by the unique Proustian spell this show, dated yet timeless, can still cast on me. Just a few bars of the score can send me back to my cousin's bedroom and those impromptu performances of half a century ago.

I felt then like we were inside the show—and the show was inside of us. And despite how much Broadway, America, the world, and those two little girls have changed since its inception, *West Side Story* can still get to me like no other musical has. Writing this book is an exploration of that phenomenon, in gratitude for it.

SOMETHING'S COMING, SOMETHING GOOD

The marquee of the Winter Garden Theatre during the original Broadway run of *West Side Story.* Courtesy of the Library of Congress.

1

WITH A CLICK, WITH A SHOCK
ENTER *WEST SIDE STORY*

For those in attendance, the performance that unfolded at the Winter Garden Theatre on September 26, 1957, was something exciting. Something unforgettable. Something radical.

For how often had a Broadway musical begun with a finger snap, instead of an overture? Or with a nearly wordless prologue, of high-kicking street toughs executing pirouettes and grand jetés in jeans and sneakers?

Since when was a Broadway tuner based on a tragic saga culminating in the violent death of its two male leads? How often did a show feature sympathetic and substantive Puerto Rican roles? Or consider urban youth violence triggered by bigotry? Or finish its opening-night performance to a response of stark silence, followed moments later by a thunderous, extended ovation?

The answer to all the above: *Never.* Until *West Side Story,* that is.

Broadway lore is chockablock with dramatic tales of opening-night triumph (and disaster). But with the arrival of *West Side Story,* something incomparable had crashed Times Square. This Shakespearean yet intrinsically American, audaciously idiosyncratic musical swept along on the raging torrent of Jerome Robbins's dances, Leonard Bernstein's music, Stephen Sondheim's lyrics, and playwright Arthur Laurents's Manhattan mean-streets adaptation of *Romeo and Juliet.*

The show blended a sense of gritty realism with emotional heft and aesthetic dynamism. It was an idealistic collaboration by artists intent on jolting Broadway by storming the Rubicon between high-brow and middle-brow art, classical and contemporary culture. And in the words of the harbinger act 1 song "Something's Coming," it really did "come cannonballing down through the sky / Gleam in its eye / Bright as a rose" that night at the

Winter Garden, and many nights after in theaters around the world.

It is hard to imagine, decades later, that *West Side Story* was not an overwhelming crowd-pleaser. The show lasted only 732 performances in its first New York stand at the Winter Garden and Broadway theatres, then returned to the Winter Garden and Alvin theatres for a post-national-tour run of 249 performances.

That was quite respectable for the time but a far shorter tenure (with fewer sold-out houses) than two other "golden era" hits playing in the 1957–58 Broadway season. *My Fair Lady,* the witty romantic delight based on the G. B. Shaw comedy *Pygmalion* and steeped in Victorian Britannia, lasted 2,717 performances. And *The Music Man,* a picturesque, nostalgic ode to small-town Americana, had an initial run of 1,375 performances.

West Side Story won only two 1958 Tony Awards (for the choreography and sets), compared to a haul of five the same year for *The Music Man,* including the prize for best musical (an honor accorded to *My Fair Lady* in 1957, along with six other Tonys). Moreover, *West Side Story* nearly didn't make it to the Great White Way at all, due to the initial reluctance of theater investors to back such a risky enterprise. Eight years in the making, it was so dark a horse it almost didn't get out of the gate.

Yet today, a world without *West Side Story* seems unthinkable. The show has mastered the feat of being hip, cool, relevant, and entertaining to its 1950s fans, as well as to their great-grandchildren. And images from the movie are seared into our collective cultural consciousness: the vision of rugged, exuberant gang boys dancing down trashed city streets and vaulting over chain-link fences. The image of star-crossed ghetto lovers singing out their ardor on a tenement fire escape. The aural iconography of those opening finger snaps followed by an insidiously sultry sax riff.

In Japan and South Africa, Cairo and Kalamazoo, people who have no truck with any other Broadway musicals can sing a few bars of "The Jet Song" or "Somewhere." They can name the leaders of the two warring Manhattan street gangs the show focuses on, Bernardo (of the Puerto Rican Sharks) and Riff (of the Euro-American Jets). They know where the dewy and doomed lovers Maria and Tony first meet (at a dance in a community gym).

Fifty years after the show's premiere, a German high school exchange student will share her excitement at finally seeing a live staging of *West Side*

Story, after having watched the movie version a dozen times. A Broadway balcony full of antsy Bronx middle schoolers will pipe down, quit fidgeting, and give their full attention to a Broadway revival of the show.

On any given weekend, high school and college kids somewhere between Hawaii and Maine, Florida and Alaska, can be heard lustily belting out "America" in a school auditorium, or blasting a marching-band version of "Gee, Officer Krupke" during halftime at an intramural football game.

According to Music Theatre International, the company that licenses the global rights to *West Side Story,* by 2010 the show had logged roughly 40,000 different productions, resulting in well over 300,000 performances. It had been translated into Serbo-Croatian and Turkish, mounted in Latvia and Lebanon, hailed in Johannesburg and Manila and Tel Aviv.

The 1961 Oscar-honored movie version is, next to *The Sound of Music,* the most popular live-action movie musical ever made. A giant box office success in its initial engagements, it is still frequently shown on TV and at film festivals and has sold millions of copies in video, DVD, and computer-streamed formats.

And then there is the unquantifiable subliminal effect of the show, and its infiltration into global pop culture. *West Side Story* has been recorded, adapted, translated, and parodied countless times, and allusions to the show routinely arise in other stage musicals, in pop songs, in movies, and on the Internet.

The show was also a watershed in the careers of its featured performers and those of its four principle creators—each of them creative mavericks, whose collective artistic contributions have enriched the cultural life of several American generations.

The magnitude of *West Side Story*'s impact over the years was surely not expected by Robbins and Bernstein, Laurents and Sondheim, during the years they spent devising, perfecting, and shepherding the show. On that premiere night in 1957, they gathered at Sardi's restaurant for the traditional Broadway post-premiere shindig with their dedicated cast and crew, their forward-thinking producers, and a circle of professional and personal well-wishers to anxiously await the verdict newspaper critics would deliver on *West Side Story.*

In that era, New York still had a half-dozen daily newspapers, and their opinions could swiftly make or break a Broadway show. That night, and in the ensuing days and months, drama critics scoured their vocabularies to describe and analyze exactly what they had witnessed on the Winter Garden stage when *West Side Story* emerged.

Most were impressed by the sheer gutsiness of the endeavor. Some were ambivalent about the outcome. A few (most notably Harold Clurman, of *The Nation,* and *New York Times* dance critic Howard Taubman) were blatantly hostile. Some took in the show a second time, to clarify their impressions of such a provocative, unusual effort and to write follow-up pieces.

The *New York Times* held a lot of sway back then (as it would fifty years later), and the crowd at Sardi's was thrilled with frontline *Times* reviewer Brooks Atkinson's critique of *West Side Story.* Atkinson reached for nothing less than a nuclear metaphor to describe the work. "The radioactive fallout from 'West Side Story' must still be descending on Broadway this morning," he wrote. "The show rides with a catastrophic roar over the spider-web fire-escapes, the shadowed trestles, and the plain dirt battlegrounds of a big city feud."

Atkinson went on, "The fundamental distinction of 'West Side Story' is the courage with which it adheres to its artistic convictions and its unwillingness to make concessions to popular taste. The artists are playing for keeps."

When a West End run was launched in London the next year, the reception was as enthusiastic, and more. "'West Side Story' struck London last night like a flash of lightning set to music," proclaimed Cecil Wilson of the *Daily Mail,* terming the imported show "the most dynamic, dramatic, operatic, balletic and acrobatic of all those epics from Broadway."

And even if the highly respected English critic and theater hand Kenneth Tynan pointed out some shortcomings (he thought the Jets and Sharks were "too kempt" and wholesome to be convincing as street toughs), he also comprehended the originality of *West Side Story* and its bracing electroshock effect on the senses.

"The Bernstein score is as smooth and savage as a cobra; it sounds as if Puccini and Stravinsky had gone on a roller-coaster ride into the precincts of modern jazz," wrote Tynan in the *Manchester Guardian.* "Jerome Robbins . . . projects the show as a rampaging ballet, with bodies flying through the air as if shot from guns, leaping, shrieking and somersaulting."

The critical establishment at large knew that *West Side Story* was not just another charming tuner on the rialto, but a force to be reckoned with.

It was an attention-grabbing upstart that sparked controversy and had the potential to alter audience expectations of what commercial musical theater could be—in ways the Gershwin brothers had aimed for twenty years earlier with *Porgy and Bess,* a sublime masterwork greeted with far less critical and commercial success.

Yet there were nightly walkouts at *West Side Story,* more than a few. Though not a curse word was heard on the stage, nor a naked breast glimpsed, some found the show unsavory, immoral, or just grimly upsetting. If you didn't know what you were in for, it was like ordering an ice cream sundae and finding a razor blade in it.

To gauge public opinion, the *New York Journal-American* took a then-unusual step of sending out a reporter to get instant (and, as it happened, overwhelmingly positive), person-on-the-street, post-show reactions from audience members. For *West Side Story* was an event that not only belonged in the entertainment section, it was actually *newsworthy*—a rare feat for a Broadway tuner in 1957.

INNOVATIONS AND ARGUMENTS

This book will examine the phenomenon of *West Side Story* from its genesis and development into a Broadway classic, and from other angles as a multifaceted cultural icon: as an adaptation of a Shakespeare tragedy; as a cinematic classic; as a controversial mirror of attitudes of about ethnicity, immigration, and injustice; as a recording-industry event, a 1950s time capsule, and a harbinger of new musical-theater trends.

But one can't ignore the original lingering debates over the show, either: they are part of the story. Despite its secure position in the musical-theater canon later, and the general consensus now that it's been a touchstone for several generations of audiences and artists, *West Side Story* can still engender strongly opposing responses—like the two polar-opposite headlines for reviews of a 2008 London revival: "It seemed exhilarating 50 years ago, but Bernstein's classic musical is far from the best of its generation," groaned one British newspaper. Another cheered: "No signs of age as pioneering West Side Story hits 50."

At first, the main controversy of *West Side Story* was over its innovations—starting with the violent content that was in such contrast to the sunnier subject matter of most Broadway musicals of the day.

A review in the *New York Journal-American* branded the show "a musical mugging." And patrons were often stunned by the ending. Often, gasps and weeping were heard in the audience when Tony and Bernardo met their doom in their youthful prime.

As Brooks Atkinson pointed out in a 1960 *New York Times* think piece, "[To] persons whose idea of the musical is conditioned by 'My Fair Lady,' the severity of 'West Side Story' came almost as an affront. Boy does not get girl. Neither boy nor girl is glamorous . . . In 1957 who would have thought that a harsh drama about juvenile crime on the scabrous sidewalks of New York would win the respect and admiration of so many thousands of theatergoers, not only in America but abroad?"

The production also upset the standard Broadway musical formula by imparting much of its story through physical movement—jagged, athletic, hypercharged dance and gesture in an exhilarating mongrel hybrid of ballet, social dancing, and cutting-edge modern dance. The score, while clever and catchy, was also novel in its synthesis of Tin Pan Alley, jazz, Latin grooves, and modernist symphonic effects that landed hard on some ears unaccustomed to dissonance and asymmetrical rhythms.

West Side Story was a true ensemble effort, with no stars featured, in a Broadway milieu dominated at the time by prominent film and stage performers: Robert Preston, Rosalind Russell, Judy Holliday, and Lena Horne were all headlining in shows at theaters nearby. And the show ruffled some feathers in its tight focus on the desires and torments of poor and unruly adolescents—with the few adult, responsible characters banished to the sidelines.

Then there was the matter of authenticity. *West Side Story* grew out of real-life, snatched-from-the-headlines events, and frightening crime stats, and it crackled with the raw energy of adolescents in extremis as it ripped along. But the travails of the Sharks and Jets paled next to the real street battles waged from the 1950s on in decaying inner-city neighborhoods.

There was a believability issue from the jump with hoodlum characters who didn't smoke, drink, or consume narcotics, who didn't appear to indulge in petty crimes such as shoplifting, car theft, muggings. To Tynan and others, the Jets and Sharks were just too "nice" to seem dangerous.

Other cavils have resurfaced periodically about the show's treatment of

Latinos—are they made out to be the villains? Are they accurately Puerto Rican? Does the piece condemn bigotry—or unconsciously promote it?

West Side Story was concocted by artists of social conscience, but they were no band of Greenwich Village firebrands. They were mainstream players, equipped with a big budget raised from backers who wanted a return on their investment. And the show was a well-tooled showbiz product conjured by canny Broadway insiders who were not above borrowing vintage shtick from operetta, vaudeville, melodrama, and Borscht Belt comedy to keep their audiences engaged and entertained.

So does *West Side Story* still fulfill a more basic mandate? Is it truly timeless, in the sense that, well, an *Oklahoma!* or a *Guys and Dolls* is?

That can be determined only by seeing numerous *West Side Story* productions (in my case, more than a dozen) in large theatres and small, professional and amateur, in venues ranging from Broadway show palaces to high school multipurpose halls.

When the Jets and Sharks are in gear, and all their cylinders are clicking, *West Side Story* remains one of the most thrilling, enthralling, and poignant of Broadway musicals—still vital and reverberant in its blend of velocity and pathos.

But the show's inherent production demands are not easily met. And with an ill-conceived design, inadequate musical accompaniment, poor singing voices, drab choreography, an ill-cast performance or two, even if other elements are exemplary, the magic can evaporate.

Tapping the full potential of *West Side Story* remains a sizable challenge for even first-class professional companies, as its several Broadway revivals have demonstrated. And yet, paradoxically, a basic, unpolished, but energetic and heartfelt rendering by high school kids in Anywhere, USA, with no professionals onstage and a slapdash set, can sometimes blow you away—and break your heart.

And when young people of different races and classes and cultures are exposed to *West Side Story* live or on film, many invariably will identify with the gang kids and their dilemmas—star-crossed love, street violence, and the ongoing predicament of new immigrants to the United States who face bigotry and xenophobia in their adopted homeland.

"[The show] was written in 1957, yet it describes most metropolitan cities today just as accurately as it did then," argues theater director

Scott Miller in his book *From Assassins to West Side Story*. "In a country where hate crimes multiply exponentially each year, and gang warfare has turned our streets into war zones, 'West Side Story' is heartbreaking and somehow cathartic."

Yet even the men most responsible for *West Side Story* have disagreed about whether it has aged well or badly, which aspects of the piece hold up the best, and why it was a leap forward for Broadway.

COMPETITION ON THE RIALTO, 1957–58

In 1957, Broadway ticket prices were a bargain by today's standards. The best orchestra seat to the first run of *West Side Story* topped out at $7.50 (or about $58 in 2010). Attending Broadway shows was a very popular and democratic pastime, accessible to the middle and lower-middle class. But competition for patrons was fierce, nonetheless.

There were some sixty productions on the Great White Way during the 1957–58 season. The majority were fleeting, but the following are some of the notable new works on the Broadway boards when *West Side Story* opened:

MUSICALS:

The Music Man by Meredith Willson
My Fair Lady by Frederick Loewe and Alan Jay Lerner
Bells Are Ringing by Betty Comden, Adolph Green, and Jule Styne
    (direction by Jerome Robbins)
Jamaica by Harold Arlen, E. Y. ("Yip") Harburg, and Fred Saidy
Damn Yankees by George Abbott, Douglass Wallop, Richard Adler,
    and Jerry Ross
Li'l Abner by Norman Panama and Melvin Frank, Gene De Paul,
    and Johnny Mercer
Most Happy Fella by Frank Loesser
New Girl in Town by Bob Merrill and George Abbott

PLAYS:

Auntie Mame by Jerome Lawrence and Robert E. Lee
Long Day's Journey into Night by Eugene O'Neill
Look Homeward, Angel by Ketti Frings
Two for the Seesaw by William Gibson

Sondheim took swipes at *West Side Story* over the years (especially his own contributions to it), naming "over-writing, purpleness in the writing and in the songs" as its "severe flaws." Yet he came to publicly recognize and validate its importance and innovations—which, for him, had more to do with "theatrical style" than subject matter. "We were influenced by the movies," he reflected; "there was a fluidity in the staging which had a cinematic quality. No other [Broadway] show has ever been staged . . . or conceived this way as a fluid piece which called on the poetic imagination of the audience." (That fluidity would be a hallmark of Sondheim's subsequent Broadway musicals, as well.)

Laurents, in his memoirs, attacked what he felt were the work's flaws, and he set out to remedy some of them in a revisionist 2009 Broadway revival he staged. But he, too, has acknowledged the sheer force of *West Side Story*—though, contrary to Sondheim, he attributed it to thematic *substance* rather than style.

"Many say 'West Side' forever changed the American musical . . . because of its use of dance and music," Laurents wrote in his book *Mainly on Directing*. "To me, it used those elements better than they had ever been used before; but what it really changed, what its real contribution to the American musical theatre was, was that it showed that any subject—murder, attempted rape, bigotry—could be the subject of a popular musical."

Bernstein felt no need to disparage the show but privately winced when it seemed to overshadow all of his subsequent compositions. Touchingly, in *The Making of West Side Story,* a documentary film of the aged composer conducting his first recording of the full score, Bernstein muses that the musical "lasts the way a poem lasts . . . in its funny little crazy way, it's a classic." He also assesses the music with a poignant mixture of humility and pride: "It's not Mozart. But who is in *that* company?"

Robbins was perhaps the least ambivalent about what was achieved in *West Side Story.* He soaked in the glory the show and film brought him but also kept tinkering with his choreography to further "perfect" it—in revivals, in a ballet suite, and in his crowning Broadway achievement, the anthology musical *Jerome Robbins' Broadway.*

The contradictions and suggested shortcomings of *West Side Story* are, to this critic, an intrinsic part of its mystique. The tension between romanticism and realism keeps the musical vibrating between the rough and the tender, the melodramatic and the sardonic, the documentary and the mythic, the make-believe of danced rumbles and the reality of mindless bloodshed.

And dismissing *West Side Story* as simply sentimental and simplistic, naïve or dated, is missing something essential: Like most other enduring works of musical theater, *West Side Story* was never intended to be a graphic sociological docudrama.

It is an act of imagination.

From that first finger snap, to its last dying moments, *West Side Story* (like its inspiration, *Romeo and Juliet*) envelops us in a mythic world of its own design. No less than the great South American writer Jorge Luis Borges understood this. Borges (who happened to be blind) was a devoted fan of *West Side Story.* His friend Alberto Manguel recalled attending the movie of the show with the novelist: "He has sat through it several times and never seems to tire of it. On the way, he hums 'Maria' and remarks on how true the fact that the name of the beloved changes from a simple name to a divine utterance: Beatrice, Juliet, Lesbia, Laura."

West Side Story is faithful unto itself, though informed by the Broadway, the Manhattan, and the United States of America it emerged from and the Elizabethan theatrics it borrowed. It has its own sense of truth and sticks by it.

In a 1985 Dramatists Guild symposium, during which the show's four instigators discussed their collaboration candidly and in some detail, Sondheim addressed the notion of theatrical truthfulness. He remarked that while working on the musical he learned "that theatrical truth, theatrical time has nothing to do with real truth, real time . . . Generally you try to make it true on both levels, because it's richer that way."

The inherent richness of *West Side Story,* its multiple layers and pleasures, have overridden its flaws to keep the piece viable and vital—live and onscreen. A journey through the genesis, creation, and long, eventful life and afterlife of this theatrical powerhouse can help us appreciate how and why it remains so.

EARLY REVIEWS OF *WEST SIDE STORY*

The initial reviews of *West Side Story* fell into three camps: (1) glowing raves that recognized the show's genius and touted its innovations; (2) mixed and ambivalent notices that praised some aspects of the work but were much more critical of others; and (3) the few out-and-out pans.

Reviewers of the pre-Broadway runs in Washington, D.C., and Philadelphia and of the British premiere tended to express more unalloyed enthusiasm for the show than their New York counterparts. But just about every notice singled out at least one major element in the show for applause—often the score, or the dances—while faulting others.

Common criticisms were (1) the story was implausible; (2) the gang members were not tough or realistic enough; (3) the musical failed to include key elements of *Romeo and Juliet* (i.e., the nature of fate); (4) the music was not up to the quality of the choreography, or book was inferior to the score, or some other combination of lopsidedness. (To the chagrin of the whole company, Stephen Sondheim's name was not even mentioned in the *New York Times* notice.)

Even critics with strong reservations tended to agree that the totality of the show, the synergistic combination of each aspect in relation to the whole, advanced the integration of story, dance, and score a few steps further than previous Broadway musicals.

There were, one should add, plenty of advocates to cheer *West Side Story* on. And the show's critical reputation would gain more luster over time.

Here are a few voices from the 1957–58 critical chorus of yeas, nays, and maybes:

> *"'West Side Story' is a work of art . . . Watching the stage at the National we are moved, and tremendously moved, by a uniquely cohesive comment on life. It may not be our personal comment on life, but it is a vibrant memorable viewpoint."*
>
> *And from a follow-up review: "'West Side Story' is the sort of work that cries for definition because in our normal laziness we are far too tempted to pigeonhole anything as this or that. This fits into many categories, not just one."* —RICHARD L. COE, *Washington Post* (1957)

"This is a bold new kind of musical theater—a juke-box Manhattan opera. It is to me, extraordinarily exciting . . . the manner of telling the story is a provocative and artful blend of music, dance and plot— and the music and the dancing are superb."

—JOHN CHAPMAN, *New York Daily News* (1957)

"There are so many fascinating aspects to this exciting and adventurous work . . . [A] striking impression conveyed by the work is its capacity for riveting one's attention. . . . [T]he dance is fully as important here as the spoken word in carrying the taut story line; and the exciting musical score complements both extremely well.

"The love story is genuinely affecting, with its balcony scene on a tenement fire escape . . . [The songs] have more distinction that the average musical-show number, which can be disengaged from the score and slid into a coin phonograph with the greatest of ease."

—UNSIGNED REVIEW, *Theatre Arts* (1957)

"Gang warfare is the material of West Side Story, which opened at the Winter Garden last evening, and very little of the hideousness has been left out. But the author, composer and ballet designer are creative artists. Pooling imagination and virtuosity, they have written a profoundly moving show that is as ugly as the city jungles and also pathetic, tender and forgiving.

Everything in 'West Side Story' is of a piece. Everything contributes to the total impression of wildness, ecstasy and anguish. The astringent score has moments of tranquility and rapture, and occasionally a touch of sardonic humor. And the ballets convey the things that Mr. Laurents is inhibited from saying because the characters are so inarticulate."

—BROOKS ATKINSON, *The New York Times* (1957)

"My opinions of 'West Side Story' are, I have to admit, very mixed. The plot, though certainly racking, seems to me strangely empty of real emotional content. Partly, this may be due to Shakespeare's ideas of what is permissible in the way of dramatic coincidence aren't easy to accept today, and it is hard to escape a feeling of patness and

contrivance in the way each fatal encounter is arranged.

"[The Sharks and Jets] are capable of murder in moments of great stress, but it is impossible to suspect them of rape, mugging, perversion, drug addiction, torture or any other practices that would naturally be repugnant to the normal American boy. . . . Asked to believe that significant tragedy and tender, doomed, not unliterary romance frequently exist among juvenile delinquents, I remain, I'm embarrassed to say, incredulous and unstirred.

—WOLCOTT GIBBS, *The New Yorker* (1957)

""West Side Story"" is not so much a musical as a ballet-opera. It uses dance-acting and rhythm to such an extent that the words and singing seem almost incidental . . . [Laurents] puts an amazing amount of teen-age jargon onstage without forcing it. And, more importantly, he penetrates the problem of juvenile delinquency in a way that should give all of us pause . . . The Puerto Rican situation is a touchy one to present and 'West Side Story' does it without direct sermonizing. True, it does not emphasize the utter squalor in which many Puerto Rican immigrants live. But 'America' . . . nicely describes the Puerto Rican's attitude toward his plight . . . And if the show fails rather badly when it tries to show a non-prejudiced utopia 'somewhere' it leaves a telling reminder for us at the final curtain, when we see the two gangs temporarily allied against the law enforcement officers." —HENRY HEWES, *The Saturday Review* (1957)

"The near success of 'West Side Story' certainly derives from the dancing. . . . [The] romance almost everywhere falls short of the gang warfare. Shakespeare's High-Renaissance ardors and angers do not translate into the barbarism . . . anymore than Greek-tragedy incests and betrayals into the primitivism of Arthur Miller's 'A View From the Bridge.' . . . Composer Bernstein does better with his harsh, tingling music for the dancers than with his lyrical duets for the lovers, and Arthur Laurents' libretto catches rasping, inarticulate hate better than yearning, inarticulate love."

—UNSIGNED REVIEW, *Time* (1957)

"The reason for the show's immediate success is that it is not only a highly expert production . . . it may legitimately claim some originality in its domain. For though a 'musical,' it is not a musical comedy and though it is almost more ballet than play and in some of the duets and 'choral' writing approaches the operatic, it remains close enough to the conventional musical comedy form.

"Although I appreciated the show's merits—and sat in a theatre echoing with 'bravos'—I did not enjoy it. In fact, I resented it: I thought it a phony . . . I do not like intellectual slumming by sophisticates for purposes of popular showmanship. It is vulgar, immature, unfeeling."   —HAROLD CLURMAN, *The Nation* (1957)

"Mr. Bernstein has permitted himself a few moments of graceful, lingering melody . . . But for the most part he has served the needs of the onstage threshing-machine . . .

"The show is, in general, not well sung. It is rushingly acted . . . And it, apart from the spine-tingling of the dances, is almost never emotionally affecting."   —WALTER KERR, *New York Herald Tribune* (1957)

"The American hit musical 'West Side Story'—flick-knives and delinquency on a theme by Shakespeare—burst on Britain last night. Furiously, fabulously, sensationally, it gave the Opera House, Manchester, a European premiere it will never forget. . . . [It is] a great musical—the greatest musical I've ever seen. It's pugnacious— yet it has poetry in it. The ballet is convulsive—but it has classic style and power."   —DONALD ZEC, *London Daily Mirror* (1958)

"A total work that demands comparison not with musical comedy as we have known it but with Menotti's operas or with 'Porgy and Bess.' Even so it is a new kind of thing: not so grand in its music as 'Porgy,' weaker in vocal resource than [Menotti's] 'The Medium,' but taken straighter out of life than either."   — J. R., *Manchester Guardian* (1958)

The *West Side Story* team: (left to right) Stephen Sondheim, Arthur Laurents, Harold Prince, Robert Griffith, Leonard Bernstein, and Jerome Robbins. Courtesy of Photofest.

2

NOW IT BEGINS, NOW WE START
WEST SIDE STORY
FROM BRAINSTORM TO
BROADWAY PREMIERE

I
t is in the nature of the beast: every Broadway musical has a challenging birth. And each is challenging in its own way.

The birthing of *West Side Story* is a testament to the power of passion, creativity, collaboration—and, not least of all, tenacity. The show was forged over eight years by some of the brightest lights of the 1950s entertainment world, during prolific periods in their long careers. En route there were long delays, gaps, clashes of temperament and aesthetics, near-derailments, patches of agony and ecstasy, and finally relief, pride, and reward.

Choreographer-director Jerome Robbins instigated the musical and was its primary catalyst. But the combined firepower of his artistic skills, instincts, and ferocious work, with those of composer Leonard Bernstein, playwright Arthur Laurents, and lyricist Stephen Sondheim, was truly formidable.

THE DREAM TEAM

This four-member "dream team" shared striking similarities of background and sensibility. All were East Coast natives and Manhattan residents, of immigrant Jewish stock. All were homosexual or bisexual. Three were born in 1918, which made them barely thirty when they began in 1949 to forge what would become *West Side Story* and just shy of forty when they completed it in 1957. (Sondheim, the sole Broadway novice among them, wasn't recruited as lyricist until 1955, at age twenty-five.)

The foursome were all ambitious and industrious, and well connected within the inner power circles of New York's arts and entertainment sphere.

By 1957, Robbins, Laurents, and Bernstein had racked up impressive accomplishments—alone, together, with other A-listers. Robbins had risen up the ballet ranks from dancer to dance-maker and established himself as a double-threat choreographer-director on Broadway with several box office hits to his credit. Laurents had penned successful Hollywood movies and Broadway plays. Bernstein was the assistant musical director (soon to be promoted to musical director) of the highly regarded New York Philharmonic Orchestra. He was also on the faculty of the prestigious Tanglewood summer music festival in the Berkshires, an in-demand freelance conductor sought out by symphonies around the world, a respected composer, and a magnetic media celebrity who brought musical appreciation to the American masses via the expanding medium of television.

If Sondheim's résumé was lighter, that was understandable. He was still an undergrad at Williams College in 1949 when the idea for *West Side Story* was first hatched, but Sondheim, too, was a precocious striver. Like Bernstein and Robbins, his talents were recognized early and encouraged by master mentors. And by the time the composer-lyricist reached forty, in 1970, he was poised to helped reinvent the American musical yet again.

These men were all multitalented, versatile cross-over artists active in more than one cultural arena. And their similar backgrounds and sensibilities gave them a common language and aesthetic rapport. Moreover, they shared a rebellious attitude toward the Broadway establishment and were eager to break down the boundaries between art and entertainment and social commentary.

They clearly diverged, however, in terms of temperament and working style—in ways, we shall see, that proved both fractious and complementary. (A largely unspoken but painful fracture occurred as the result of Robbins's "friendly" testimony in 1953 before the notorious congressional House Un-American Activities Committee.)

It's telling also that *West Side Story* came about in an era when New York City, and the country at large, was undergoing a cultural and socioeconomic redefinition. The post–World War II economy was flourishing. A growing middle class with more leisure time had increasing access to higher education and culture enrichments. Broadway was booming. And in Midtown jazz clubs and Greenwich Village coffeehouses, Off Broadway lofts and theater labs, it was a heady period of freewheeling experimentation.

The *West Side Story* team was not, as mentioned earlier, a cabal of bohemians. But they were restless and adventuresome idealists.

"I didn't like the idea that we had to separate ourselves in two halves, one the commercial half, one the classical half," Robbins later reflected. "For me what was important about 'West Side Story' was our aspiration. I wanted to find out at that time how far we, as 'long-haired artists,' could go in bringing our crafts and talents to a musical. Why did Lenny have to write an opera, Arthur a play, me a ballet? Why couldn't we, in aspiration, try to bring our deepest talents together to the commercial theater in this work?"

In his journal entries about the making of *West Side Story* (entries he actually wrote, from reconstructed memories, after the show's Broadway debut), Bernstein envisioned "a bigger idea" of "making a musical that tells a tragic story in musical-comedy terms, using only musical-comedy techniques, never falling into the 'operatic' trap. Can it succeed? It hasn't yet in our country."

For all those involved, *West Side Story* was a joint mission—not merely an attempt to hatch another hit.

"There was this wonderful mutual exchange going on," Robbins reflected during the 1985 Dramatists Guild panel discussion involving all four collaborators. "The essence of it was what we gave to each other, took from each other, yielded to each other, surrendered, reworked, put back together again, all those things."

"We all had real respect for each other and, without doing it overtly, challenged each other to do our best," seconded Laurents. "That's all we thought about—doing our best." On the same occasion, Bernstein suggested their mutual commitment gave them the courage to defy convention. "If you want to be polite you say 'bravery,'" he explained. "If you want to be impolite you say 'chutzpah' . . . [It] was a kind of bravery in which we all fortified one another."

And when *West Side Story* finally came to fruition, they were all shareholders in its success. "The opening last night was just as we dreamed it," Leonard Bernstein wrote in an entry in his journal dated August 20, 1957, the day after the show's pre-Broadway world premiere at Washington, D.C.'s National Theatre. "All the . . . agony and postponements and re-re-re-writing turn out to have been worth it. There's a work there; and whether it finally succeeds or not in Broadway terms, I am now convinced that what we dreamed all these years is possible; because there stands that tragic story, with a theme as profound as love versus hate, with all the theatrical risks of death and racial issues and young performers and 'serious' music and complicated balletics."

How did all this come to pass? Let us start at the beginning, a very good place to start.

1948–49: "EAST SIDE STORY"

No one disputes that Jerome Robbins originated, planted, watered, and avidly tended and sheltered the seedling of an idea that ultimately blossomed into *West Side Story*. He often recounted that the show's original concept (for which he insisted on receiving full credit and billing) came to him as the result of a conversation with an actor friend—most likely his sometime-lover Montgomery Clift. In Robbins's recounting, his (unnamed) friend was preparing to tackle the role of Romeo in a scene class at the Actors Studio and wanted advice on how to portray the character.

In the late 1940s, Clift and Robbins were members of the Actors Studio, where they studied "the Method"—an experiential, quasi-psychoanalytical approach to acting and directing that informed the work of a generation of charismatic stage and film performers—and others to follow. The Actors Studio was, in the 1950s, a breeding ground for such earnest and idolized thespians as Marlon Brando, James Dean, Paul Newman, and Marilyn Monroe.

The Method teachings encouraged actors to pour "sense memories" of dramatic personal experiences into their roles and to analyze scripts in terms of psychological subtext and motivations. Adapted from the philosophy of Russia's influential Moscow Art Theatre director Constantin Stanislavski, the initial American version of the technique was developed in the 1930s by the Group Theatre—a company of actors, directors, and writers who also endeavored to make Broadway a forum for serious,

American-tooled theater artistry—though in their case, it was through naturalistic ensemble acting and hard-hitting new dramas.

After the Group disbanded in 1940, some of its leading members became prominent teachers of their own interpretations of the Method, including Actors Studio co-founder and guru Lee Strasberg and (in their own schools) Sanford Meisner, Robert Lewis, and Stella Adler.

Robbins was intrigued by their techniques, eager to experiment with them, and they had a pronounced effect on his direction of *West Side Story* and subsequent shows. "Jerry's performance experience was rooted in a sense of form," recalled Robert Lewis. "He was a superb young dancer now wishing to explain what the difference was in the source of expression for acting as opposed to dancing."

According to Robbins, in 1948 or early 1949 his friend (Clift) complained that Romeo seemed a very passive character and sought his counsel. "So I asked myself," recounted Robbins, "if I were to play this, how would I make it come to life?"

At the time, Robbins had begun to successfully branch into choreography and stage direction. (Coincidentally, he had also danced the role of Benvolio in Anthony Tudor's *Romeo and Juliet* ballet at New York City Ballet.) He encouraged his actor friend to imagine Romeo "in terms of today," against a backdrop of "the gangs of New York." It would be a more current, more accessible way into the character than trying to replicate the mindset of Shakespeare's warring clans of ancient Verona.

His approach was also colored by the steady drumbeat of news about post–World War II juvenile delinquency in New York City. Robbins was well aware it was on the rise. In 1949, he created for the New York City Ballet an abstract ballet, *Guests,* about forbidden love between members of two antagonistic social groups.

The idea of a modern Romeo tantalized Robbins, so in that same year he proposed to Bernstein making it the basis of a Broadway musical drama. The two had recently collaborated on two very successful works: *Fancy Free,* an innovative story ballet scored by Bernstein about ebullient wartime sailors on leave in New York, and the Broadway hit *On the Town,* which expanded the sailors' lark into a hit musical comedy.

Since both Bernstein and Robbins were Russian American Jews with immigrant roots, it was not surprising that Robbins's first impulse was to set their *Romeo and Juliet* story in the Lower East Side, amid clashes between immigrant groups of gentile and Jewish youths. (Such tensions led to bloody clashes in the early 1900s, fueled by anti-Semitism.)

Bernstein's journal entry dated January 6, 1949, elaborated. "Jerry R. called today with a noble idea: a modern version of 'Romeo and Juliet' set in slums at the coincidence of Easter-Passover celebrations. Feelings run high between Jews and Catholics. Former: Capulets; latter: Montagues. Juliet is Jewish. Friar Laurence is a neighborhood druggist. Street brawls, double death—it all fits."

For a suitable librettist for the nascent project (working title: "East Side Story"), Robbins suggested Arthur Laurents, whose recent play *Home of the Brave* had boldly depicted anti-Semitism in the U.S. military. He and Robbins met and became friends while Laurents was still in uniform serving out a U.S. Army stint in New York writing scripts for military radio shows.

Though Bernstein hadn't yet met Laurents, an entry in his reconstituted journal has him telling Robbins, "I do know 'Home of the Brave,' at which I cried like a baby." And in his memoir *Original Story By,* Laurents recalled that it was Bernstein who most convinced him to join the project. Bernstein's "ache to compose something for the theatre was so exposed," he wrote, " I wanted to please him. And I wanted to work with him."

The next step was to start sketching out the show's Lower East Side plot together, with all three men pitching in ideas for the story and score. Evidence of their early handiwork is preserved in the Library of Congress and in Robbins's papers. One telling item is Bernstein's personal paperback copy of *Romeo and Juliet,* with his handwritten annotations. On the first page, he identified an overarching theme for the musical: "An out and out plea for racial tolerance." Other notes indicate there should be a song about anti-Semitism ("It's the Jews") for the show's depiction of warring Jewish and Italian Catholic kids, and that Shakespeare's short prologue to the play would in the musical "be interrupted by a street fight."

Also preserved are typed pages of Robbins's early rundown of scenes (with Bernstein's feedback penciled in) for "East Side Story," with a Passover seder and a "street carnival" among the settings; a detailed six-page plot synopsis by Laurents; and a scrawled flowchart by Bernstein, indicating spots where specific kinds of music would be used.

With three of Broadway's best and brightest young turks involved, word of the project traveled fast. On January 27, 1949, the *New York Times* published an item by showbiz reporter Louis Calta about their plans for "a modern musical drama, as yet untitled, based on 'Romeo and Juliet.'" While "still in the preliminary stages," wrote Calta, "according to the present scheme of things, the musical will arrive in New York next season." So much for that scheme: the *Times* was seven years off in its prognostication.

In fact, soon after the item appeared, "East Side Story" hit a snag. Reading Laurents's draft of the opening scene, Bernstein objected to its "too angry, too bitchy, too vulgar tone." He later described that preliminary draft as "very good and very harsh, but harsh in the wrong way. It didn't have its own kind of magic language, which Arthur developed later." Bernstein also fretted about how little time he had to work on the show in a schedule packed with out-of-town U.S. and foreign guest-conducting jobs and other commitments. One of his diary entries bemoans that "this remote-control collaboration isn't right. Maybe they can find the right composer who isn't always skipping off to conduct somewhere."

Laurents had his own reservations. He worried that "East Side Story" would settle into a musical version of the 1922 play *Abie's Irish Rose,* a schmaltzy interfaith romantic comedy about Irish Catholics and Jews by Anne Nichols. It lingered on Broadway for five years (and was mercilessly mocked every week in the *New Yorker* theater listings by humorist and drama critic Robert Benchley). What could be less *au courant* than that?

Additionally, Laurents was concerned that Bernstein's symphonic ambitions as a composer would produce a grandiose music score that would overwhelm their dramatic piece. At a meeting with Robbins and Bernstein, he didn't mince words: "I want to make one thing clear before we go any further, and that is that I'm not writing any fucking libretto for any goddamned Bernstein opera!"

Though impressed with the outline of "East Side Story," American Ballet Theatre dancer Nora Kaye (a good friend to all, whom Laurents dubbed "our part-time witch"), foresaw more trouble ahead. "You'll never write it," she predicted. "Your three temperaments in one room, and the walls will come down."

As Laurents went off to Hollywood to toil on films, and Robbins and Bernstein juggled other assignments, work on "East Side Story" was suspended—indefinitely. "We had another meeting in New York and decided to give it up," recalled Bernstein. "We didn't bury it, but we decided to sleep on it."

It was a big sleep.

1955–1956: "ROMEO"

During Robbins and company's long hiatus from the project, violent clashes among New York slum gangs increased and media coverage of them intensified. The trend alarmed New Yorkers (and paralleled upticks in youth crime in other big American cities). And it inspired Robbins to dust off the long-shelved "East Side Story" idea. He urged Laurents and Bernstein to get back to the drawing board with him while the topic was hot.

They agreed. In September, Laurents took the time to work up a new outline for the show, which dropped the religious overtones in the story in favor of a more timely focus on street gangs. But what kind of gangs? There had been a flurry of Jewish gang activity from the 1880s to the end of Prohibition. But that had died down. And whatever violent Jewish thugs were still on the rampage were most likely to be adult mobsters of the Meyer Lansky breed. Hooliganism by poor Irish Catholic youth remained a problem in 1950s New York, but anti-Semitism wasn't a prime motivation for it.

Then, a thunderclap: in August, Laurents and Bernstein had a fortuitous brainstorm. They were discussing their languishing project about poor kids in love and trouble, while hanging out (irony of ironies) by the pool at the tony Beverly Hills Hotel in Los Angeles.

Bernstein was in town to conduct at the Hollywood Bowl, and Laurents was toiling on a remake of the Greta Garbo movie *The Painted Veil* (from which he later withdrew). Both were gigs taken primarily for the cash— "tax-paying" jobs, as Laurents put it—as opposed to their less commercial passion projects.

While chatting at the hotel, they spotted a headline in the *Los Angeles Times* about bloody LA gang clashes involving Chicano youths. (According to Nigel Simeone in his illuminating book *Leonard Bernstein: West Side Story*, what they likely saw was an August 22, 1955, *LA Times* news story about the gang-related death of a twenty-year old man from injuries sustained in a fistfight with a fellow Mexican American.)

"What if we did it with Chicanos?" Bernstein later recalled asking Laurents, who agreed the concept was interesting. But how about bringing it closer to home? What if their Juliet was a Latina and their Romeo a white kid? What if the opposing gangs were Puerto Ricans (who were then migrating to New York City in unprecedented numbers)? And what if their rivals were Anglo toughs, enraged that their turf was being invaded by darker-skinned interlopers?

The topicality of the theme, and the prospect of weaving Latin musical motifs into his score, excited Bernstein. "I hear rhythms and pulses, and—most of all—I can sort of feel the form," he wrote in his journal. He adored Latin music, which he sought out on numerous visits to Latin America and South America. (His actress wife Felicia Montealegre Bernstein, hailed from Chile.)

In an entry dated September 6, 1955 (a few days later), Bernstein enthusiastically noted Robbins's reaction to the new plan: "Jerry loves our gang idea. A second solemn pact has been sworn. Here we go, God bless us!" But their intention to begin toiling in earnest on the show, now under the working title "Romeo," was delayed yet again, when Laurents got a lucrative offer from Hollywood to script the Ingrid Bergman movie *Anastasia.*

Though Robbins was irritated by this development, the delay proved professionally advantageous to him too. He was, at the time, neck deep in preparations for the Broadway debut of the new musical *Bells Are Ringing,* which he was directing and co-choreographing with the young Bob Fosse. In fact, the delay allowed all three men to complete significant projects—and likely enriched their joint enterprise once they returned to it.

During 1955 and 1956, Bernstein, Robbins, and Laurents perfected the art of multitasking. As the busy trio developed other new musicals—composed and choreographed and wrote and directed and conducted and traveled—somehow they scrounged the time to reenvision the renamed project, "Romeo." Their latest plan for it was summarized in a new six-page outline by Laurents that had the star-crossed tenement lovers (now Puerto Rican and Anglo-American) dying at the end of a three-act work. (A detailed analysis by Simeone revealed pronounced differences, but also some key similarities, between the scenes described in this outline and those that appear in Laurents's finished text for *West Side Story*.)

In Hollywood staging his much-lauded ballet "The Small House of Uncle Thomas" for the movie of *The King and I* (based on his choreography for the hit Broadway version), Robbins relished the chance to study how filmmakers shoot and then edit a multitude of different camera shots into a fluid cinematic narrative.

He wanted to create a similar sense of seamless motion in the theater and dashed off a note to his cohorts urging that "Romeo" be compressed into two acts rather than the planned three, and that the plot have a sweeping momentum. Robbins also dashed off a detailed critique of Laurents's latest draft of the scenario, encouraging the dramatist to resist "the intimidation of Shakespeare standing behind you" by writing "in your own style with your own characters and imagination."

But a new delay arose. Bernstein had another complex and unorthodox musical in the works, *Candide* (based on the Voltaire novel, as adapted by leading Broadway playwright Lillian Hellman). After a period on hold, the project had found backers and was slated for imminent production. "Maybe it's all for the best," Bernstein wrote in his reconstructed journal. "By the time ['Romeo'] emerges it ought to be deeply seasoned, cured, hung, aged in a wood. It's such a problematical work anyway that it should benefit by as much sitting time as it can get."

Bernstein also was realizing that even he, a seemingly tireless artistic dynamo, didn't have enough hours in the day to concoct the complex semi-operatic score for *Candide* while summoning up the music and all the lyrics for "Romeo." The answer was to find a co-lyricist—but who? Likely suspects Betty Comden and Adolph Green (who wrote the book and lyrics for *On the Town* and contributed lyrics to the Robbins-staged hit musical *Peter Pan* starring Mary Martin, which Robbins directed) were tied up working on—wouldn't you know it?—that other Robbins project, *Bells Are Ringing*. And Laurents was convinced their breezy, snappy style wasn't right for "Romeo" anyway.

Then one evening, by sheer serendipity, Laurents attended an opening-night party for the New York debut of avant-garde Italian playwright Ugo Betti's *Crime on Goat Island,* where he bumped into Oscar Hammerstein's young protégé Stephen Sondheim. As Sondheim recalled fifty years later, in an onstage interview with *New York Times* columnist critic Frank Rich, Laurents had earlier heard him play his original songs from an unproduced musical, "Saturday Night," for a different project. At the Betti soiree, the playwright "literally smote his head" when it occurred to him Sondheim might be just the right co-lyricist for *West Side Story.*

Sondheim auditioned with his original "Saturday Night" show tunes, and though Bernstein wasn't impressed with the music, he "went wild" for the sophisticated lyrics and thought, "here was a real honest-to-God talent."

When invited to come aboard, however, Sondheim hesitated. The distinguished modern composer Milton Babbitt, one of his musical mentors, later observed, "Steve had always regarded himself as primarily a composer and for a long time he felt humiliated a little bit" by assuming what he considered to be a secondary role on *West Side Story.*

Unlike his older colleagues, Sondheim felt his upper-class New York Jewish background did not equip him for the assignment. "I've never been poor and I've never even known a Puerto Rican," he reportedly told his agent, Flora Roberts. But she, Hammerstein, and others urged him to take the golden opportunity to break onto Broadway in the company of such illustrious colleagues. He saw their point.

Though at first Sondheim was signed on as Bernstein's co-lyricist, the composer soon realized that his colleague was perfectly capable of writing all the lyrics needed. Bernstein wanted to preserve a few lines he'd already penned for the score, but he magnanimously insisted Sondheim be credited as sole lyricist. (Sondheim later regretted that he was so gratified, and so green in the business, that he declined Bernstein's offer of an additional share of the royalties—which, given the fortune raked in by the *West Side Story* movie, amounted to a tidy sum.)

The four-way partnership was complete, and for the most part it was harmonious. "When Steve came into the picture and we began working together, he became part of the team and the contribution he made was just enormous," stated Bernstein, according to Craig Zadan's book *Sondheim & Company.*

Despite some retrospective misgivings about some aspects of *West Side Story,* Sondheim told this author his involvement in the show was a "huge" professional opportunity and experience—"the beginning of everything."

Once the creative team was in place, "we would work on [the show] wherever we could, depending on our schedules," Robbins noted. "Arthur would come in with a scene. The others would say they'd do a song on this material. I'd supply, 'How about if we did this as a dance?'" Said Laurents, "Without any consciousness of it, we were all just high on the work and loving it."

The next step was capitalizing the production. But despite the backstage star power fueling the venture, the money chase was not just disappointing, it was dispiriting. None of the usual "angels" understood the new breed of dance–theater–music hybrid as a worthy investment at first. Not even those who had prospered from earlier Bernstein–Robbins musicals.

Bernstein recalled in Jonathan Cott's book of composer interviews *Back to a Shadow in the Night,* "Everybody told us that the show was an impossible project. Steve Sondheim and I auditioned it like crazy, playing four-hands in order to convey a quintet or the twelve-tone 'Cool' fugue. But no one, we were told, was going to be able to sing the augmented fourths—as with 'Ma-ri-a' [C to F-sharp]. Also, they said the score was too 'rangy' for pop music—'Tonight, tonight'—it went all over the place. Besides, who wanted to see a show in which the first-act curtain comes down on two dead bodies lying on the stage?"

The project needed "angels" who would take a gamble with these A-list artists. And highly enthusiastic lead producers who could rustle up the cash.

1957: "GANGWAY!" AND *WEST SIDE STORY*

The respected Broadway veteran Cheryl Crawford agreed to produce the show, with assistance from a young businessman–theatrical investor (and future chairman of the John F. Kennedy Center for the Performing Arts), Roger L. Stevens—but only "after it was turned down by everybody else," Laurents noted. "Everybody else" included such heavy-hitter Broadway producers (and longtime colleagues and friends of the artistic team) as George Abbott, Richard Rodgers, and Leland Hayward.

Relying on Crawford to shake the money tree was a problematic setup from the get-go. She had a gilded record of producing daring and historically important works of the Provincetown Players, the Group Theatre, and the Theatre Guild, and independently producing the premiere of *Porgy and Bess* and landmark shows by Bertolt Brecht, Tennessee Williams, and other great playwrights. She also co-founded the Actors Studio.

But Crawford was not on the same wavelength with Robbins and his renegades. She balked at the "exorbitant" budget for the production (which covered an essential but unprecedented eight-week rehearsal period, twice the standard length). To her ears the music was too difficult for theater singers, and the book was "thin somehow . . . and really, there wasn't any leavening, any humor." (The comic setpiece "Gee, Officer Krupke," was added later.)

And for Crawford, the show's treatment of social issues was a case of too much, but not enough. She criticized the scenario as belonging to a dated "ash can" school of faux-realism—at the same time demanding that it provide the audience with a more specific, detailed sociological rationale for the alienation and brutality of the gang members. Her lack of enthusiasm helped to explain why investors were not clamoring to get a piece of the action. As the starting date of rehearsals loomed closer, the financial situation grew dire. It all came to a head after a backer's audition that became the stuff of Broadway legend.

On an unseasonably sweltering April afternoon, Robbins and company performed the songs and outlined the plot of *West Side Story* for a group of well-heeled but clearly uninterested potential investors gathered in a posh Manhattan living room. The periodic squawk of tugboat horns on the East River punctuated the presentation of excerpts from the Bernstein–Sondheim score. It was a grim outing, and according to Laurents, "We didn't get a nickel."

Shortly afterward, Crawford called a meeting of the team to announce she was withdrawing from the production—leaving it without a producer, or funds, a mere six weeks before rehearsals were due to start. "I said, 'Cheryl, you're an immoral woman,'" Laurents remembered, countering her reputation as a Broadway titan of the highest ethical standing, "and we all got up and walked out and went to the Algonquin [Hotel] to have a drink. . . . We were so desperate we were talking of having it done for two weeks at City Center." Noted Bernstein, "We thought at that point it would not go on. Everybody begged us to stop. They all said it was suicidal."

In a last-ditch effort to rescue the project, the creative team placed an emergency transatlantic call to Stevens, then visiting Paris. He heard their distress and agreed to make a bridge loan—a lifesaver. Enter the astute and savvy young Broadway producer Harold Prince, a social friend of Sondheim's, and Prince's partner Robert Griffith. Prince and Griffith had with director George Abbott co-produced the hits *Wonderful Town* and *The Pajama Game* (with Robbins's creative involvement) and the winning 1955 baseball musical *Damn Yankees.*

In the spring of 1957, they were busy with Abbott mounting another new musical (*New Girl in Town,* based on Eugene O'Neill's *Anna Christie*), and Prince called Sondheim to kvetch about the troubles they were having in tryout. But the twenty-seven-year-old impresario (and future director of many a Sondheim musical) was not as risk-averse as Crawford and Broadway's other old guard. And after listening to Sondheim's tale of woe, he and Griffith flew in from Boston for a confab.

"Now I had heard the entire score of 'West Side Story,'" Prince recounted later. "I knew every note of it, because Steve would play it at home or up at my apartment. But he said, 'Don't give me away, I'm not supposed to have played any of this music for anybody!'. . . About halfway through the audition, I started to sing along with the material. And Lenny stopped and said, 'Oh, that's what I've always wanted, a producer who's musical!'"

Prince agreed to tackle the show. He also quickly established himself as a hands-on producer, by opining that the opening gang song, "Mix," hit "the wrong note to begin with" and should be cut.

Out it went (by consensus), and Prince and Griffith swiftly rustled up the show's entire budget of $350,000 (the equivalent of about $2.7 million in 2010) from 173 individual backers—including actress Thelma Ritter, famed classical violinist Mischa Elman, and the lyricist's father, Herbert Sondheim, as noted in the papers of Stevens (who continued to lend his support to the effort).

Casting was next (not an easy process, but a fulfilling one, that will be discussed later). The lengthy, intensive, and revelatory rehearsal period for the musical, under its (short-lived) working title of "Gangway!" (which Laurents said he suggested as a gag), commenced on June 24, 1957, at the Chester Hale Studio in Manhattan.

Fast-forward to the first full performance of the show soon to be renamed *West Side Story.* It was a traditional Broadway "gypsy run-through" for invited theater colleagues. The cast performed in practice clothes, with dummy props and no orchestra. But the response was tremendously positive and a precursor of things to come.

Remembered Prince, "All the kids on Broadway from other shows came, and friends, and they were knocked sideways by it. Just the sound of it, and the movement, and just the whole thing was something no one had ever seen before." Carol Lawrence, who played Maria, was stunned that "people like Lena Horne were screaming 'Bravo' at the end and putting their arms around you and crying and sobbing."

West Side Story had another rapturous reception in the initial tryout run at Washington, D.C.'s National Theatre, as recorded in Bernstein's chatty letters to his wife Felicia. After a stellar opening on August 19, 1957, before an audience studded with members of the Washington elite ("even Nixon and 35 admirals"), the composer attended a luncheon at the Eisenhower White House, where *West Side Story* was a hot topic. He wrote of the high morale of the production team and "long lines at the box office" but cautioned, "it's only Washington, not New York—don't count chickens."

But the company's continuing euphoria and good fortune are well evident in his after-the-fact log. "I laughed and cried as though I'd never seen or heard it before," Bernstein marveled about the premiere. "And I guess that what made it come out right is that we all really *collaborated;* we were all writing the *same* show. Even the producers were after the same goals we had in mind. Not even a whisper about a happy ending has been heard. A rare thing on Broadway. I am proud and honored to be a part of it."

The reviews and crowd reaction for the second tryout run, at the Erlanger Theatre in Philadelphia, were also extremely positive. That revved up the company for the all-important Broadway opening at the Winter Garden Theatre on September 26.

As mentioned earlier, it was not immediately apparent if the *West Side Story* team had a bona fide hit on its hands—much less a show for the ages. The Broadway audience of critics, showbiz celebrities and insiders, and other first-nighters "sat on their hands" at the start, reported Lawrence in her memoir *Carol Lawrence: The Backstage Story,* as they were "looking at kids in blue jeans and sneakers killing each other with switchblades and singing opera and dancing too much."

But the responses perked up during the vivacious "America" number, which "stopped the show cold." And from then on, the crowd was electrified. At the finale, as Lawrence weepingly followed the Jets and Sharks bearing the inert form of Larry Kert (Tony) into the wings, the actress heard only dead silence as the curtain came down.

As she described it, the actors quickly assembled onstage for the curtain call, and the audience stayed so silent she worried, "They hate it. They didn't get it. It's a bomb . . . And then, as if Jerome Robbins had choreographed it, they leapt to their feet, screaming and sobbing and stamping their feet and applauding. . . . And they would not, would not, stop."

West Side Story had arrived. It had proved all the doubters wrong. If the show did not receive unanimous critical raves, if it did not please every ticket holder, or match the box office receipts of *My Fair Lady,* if Prince prematurely interrupted that debut run by unwisely sending the production on the road (and returning it to Broadway, for a second and shorter engagement), in the big picture it mattered little.

A new American masterwork had been launched and recognized. Something came, some good. And in the great trove of Broadway musical theater, and the whirligig of American culture, it was here to stay.

TOP CATS IN TOWN: 1949–57

Though *West Side Story* took eight years to realize, from the idea stage to opening night, its instigators were not putting all their artistic eggs in one basket, to say the least. They collectively kept busy during that period with a slew of other prime creative projects that enriched Broadway, Hollywood, and concert halls, further honing their crafts and at times collaborating with one another on memorable efforts. (Since Sondheim was a decade younger, and still a Williams College student in 1949, his list of doings was understandably slimmer.)

1949 PROJECTS

Symphony No. 2, "The Age of Anxiety"—composed by Bernstein

Home of the Brave (movie)—screenplay by Laurents

Caught (movie)—screenplay by Laurents

Anna Lucasta (movie)—screenplay co-authored by Laurents
   (with Philip Yordan)

1950

The Bird Cage (Broadway play)—by Laurents

Call Me Madam (Broadway musical)—choreographed by Robbins

Peter Pan (Broadway musical)—songs and incidental music by Bernstein

1951

The King and I (Broadway musical)—choreographed by Robbins

The Cage (ballet)—choreographed by Robbins for New York City Ballet

1952

Trouble in Tahiti (opera)—composed by Bernstein

Time of the Cuckoo (Broadway play)—by Laurents

1953

Wonderful Town (Broadway musical)—composed by Bernstein;
directed and choreographed by Robbins

Saturday Night (unproduced musical)—score by Sondheim

Topper (TV show)—Sondheim wrote episodes

1954

The Pajama Game (Broadway Musical)—directed and
co-choreographed by Bernstein

On the Waterfront (soundtrack, movie)—composed by Bernstein

Serenade (musical based on a James Cain novel, shelved)—Bernstein
was to compose; Robbins to direct

The Lady and the Tiger (unproduced musical)—Sondheim
co-wrote and composed (with Mary Rodgers)

Serenade (After Plato's Symposium) (orchestral work)—composed by Bernstein

Peter Pan (Broadway musical)—directed and choreographed by Robbins

1955

The Girls of Summer (Broadway play by N. Richard Nash)—incidental
music composed by Sondheim

The Lark (Broadway play by Lillian Hellman)—incidental music
composed by Bernstein

Summertime (film)—screenplay by Laurents, based on his play *The Time of the Cuckoo*

1956

A Clearing in the Woods (Broadway play)—by Laurents

Bells Are Ringing (Broadway musical)—directed and
  choreographed by Robbins

Candide (Broadway musical)—composed by Bernstein

IN THE SHADOW OF THE BLACKLIST

Did the anti-Communist fervor of the early 1950s, led by U.S. Senator Joseph R. McCarthy and other right-wing zealots, have any impact on the creation of *West Side Story*?

Not directly, perhaps. But the dark and tangled web of accusation and the punishing blacklists of the period entrapped many Americans in the entertainment field and impinged on the lives and careers of Bernstein, Laurents, and Robbins, and (to some degree) their relationships with one another during the time of *West Side Story*'s development.

All three had, like many of their liberal Jewish American peers in the arts world, been engaged to varying degrees in peace, civil rights, and other causes since their youths. And Robbins was among the many young idealists who joined the Communist Party and, after becoming disillusioned, later abandoned it. As prominent cultural figures, Robbins as well as Bernstein and Laurents landed in the government files that J. Edgar Hoover's FBI doggedly kept on alleged "subversives." And in the late 1940s and early 1950s, their progressive political views and associations cast them under a diffuse, toxic cloud of suspicion that threatened to harm their reputations and careers. But each man was targeted in a different way by the forces of fearmongering, and each reacted differently.

Leonard Bernstein's FBI file reveals that in 1949 he became the subject of a security investigation ordered by the White House prior to a concert he conducted in honor of Chaim Weizmann, the first president of Israel. It was an event U.S. President Harry Truman had originally planned to attend.

According to documents later declassified, the FBI when consulted made no recommendation on whether Truman should appear at this event (the concert went on, but without him). However, in an internal memo to Hoover, Bernstein was tarred as "connected, affiliated, or in some manner associated" with Communist front groups, because he had lent his name to support various liberal causes. In 1950, he was named in the scurrilous witch-hunting publication titled *Red Channels.* Created by three former FBI agents, it named 151 professional writers, directors, and performers in the entertainment industry, implying they were "Red Fascists"–that is, Communist sympathizers. (The list also included such artists as Pete Seeger, actor Orson Welles, and writer Dorothy Parker.)

Being named in *Red Channels* put a chill in Bernstein's once hot-as-a-pistol career. And astonishingly, in 1951 he was placed on the "prominent individuals list" of the U.S. State Department's Security Index, which named citizens who might pose a threat to the United States in the event of a national emergency.

Though the list was abandoned soon afterward, Bernstein remained under suspicion and subject to vague insinuations made to the FBI by informants. In 1953 his passport was revoked, and to recover it was, as Bernstein put it, "a ghastly and humiliating experience," during which he had to write a lengthy affidavit declaring his loyalty to the United States and swearing he'd never been a Communist Party member.

There is also some evidence, according to Barry Seldes in his illuminating book *Leonard Bernstein: The Political Life of an American Musician,* that the maestro was blacklisted from appearing on the CBS television network during the early 1950s. The ban was lifted in time for the network to launch Bernstein's historic, Emmy Award–honored musical series *Omnibus* in 1954. But he was never called before the infamous congressional House Un-American Activities Committee (HUAC), which exerted terrible pressure on witnesses (starting with the browbeaten movie actor Larry Parks) to cough up the names of "fellow travelers"–colleagues with Communist Party ties (or suspected ones).

Arthur Laurents' political leanings and outspoken stance against the blacklists made him persona non grata in Hollywood in the early 1950s, a predicament that later inspired his screenplay for the hit film *The Way We Were* and his semiautobiographical stage drama *Jolson Sings Again.*

Laurents's so-called subversive activities were itemized in *Red Channels* also. That effectively dried up his Hollywood movie employment, and he did not receive a film-writing credit again until 1956.

Without screenwriting gigs on the horizon, in 1950 Laurents took a lengthy sojourn in Europe. But when he first applied for a passport, his application was denied on political grounds.

To be issued a passport, Laurents hired a lawyer–who turned out, unbeknownst to him, to be an FBI informer. "The lawyer grilled me for hours, pressing for the names of people in a Marxist study group I was part of," he told this author in a 1995 interview for the *Seattle Times*. "I gave him no names, though I was dying to tell him just one to see his reaction. It was Ava Gardner!"

After finally securing his passport, Laurents spent more than a year abroad and then returned to New York to focus on writing plays for Broadway, where the blacklists held little sway.

But the person whose life was the most damaged by the "witch hunts" was Robbins. He had followed friends and colleagues into the Communist Party in the early 1940s, and that affiliation returned to haunt him.

Robbins's ordeal began in 1951, the year he was working on staging musical numbers for *The King and I* and was named in "Counterattack," another damning list of alleged "Reds." Around the same time, Robbins biographer Amanda Vaill uncovered, the TV variety show host, showbiz gossip columnist, and fierce Communist-hunter Ed Sullivan went after Robbins in a column that appeared in the *Philadelphia Inquirer.* "I'd suggest that the House Un-American Activities Committee subpoena [*sic*] ballet star and choreographer Jerome Robbins," Sullivan wrote. "Robbins can give the Committee backstage glimpses of the musical shows which have been jammed with performers sympathetic to the Commie cause" and identify "conspirators who hide behind the music racks, ballet bars and musical comedy billing" of Broadway.

With the help of his lawyers, Robbins was able to prevent the item from running in the New York and Los Angeles papers. But Sullivan had done his dirty work: for the next several years, Robbins was pressured by the FBI to testify before HUAC. Fearing that revelations of his party membership and bisexuality would destroy his career, Robbins finally relented. In an hourlong committee session in New York on May 5, 1953, an anxious, obsequious Robbins recanted his own involvement in the Party and implicated eight friends and colleagues. (The list included writer Jerome Chodorov, who penned the book for the Bernstein–Comden–Green musical *Wonderful Town,* which Robbins had only recently choreographed.)

After he testified, the FBI hounding and the fear of exposure in a time of intense homophobia and demagoguery lifted off Robbins. And in 1958, Sullivan granted Robbins's world-touring troupe Ballets: U.S.A. *two* appearances on his TV show, with glowing introductions from the host.

But Robbins could not evade the personal repercussions of his betrayal of cohorts or wipe clean the permanent stain on his reputation. Laurents recalled Robbins telling him after the HUAC hearing, "It'll be years before I know whether I did the right thing." To which Laurents responded, with typical directness, "I can tell you right now, you were a shit."

The people Robbins named, and many of his other colleagues, were horrified by his caving to HUAC. Some shunned or avoided him for the rest of his life. Robbins also faced the ignominy of being identified, in virtually every historical account of the McCarthy Era blacklists, as one who named names.

The incident tormented Robbins, and he was still trying to reconcile his actions near the end of his life. An autobiographical dance-theater work he drafted titled "The Poppa Piece," in which the HUAC hearing would be reenacted, was never completed. He wrote to a friend, "Maybe I can't—will never find a satisfying release from the guilt of it all."

While Laurents and Bernstein disapproved of his actions, they didn't shun him—socially or professionally. Why? Perhaps for the same reasons artists who abhorred the witch hunts (including Bernstein) were still willing to collaborate with stage and film director Elia Kazan, who also betrayed close associates to HUAC: Like Kazan, Robbins was a difficult but brilliant and inspiring collaborator on works they wanted to create with him.

And, no matter how destructive Robbins's testimony was, Bernstein and Laurents fully understood the horrible pressures of a period Lillian Hellman called the "scoundrel time."

"Since then, looking back," Laurents told National Public Radio, "I'm not very proud of myself for ignoring the fact that Jerry informed, because that validated him. And I had to face that. I can explain what I did; I don't condone it. We were all so involved in the making of [*West Side Story*] that extra-curricular affairs, as it were, didn't enter into it. There were no fingers pointed. It was not a good time. Anybody who went through it, it still comes up almost every day, and it's us, and it's them."

There is no direct parallel to Robbins's HUAC troubles in *West Side Story*. But at least one exchange in Laurents's dialogue must have hit a related nerve. Trying to squeeze information out of the gangs about who began the fight in "The Prologue," Lt. Schrank asks, "Didn't nobody tell ya there's a difference between bein' a stool pigeon and cooperatin' with the law?" Riff promptly answers: "You told us the difference, sir. And we all chipped in for a prize for the first guy who can figure it out."

The original Tony and Maria, Carol Lawrence and Larry Kert. Courtesy of Photofest.

3

^^^^^^^

A TIME AND PLACE FOR US
THE BOOK AND CHARACTERS
OF *WEST SIDE STORY*

West Side Story erupts from a concrete jungle and then moves like a speeding bullet through two acts and fifteen scenes—piercing through comedy, romance, and violent conflict before striking its final destination of plaintive tragedy.

With the innovation of conveying much of the action (and emotion) in dance and other physical movement (like a ballet), and suffusing, driving the action with music (like an opera or symphony), Arthur Laurents knew his book for the show had to be tightly compressed. It also had to be a sturdy platform for the dance numbers and songs to blast off from. And it had to make the most, in contemporary urban terms, of its *Romeo and Juliet* template without becoming a stilted update or pretentious imitation of Shakespeare.

"The book is remarkable not only because it's so brief but because so much happens in it," Sondheim has pointed out. "'Romeo and Juliet' is, after all, a melodrama with something extraordinary happening in every scene. . . . [The plot] drives our show even when it isn't well sung or well danced—the plot is still exciting."

Though Laurents's streamlined text tends to be overshadowed by the work of his collaborators, it is vital to the cohesive totality of *West Side Story*. One can certainly question the lack of memorable poetic language, or the mock-slang dialogue of the gang boys, or the slightness of conventional character development in the text. (The latter complaint has also been lodged over the centuries at Shakespeare's *Romeo and Juliet,* by the way.)

But Laurents's *West Side Story* partners always heaped high praise on him, saying his book was invaluable to the whole enterprise. Said Robbins, "We could make our poetry out of the music, the dancing, the song lyrics, but Arthur had the burden of making his text go along with 'Romeo and Juliet' and still communicate some of the poetry, the argot, the drives and passions of the 1950s."

From the show's first gasps of life, the book provided the backbone, the blueprint for every other element of the piece. Yet like all aspects of the production, it was subjected to constant group think and rethink, debate and amendment.

Over the different phases of *West Side Story*'s development, not only was there the important shift of its ethnogeographical setting, from a Jewish and Catholic neighborhood on Manhattan's Lower East Side, to a Puerto Rican and European American community on the Upper West Side. There also were, over time, significant alterations of content and format.

What would *West Side Story* have been like if, as some early drafts proposed, Maria committed suicide with poison and Tony lived on? Or they both died together? Or if a Jewish Juliet's *tante* (aunt) joined in on the balcony scene? Or, in "The Prologue," the Jets and Sharks sang a breakneck lyric to Bernstein's thundering music, as they pummeled each other?

But there was early agreement on some core questions raised by the material. In a witty, revealing 1957 piece for the *New York Herald Tribune,* Laurents listed the overarching concerns the entire team had pondered and tackled as the scenario was hammered out: "Should the play follow Shakespeare closely, almost paraphrase the original? Should it keep only key scenes and characters? Or should it simply use the original as a reference point and let the story wind its own way, led by the character of today's youth?"

The answers were thrashed around for years in outlines, in sketches of scenes, and in letters, memos, phone calls, meetings. But there was easy consensus on what should *not* be in the show.

"Neither formal poetry nor flat reportage; neither opera nor split-level musical comedy numbers; neither zippered-in ballets nor characterless dance routines," wrote Laurents. "We didn't want newsreel acting, blue-jean costumes or garbage can scenery any more than we wanted soapbox pounding for our theme of young love destroyed by a violent world of prejudice."

What Laurents aimed for, and often achieved, was cogent storytelling and, as he put it, "a theatrically sharpened illusion of reality"—what Picasso famously described as "the lie that makes us realize the truth." The playwright deliberately emphasized "character and emotion rather than place-name specifics and sociological statistics" and had the young toughs speaking "my translation of adolescent street talk . . . it might sound real, but it isn't."

Though this was his first musical drama, Laurents's training and experience as a director, and his years of crafting radio and film scripts, where verbal economy is essential and words are all but synonymous with actions, are evident in the jet-propulsion narrative of *West Side Story.*

The dramatic arc of romance, disorder, disillusion, and death in the show essentially obeys Aristotle's "unities." The entire story happens between 5:00 p.m. one evening and around midnight the next. (Aristotle's dictum was twenty-four hours, but who's counting?) Apart from a single fantasy/reverie (the "Somewhere" ballet) and a timeout for comedy ("Gee, Officer Krupke"), the action occurs in a straight shot, within a few short Manhattan blocks. There are no subplots, no tangents, no optional "supporting characters." Every incident and musical interlude is fused into a single narrative strand, designed to motivate and portend what happens next.

Laurents became adept, he later noted, "at providing the briefest of lead-ins to a song or number." His various outlines, and the book in its finished form, boast the pungent description and detail of a good screenplay, as well as the crisp motivational "beats" of a well-made play.

For instance, in an outline for the show when its tentative title was "Romeo," he sketched a scene in a tenement alleyway (with Shakespeare character names as markers), this way: "Gang tears wildly through alley, under fire escape, seeking Romeo, fun, trouble. After they go, Romeo comes out of shadows. Balcony scene between Romeo and Juliet on fire escape."

Though *Romeo and Juliet* was the primary inspiration for *West Side Story,* and the work contains many obvious and subtle parallels to the classic tragedy, on a more subliminal level there are also echoes of *Peter Pan*—the classic J. M. Barrie tale, which had recently been theatricalized by Robbins and Bernstein in two separate Broadway musicals and was a major influence on the 1955 James Dean film *Rebel Without a Cause.* The

Barrie story depicts a gaggle of brash, ragtag adolescent males whose refusal to grow up (or straighten up) is a badge of honor. Like the Jets and Sharks, they try to nurture and protect one another and fill in for absent, indifferent, or preoccupied parents by forging an alternative family. But life for the Jets and Sharks is even more dangerous than a place terrorized by Captain Hook and his pirates. From this Manhattan Never Never Land, there is no way out.

THE ART OF COLLABORATION

The accounts of Laurents and his colleagues, and the surviving paperwork (outlines, letters, memos, music sheets) charting the progress of *West Side Story,* make it clear that the book was a genuinely collaborative effort.

Bernstein had considerable input into the text. Sondheim offered feedback and ideas in its later phases. And Robbins functioned as a demanding editor, combing over drafts and giving incisive criticism, suggestions, and (when he felt Laurents had nailed something) praise and reinforcement.

Confident in his own vision of the piece, Robbins drew on his experience as a sought-after script doctor of musicals and perhaps his awareness of how Broadway mentor George Abbott and such "Method" directors associated with the Actors Studio (Harold Clurman, Elia Kazan) worked with leading dramatists including Tennessee Williams and Arthur Miller. These directors didn't just stage completed scripts, but also functioned as dramaturges and, in a loose and uncredited sense, even co-writers.

Laurents welcomed Robbins's input but in general viewed the Actors Studio approach with more skepticism. And unsurprisingly, his own directorial instincts and priorities sometimes clashed with Robbins's as their roles overlapped during rehearsals.

Robbins demanded that anything violating his conception of the show be axed. He was particularly hypersensitive and reactive to what he considered conventional musical-theater shtick. In one memo, he objected strongly to Laurents's depiction of the character of Anita in an early draft of "Romeo" as older than the other gang-related characters and what Robbins viewed as a "typical downbeat blues torchbearing 2nd character" who "falls into a terrible cliché."

"You are away off the track with . . . Anita," he advised Laurents. "If she's 'an-older-girl-kicked-by-love-before-experiencing-the-worst' (and I'm quoting you) she's much too experienced for the gang, or else is sick, sick, sick to be so attached emotionally and sexually to a younger boy of a teenage gang."

Robbins was by all witnesses usually hell-bent on getting his way, and he resorted to bullying and worse until he wore an opponent out. His colleagues, even those as accomplished and self-assured as Laurents and Bernstein, often yielded to him—not just to avoid a nasty scrap, but because his finely tuned aesthetic insights and instincts were so often correct.

In his memos, Robbins could distill the essence of the task before the team and help everyone keep their eyes on the prize. Considering how to best handle the tragic dimension of *West Side Story,* he wrote to Laurents and Bernstein on October 15, 1955, "As for the overall picture, we're dead unless the audience feels that all the tragedy can and could be averted, but there's hope and a wish for escape from that tragedy, and a tension built on that desire." (That's *Romeo and Juliet* in a nutshell, too.)

However, in the rough-and-tumble of give-and-take, Laurents was no slouch either. When Robbins suggested, "If you keep each scene down to strict story points (outside of Romeo and Juliet themselves) you will be writing perfectly for this type of show," Laurents retorted that if he "pared the script to story points, then we will have a conventional musical with two-dimensional characters. Furthermore the gangs will be unsympathetic because there will be no understanding of their characters or feeling."

Laurents was fully aware that he was not writing a typical Broadway musical. And since he had never written one of any sort, he had little baggage and no wariness about breaking the unwritten Broadway rules. "We were telling much of the story through dancing and singing; it was a natural way to us, consequently it was natural," he explained in his book *Mainly on Directing.* When it served *West Side Story,* he agreed movement and music would replace dialogue, and lines from his speeches would be appropriated for songs. On the flipside, he agreed for the dummy speech he wrote for Maria as she excoriates the Sharks and Jets for their role in Tony's death to be used at the finale in lieu of a song intended for that moment.

As for "The Prologue", Laurents pointed out later that "even before I began actually writing the book of 'West Side Story,' when I was making an outline to structure the story . . . I described '"The Prologue"' as being danced with three or four spoken words. What better way to set the style, to tell the audience this story was going to be told primarily through dance and music?"

This was, said Bernstein, "a testimony to Arthur's particular generosity. He never said, 'I'm sorry, that's got to being spoken. What's going to happen to my scene?' He gave wherever he could."

Reviewing all the documentation in his scrupulous study *Leonard Bernstein: West Side Story,* Nigel Simeone uncovered the constant interplay of fresh ideas, variations, alternatives—a working style in which constructive criticism and continual alteration was an essential dynamic. Songs scrapped? Scenes scrapped? Locales changed? That left room for new and better ideas to emerge. This kind of organic show-making process requires enormous respect and trust from the co-creators and illustrates why a piece of ensemble art can take years to come to fruition.

Laurents and company were also supported by a "village" of advisors— an elite inner circle of Broadway directors, producers, and artists from whom suggestions could be solicited and incorporated. But not all the feedback from this select club was accepted. And the objections Laurents fielded and rejected from initial *West Side Story* producer (and consummate Broadway insider) Cheryl Crawford may have helped sharpen his own convictions about what the show should become.

In an April 11, 1957, letter to Laurents, Crawford worried that too little of the Bernstein–Sondheim score had been finished, that "the story at present has no real depth or urgency," and that Tony and Riff were not profound or universal enough characters whose "yearnings are strong and shared by youths all over the world and in other sections of society."

In his pointed written response, Laurents agreed the show needed more dramatic urgency and said he was working toward that goal. But he countered her suggestions that "tend toward a social opera about today's youth, with the minor story of two lovers. This is not the show we intended to do." He underscored that the artistic team was forging "a strong love story against a heightened, theatricalized, romanticized background based on delinquency," and the "reality would be an emotional, not a factual one."

THE WEST SIDE STORY CHARACTERS

The main roles in *West Side Story* are inspired by parallel figures in *Romeo and Juliet,* as are aspects of the plot. But there are many departures—most essentially, Maria's survival at the finale, in contrast to Juliet's suicide.

Here are Laurents's scripted descriptions of the major characters (in italics), with comments on how they serve the story:

CENTRAL FIGURES

TONY. *"A good-looking sandy-haired boy."* A mid-20th century, urban Romeo, Tony (nee Anton) has outgrown his wild days as a founding member of the Jets gang, and now works a "straight" job at Doc's neighborhood drugstore. Once a tough street scrapper, Tony now dismisses those antics as kids' play. But he remains close to the crew's current leader Riff, who (for reasons unexplained) has lived with Tony's family for four years and is like a brother to him. As he toils at a regular job at Doc's drugstore, Tony senses that something better than gangbanging, something magical and life-transforming, is just "around the corner" for him—though he's uncertain what it could be.

Tony is generally considered the most straightforward (or simplistic) principal character in the musical. He is the son of poor Polish immigrants, and is trying to "go straight." He is as vulnerable as Romeo to sincere and moony infatuation (though unlike with Romeo, we hear nothing of his previous girlfriends). And his brotherly bond with Riff is so close, he will destroy his own life and the life of another, to avenge him.

That is enough to build a characterization on, if one can also sing those feelings expressively. Because much of Tony's journey is expressed musically. As the show begins, he has already moved away from innocence toward manhood by recognizing that gangs and rumbles are juvenile and unproductive. He no longer gets the "kick" from them he once did. But when he finds a new raison d'être, in his love for Maria, he ironically winds up reverting back to his earlier gang identity and loses everything—his love, and his life.

Is Tony a hero? A victim? A natural-born killer? One of the cornerstones of "West Side Story" is that it does not impose such a rigid moral judgment on him or his peers. But an actor needs to reach beyond the obvious with Tony, to match his male ingénue romantic swoon with the grit and toughness that made him form the Jets with Riff in the first place—and, reflexively but reluctantly, still live by the gang code.

RIFF. *"Glowing, driving, intelligent, slightly wacky."* Like Shakespeare's Mercutio, Riff is the raffish leader of the pack—"the gold medal kid with the heavyweight crown," as he crows in "The Jet Song." He calls the shots for the Jets, giving orders, commanding respect, and keeping them in line, and flaunts his power and his brassy girlfriend.

Sharp, cocky and street-savvy, Riff sees no other life beyond the one he has found in the patch of cement turf he rules. His natural leadership ability, his charisma and "cool," are funneled into his gang's struggle for dominance. He sees no other outlets for his energy and talents, nowhere to excel but the streets, no other goal but to make the Jets "Number One, to sail, to hold the sky!"

But Riff has some vulnerability. He isn't quite the acerbic cynic that Mercutio is. He's a little hurt and very mystified that his surrogate brother Tony deserted the gang—because "when you're a Jet, you stay a Jet." He's the Lost Boy who inherits the mantle of Peter Pan when Peter moves on—but he's still lost, and without his closest comrade.

Riff's pride and machismo prevent him from showing neediness ("I never asked the time of day from a clock"), but he needs Tony at the rumble for both a show of force and for emotional support. Ironically, it is Tony's much-desired presence at the dance, and the fight, that seal Riff's doom.

MARIA. *"Extremely lovely, extremely young...an excited, enthusiastic, obedient child with the temper, stubborn strength and awareness of a woman."* Beautiful, virginal, charmingly feisty too, this barrio Juliet chafes at her family's strict rules to guard her innocence, as enforced by her doting older brother Bernardo and his girlfriend Anita. As a new immigrant and blossoming adolescent, she is hungry for experience and autonomy. Spreading her wings by attending the dance "as a young lady of America" is an important rite of passage for her.

Her girlishness begins to fade when she falls in love with Tony. She's forced to grow up very quickly to cope with a world of bigotry and warfare entirely new to her. But for as long as possible Maria clings to her starry idealism, her belief that love can conquer the hatred churning around her. She unknowingly fails Tony, and her brother Bernardo, by misjudging the depth of that hatred.

As an archetype, Maria is a triptych of innocent child, enamored young woman and, finally, bereft widow. (The image of her final moments cradling the dying Tony in her arms, as staged by Robbins, resembles the grieving Mary cradling the martyred Jesus, in Michelangelo's Pieta.)

Like Tony, the role of Maria can be easily underestimated and underplumbed. She has moments of sharp insight, and a code of righteous justice as well as a naiveté that furthers the tragedy. But in the end she matures the most of all the youths—first in her forgiveness of Tony, then in her angry comprehension of the endemic violence that shatters her world. While her final speech strains credulity, with its high-minded rhetoric delivered by a neophyte English-speaker, it can be deeply moving nonetheless—especially as it is followed by Maria's dignified, funereal march offstage to an adult path paved in grief and disillusionment.

ANITA. *"A Puerto Rican girl with loose hair and slightly flashy clothes . . . knowing, sexual, sharp."* The juiciest role (and often the best, as a performance vehicle), Anita is a far distant relation to the hovering, meddling old nurse in *Romeo and Juliet.* A clever, high-spirited gal who enjoys her status as Sharks leader Bernardo's squeeze, her sexuality and mother wit shine through much of the show. She's observant enough to know that life in neither Puerto Rico nor the United States is a bed of roses. And though more open-minded than Bernardo, she's worldly enough to realize the "taboo" union of Maria and Tony will probably end badly.

When it does, taking down her lover Bernardo with it, Anita's gusto fizzles. And her reaction is complex—molten anger, leavened with pity and empathy, then traumatized into vengeance.

Anita is certainly not free of the clichés of the "Latin spitfire" archetype—but she isn't limited by them. (She has a quick mind and a warm heart, as well as a hot body.) If Maria is not essentially a passive character, Anita is even less so. She exerts a mind of her own with Bernardo, who adores her (he leads her onto the dance floor, say the stage directions, "like she was the most magnificent lady in the world"). And their spicy sparring is a delight. When physically and verbally attacked by the Jets, she hits back—"If one of you was lying bleeding in the street I'd walk by and spit on you!"—and in an instant betrays her friend, and Tony.

Not surprisingly, given Anita's humor, dramatic circumstances and show-stopping dance numbers, those who play her well are singled out for kudos. While the actors portraying Tony and Maria have been shut out of top stage and film prizes, Rita Moreno received an Oscar for her rendition of Anita in the 1961 movie of *West Side Story,* and Karen Olivo won a 2009 Tony Award for her Anita in *West Side Story* in a Broadway revival. (Chita Rivera was, sadly, shut out of the Tonys entirely, but critically acclaimed Carol Lawrence was nominated, but lost.)

BERNARDO. *"Handsome, proud, fluid, a sardonic chip on his shoulder."* A beefed-up variation on Shakespeare's Tybalt, Bernardo is Riff's counterpoint: a natural leader admired by his gang, and a suave king to Anita's steamy queen. He's tough and calloused by necessity, from dealing daily with the virulent prejudices of not just the Jets and the cops, but bigoted New York in general. He has a sardonic streak, and is quick to call out adversaries (including the cops) on their hypocrisy. And he has no illusions about his place at the bottom rung of the social ladder, but still resents it.

Because he also cuts a romantic figure, Bernardo is often played with a kind of Rudolph Valentino-esque elegance. His treatment of "the ladies," as he calls them is macho in the courtly and protective sense. He feels an innate sense of superiority to the Jets, and chides them for their lack of manners and, well, class. But scratch his leonine poise and panache, and there's a gladiator capable of murder.

As smart and wary as Bernardo is, why does he pull a knife against Riff and turn fisticuffs into a deadly duel? This is, of course, central to the plot. And it is also in keeping with Shakespeare's Tybalt, who has a fiery temper and a feline grace. (Tybalt has the same name as a character in the medieval French allegory, "Reynard the Fox," and is derisively referred to as "King of the Cats" by Mercutio.)

Bernardo's code of honor dictates that he defend the virtue of his sister, especially from a white boy. Tony thus becomes his mortal enemy, and for Bernardo the rumble boils down to a contest between the two of them. Riff literally gets in the way of his real quarrel, and pays the price.

ADULT CHARACTERS

LT. SCHRANK. *"Strong, always in command; he has a charming, pleasant manner, which he often employs to cover his venom and fear."* This veteran New York City detective (a hard-boiled, hands-on version of Shakespeare's Prince of Verona) is an authority figure eager to "clean up" his beat. He may have once nursed a belief he could reach some of these mixed-up kids. But despite the "charm" that Laurents' stage directions endow him with (and which actors find it hard to locate and convey), he can't contain his own toxic frustrations and prejudices. They spew out: he treats the Sharks with racist contempt, and also demeans the Jets as slum "trash." Years of patrolling poor, crime-ridden precincts have jaded him, and his ineffectual attempts to establish order on the streets inspires more rebellion and ridicule than fear. He tries to prevent the Jets vs. Sharks feud, but is impotent to do so.

DOC. *"A little middle-aged man."* A sympathetic adult, but more disapproving, less avuncular than Shakespeare's Friar Laurence, this employer and friend to Tony despairs over the gang violence, and disdains the toughs who hang out at his soda fountain. Doc recalls a time when then this was a safer, more homogenous neighborhood, and his tone is sometimes folksy, sometimes preachy ("You make this world lousy!").

He disapproves of these kids, but after Tony kills Bernardo, he shelters him and gives him money to help him flee the cops. There's a wistful, vicarious (and rather schmaltzy) air about this aid ("I never had a Maria"), hinting that his own circumstances are lonely and loveless. Despite Doc's good intentions, like Friar Laurence he has a hand in the tragedy by passing along incorrect information from Anita (about Maria's supposed death), which leads to Tony's suicidal self-exposure to Chino.

KRUPKE. *"A big goonlike cop."* A buffoonish sidekick of Schrank's, and his detested enforcer, he's the "goon" the Jets love to mock.

GLAD HAND. *"A square."* A chaperone at the community center gym dance, he's a comic-relief figure of total ridicule to both gangs as he urges inter-racial mingling and dancing among the "boys and girls."

THE OTHER JETS

ACTION. *"A catlike ball of fury."* A seasoned hooligan, this is a volatile, damaged kid—alienated, edgy, racist, spoiling for a fight. He bitterly objects to being labeled a "cruddy juvenile delinquent" by adults, which gets spun into the trenchantly comic "Gee Officer, Krupke." In that post-rumble number, Action has fun playing a hapless street punk who is labeled and shuttled from social worker, to psychiatrist, to judge by a clueless establishment. His ugly darker side takes over in the drugstore scene where he leads a vicious verbal and sexual assault of Anita, unaware that by attacking the messenger Tony will never get the word from Maria that might have prevented his death.

ANYBODYS. *"A scrawny teenage girl, dressed in an outfit that is a pathetic attempt to imitate that of the Jets."* One of the first intentionally sexually ambiguous female roles in a Broadway musical, this "tomboy" outcast yearns to be one of the boys. She adopts their swagger, and volunteers for every Jets maneuver—braving a barrage of ridicule for being a Jets wannabe, and not knowing her place as a girl. (Graziella calls her "an American tragedy.") But Anybodys gets to prove her mettle by bravely helping Tony after the rumble, and by attempting to rescue him from the gun-toting Chino in the final scene.

A-RAB. *"An explosive little ferret who enjoys everything and understands the seriousness of nothing."* A foil for Action, he's the gang clown, a cut-up at every opportunity, and not quite as tough as he thinks he is.

BABY JOHN. *"The youngest member of the gang . . . awed at everything, including that he is a Jet, trying to act the big man."* A comic book–reading puppy, Baby John is the most innocent, impressionable and fearful member of the Jets. He's thrilled to be in the club, and like Anybodys tries to bluster his way to their approval. But when it comes to the rumble, he's frightened before hand, and anguished and weepy afterward. Baby John is a small but choice role, another character . . . forced to grow up too fast before our eyes.

VELMA. Riff's girlfriend, a self-styled glamour girl, a poopsie who wants to be taken seriously enough to listen in on the war council.

GRAZIELLA. *"A would be grand number."* Diesel's girlfriend, and Velma's giggly pal.

OTHER JETS. (smaller and non-speaking roles). SNOWBOY (*"a bespectacled, self-styled expert"*), DIESEL (*"Riff's lieutenant: big, slow, steady, nice"*), BIG DEAL, GEE-TAR, MOUTHPIECE, TIGER, MINNIE, CLARICE, PAULINE.

THE SHARKS

CHINO. *"A shy, gentle, sweet-faced boy."* Like Paris in *Romeo and Juliet,* Chino has been "promised" to Maria by their families. He is often portrayed as a self-effacing, meek character—that is, around women. He is also one of Bernardo's sidekicks, however, and can be a tough fighter. He is Maria's escort to the dance, and her presumptive suitor. But Maria tells Anita that when she looks at Chino there are no romantic sparks—"nothing happens." Her romantic interest in Tony makes him jealous, and when Bernardo is killed in the rumble and Maria gives away her loyalties by expressing more interest in Tony's well-being than her brother's, Chino snaps. He then has two burning reasons to seek Tony out, and gun him down on the street—to avenge the death of Bernardo, and stick it to Maria.

ROSALIA. *"More quietly dressed . . . She is none too bright."* This is the "dumb brunette" role, who is Anita's foil in "America," a number in which Rosalia guilelessly expresses her homesickness for Puerto Rico—and gets shot down, with sass, by Anita.

CONSUELA. *"A bleach-blonde, bangled beauty."* A brassy wise-cracker, who is one of the main teasers of Maria, during the "I Feel Pretty" number.

OTHER SHARKS. PEPE (Bernardo's lieutenant); INDIO, LUIS, ANXIOUS, NIBBLES, JUANO, TORO, MOOSE, TERESITA, FRANCISCA, ESTELLA, MARGARITA.

THE STORY

Setting: the West Side of New York City during the final days of summer.

ACT ONE

Scene 1: The show begins, with no musical overture but a dance number that is *"a condensation of the rivalry of two gangs,"* as the Anglo Jets and Puerto Rican Sharks taunt each other and brawl over turf in a tough, multi-ethnic Manhattan West Side neighborhood. ("The Prologue".)

After the police break up the fight and leave, Riff, leader of the Jets, and Bernardo, the Sharks captain, talk of settling their turf feud once and for all with a fight. The Sharks leave, and the Jets reassert their dominance of the turf. ("The Jet Song.")

Scene 2: Riff comes to Doc's neighborhood drugstore to try and convince Tony, who co-founded the gang but has quit to work a legit job at Doc's, to join in the rumble or at least come to the dance at the gym where he and Bernardo will be setting the terms of the fight. Tony reluctantly agrees to come by, but imagines fate has something momentous, and better, in store for him very soon. ("Something's Coming.")

Scene 3: In the Puerto Rican bridal shop where they work, the pretty teenaged Maria and her brother Bernardo's more worldly girlfriend Anita prepare to place the finishing touches on a new dress which the excited Maria will wear to her first American dance at the local gym.

Scene 4: The Jets and Sharks pour their nervous and sexual energy into an extended "challenge dance" ("Dance at the Gym"). Meanwhile, Maria and Tony enter and spot each other across the crowded dance floor. Magnetized by each other's gaze they drift toward one another, exchange a dance, a few dreamy words, and a brief kiss. A furious Bernardo interrupts them, warning Tony to stay away from his sister. Riff jumps in and gets Bernardo to agree to meet up with both gangs at a "war council" at Doc's. Bernardo storms out with his kid sister Maria in tow.

Scene 5: A dazed Tony wanders into the street, pouring out his new infatuation in song. ("Maria.") He finds Maria's tenement apartment, calls her to come out, and the two pledge their new love in a tender rendezvous on her fire escape. ("Tonight.") They agree to meet again the next evening at the bridal shop where she works.

  After the two part, Bernardo, the Sharks and their girlfriends gather nearby to tease and banter. When the men go off to meet with the Jets, the women stay behind to hold a teasing debate on merits and downsides of life in Puerto Rico vs. their new homeland in the United States. ("America.")

Scene 6: The Jets hang out at Doc's waiting for their war council with the Sharks. They're jumpy with adrenalin and spoiling for a showdown the two gangs have been building up to for months. Riff urges them to simmer down and channel their restless anger into the battle ahead. ("Cool.")

  The Sharks appear and agree to a rumble. As they are discussing weapons, Tony enters and tries to ratchet down the violence of the fight. He gets Bernardo and Riff to agree to a one-on-one, bare knuckle match between each gang's best fighter, instead of an all-out war with switchblades or zip guns. Schrank enters, sensing that a battle is imminent. He lobs a racial insult at the departing Sharks (who respond, under Bernardo's lead, by whistling a chorus of "My Country 'Tis of Thee"). Then Schrank tries and fails to get information from the Jets about where and when the rumble will happen.

Scene 7: The next evening, as the bridal shop is closing and Anita and Maria are finishing up their work, a euphoric Tony enters. Anita thinks their relationship is unwise, but agrees to keep it under wraps. When she departs, Tony and Maria sweetly rendezvous. She urges him to go to the rumble and try to make peace between the enemy gangs, and he consents. Using shop dummies as stand-ins for their parents, the two shyly fantasize and act out their future wedding. ("One Hand, One Heart.")

Scene 8: Around the neighborhood, Tony, Maria and the gangs anticipate the rumble in a mood of portentous anticipation. The Sharks and Jets blame each other for the war, and are raring to fight. Riff and Tony confirm their friendship, and Tony's presence at the rumble. Anita imagines a romantic tryst ("a private little mix") with Bernardo later. Tony and Mary separately sing of their love. ("Tonight Quintet.")

Scene 7: As the gangs gather on a dead-end street under the highway, Riff puts forth Diesel to fight Bernardo in the agreed-upon fistfight. Tony interrupts, and tries to make a truce with Bernardo, who then tries goading Tony, verbally and by punching him, to fight with him. Riff intervenes, and he and Bernardo both pull out switchblades. ("The Rumble.") The tension escalates on both sides, as the two parry and thrust. Tony tries to get between them, and as Riff hesitates, Bernardo runs his knife into him—perhaps unintentionally. Tony impetuously grabs the knife from the dead Riff's hand, and fatally stabs Bernardo in retaliation. A free-for-all breaks out between the Jets and Sharks, ended by the roar of a police siren. The gang members scatter and flee, while the stunned Tony is led away from the crime scene by Anybodys.

ACT TWO

Scene 1: Unaware of the deaths of her brother and Riff, Maria giddily cavorts with the Shark girls as she anticipates a happy reunion with Tony. ("I Feel Pretty.") As her friends leave, Chino appears to tell Maria what happened at the rumble. Panic-stricken, she demands to know if Tony was hurt, causing Chino to recoil, upbraid her and angrily stomp out.

Tony sneaks into Maria's room through a window, and in her grief she pounds his chest and calls him a murderer. But she quickly forgives him and begs him not to go to the police but to run away with her—to some haven outside the city, where they can be together in peace. ("Somewhere.") In a fantasy ballet, the Jets and Sharks reconcile and play like happy children. Then Tony and Maria's imagined wedding ends in a replay of the rumble, and the couple returns to grim reality. As the lights fade, Tony and Maria sink back on the bed, into each other's arms.

Scene 2: In an alleyway, A-Rab, Baby John and other Jets members evade the police and talk about the rumble. After a run-in with Officer Krupke, they blow off steam by complaining about being pegged as juvenile delinquents by the adult authorities and "experts," in the comic number, "Gee, Officer Krupke."

Scene 3: Tony and Maria are awakened in bed by the grieving Anita knocking at the door. After Tony leaves (promising to get money from Doc, and meet Maria later to flee the city), Maria lets in the distraught Anita. Anita can tell she's been with Tony and lashes out at her. Maria responds that she can't help loving Tony, and Anita should understand that. ("A Boy Like That / I Have a Love.") As the police show up to question Maria, Anita tells her that Chino has a gun and is hunting for Tony. She reluctantly agrees to help the couple escape by going to Doc's and letting Tony know Maria's been delayed but will come soon.

Scene 4: The Jets have gathered at Doc's, and as Anita enters they pepper her with racial insults and threaten to rape her. Rescued by Doc, in a fury she lies to them, saying Maria has been murdered by Chino.

Scene 5: Doc goes down to the cellar and breaks Anita's news to Tony, who is so distraught he runs into the street, defenseless, and shouts for Chino to "come and get me too!"

Scene 6: Tony spots Maria in the shadows, but as she calls out to him and he moves toward her, Chino shoots him. Tony dies in Maria's arms, and she grabs the gun, pointing it at the gathered gang members and policemen, threatening and blaming them for their collective responsibility for the deaths of Riff, Tony and Bernardo. She drops the gun, and as members of both gangs come together to carry out Tony's body, Maria mournfully follows them and the show ends.

ARTHUR LAURENTS BIO

Arthur Laurents was born in Brooklyn, New York City, on July 14, 1918, to Irving Laurents, a lawyer, and Ada Robbins Laurents. He grew up in a comfortable home in Brooklyn, where he got interested in theater after watching shows at a local playhouse and Broadway productions with his family. Laurents attended Cornell University, and after graduating in 1937 he took a special radio writing class at New York University and wrote his first radio drama, *Now Playing Tomorrow.* His teacher helped him sell it to the CBS network, and he became a freelance scriptwriter for numerous radio shows.

Laurents was drafted during World War II and served in the U.S. Army Pictorial Service in New York, honing his script skills further by writing military training films and Armed Services Network radio programs. In 1945 he made his Broadway debut with his provocative play *Home of the Brave,* which examined anti-Semitism in the American military, followed by *The Bird Cage* (1950), about the hard-boiled owner of a bar. Neither was a box office hit, but in 1952 he scored one with *The Time of the Cuckoo,* a study of a lonely woman teacher who has an affair with a married Italian man. (It was made into the film *Summertime,* starring Katharine Hepburn.)

Laurents embarked on a successful film career in the 1950s, composing scripts for Alfred Hitchcock 's *Rope,* as well as *Summertime, Anastasia,* and *Bonjour Tristesse.*

After the 1957 premiere of *West Side Story,* his first Broadway musical, Laurents wrote another Broadway drama (*A Clearing in the Woods*), and the libretti for the musicals *Gypsy, Anyone Can Whistle, Do I Hear a Waltz?,* the 1968 Tony Award honoree *Hallelujah, Baby!,* and two later flops, *The Madwoman of Central Park West* and *Nick & Nora.*

Laurents also carved out a successful stage-directing career, helming *I Can Get It for You Wholesale* and *La Cage aux Folles* and revivals of *Gypsy* and *West Side Story.* He penned two more movie hits in the 1970s, *The Turning Point* and *The Way We Were,* and has authored two memoirs, *Mainly on Directing* and *Original Story By.* Among his professional honors are two Tony Awards, two Oscar nominations, and a National Board of Review lifetime achievement prize. In 2010 he founded the Laurents/Hatcher Foundation Award, a large cash prize for dramatists named in part for his longtime companion, Tom Hatcher. On May 5, 2011, Arthur Laurents died from complications of pneumonia at age 93.

THE FRABBAJABBA

Thanks to Jerome Robbins, the Sharks and Jets could walk the walk. When it came to them talking the talk, Arthur Laurents had an imperative and an opportunity.

No matter how commonplace it was otherwise, profanity was anathema to mainstream American entertainment in the 1950s. For fear of offending, even inserting a "damn" or a "Hell" into dialogue was frowned upon by producers of Broadway musicals, TV programs, and Hollywood films—much less spraying four- or five-letter curse words around.

So when it came to the lyrics and dialogue in *West Side Story,* necessity prompted invention. But Laurents later maintained that he actually welcomed the task of fabricating fresh argot for the gang members. It was not only about getting around the profanity barrier without entirely robbing his hoodlums of their verbal aggression. But as Keith Garebian perceived it in his valuable book *The Making of "West Side Story,"* it was also distributing "language across a narrow sociological area in order to shift the dramatic focus from character to environment." Laurents also believed that inventing new lingo, untethered to any particular era, would help keep *West Side Story* from fossilizing.

One does hear morsels of 1950s hipster slang in the dialogue, most of which originated with African American jazz musicians before working its way into common usage. The Jets toss around the commonplace "daddy-o" and "dig" in conversation. And an entire song in the show is devoted to the business of "cool"—a kind of transcendent aplomb that has been variously defined as an aesthetic, an attitude, even a state of being. ("Cool" might be a timeless concept: art historian Robert Farris Thompson traces the term way back to the fifteenth-century West African philosophy and term *Itutu,* or "mystic coolness.")

Taking a leaf from Shakespeare (who, it is said, invented an estimated 1,700 words and expressions in his collected works), Laurents coined his own jive talk. Here's a glossary:

"Cut the frabbajabba" (Cut the crap)

"Gassin', crabbin" (Chattering and complaining, to no effect)

"Chung! Chung!" / "Cracko Jacko!" / "Pam Pam!" / "Riga Diga Tum!"
    (All utterances in the wham-bam school, indicating bursts of explosive
    energy, or the landing of a punch)

"Kiddando" (A faux Spanish term, like *kiddo,* pejoratively used by
    Bernardo against the Jets)

"Ooblee-oo" and "Ooblee-pooh" (Insouciant baby-girl talk, giggly
    verbal shorthand between Velma and Graziella)

The Sharks and the Jets meet at the gym. Courtesy of Photofest.

4

GONNA ROCK IT TONIGHT
THE STAGING OF
WEST SIDE STORY

Give me a show I want to do. Show me a show that's about something, that has got some gut feeling about it," Robbins once declared, encapsulating his overriding artistic credo. And his commitment to that credo is nowhere more evident than in *West Side Story.*

It is not enough to say that Jerome Robbins came up with the premise for *West Side Story,* and that he brilliantly staged the show and choreographed it (though originally, he wanted to concentrate solely on directing it—a plan his collaborators and producer Harold Prince immediately, adamantly shot down).

It is also true that just about every aspect of *West Side Story,* every moment of it, is imprinted with Robbins's creative DNA. The score and book, the design scheme, the performances, and the very psyche of the work reflect his conception of a piece he nursed and nudged and propelled along for nearly a decade.

Of course, he took every ounce of credit, star billing, and every royalty point he could get for *West Side Story,* at times arousing the ire of the show's other deserving architects. And his demands were not, by general consensus, out of character for Robbins, a mercurial and complicated man, to say the least.

A relentless perfectionist, autocrat, and micromanager, Robbins could be notoriously harrowing to work with. Laurents once quipped that the conflict-averse Bernstein was afraid of only two things—"God and Jerry Robbins." Bernstein himself wrote his wife Felicia during the making of the musical, "Jerry continues to be—well, Jerry: moody, demanding, hurting. But vastly talented."

The process could be excruciating with Robbins, many colleagues agreed, but the end result was usually worth the torture. Though Sondheim concurred that Robbins could be "an awful man," he added, "Some of his invention rubs off on you. You get more inventive when you work with Jerome Robbins."

Robbins's tenacity kept the *West Side Story* project alive during its lulls and lags, at least partly because he viewed the show as an opportunity "to do our best serious work within the context of the popular theater."

If anyone could figure out a way to integrate balletic dance with Elizabethan tragedy and modern angst, it was Robbins. Mused Sondheim, "He had style and substance, but he also knew how to turn it into entertainment, to bridge the gap to the audience. He had a way of dealing with the high and the low and a way of combining them."

Paying tribute to his genius, Susan Stroman (one of many Broadway director-choreographers to claim him as a major influence) reflected that Robbins was all about "making it believable" that characters would burst into dance. In *West Side Story,* he also made damn certain they had good reason to sing, and love, and laugh, and kill, and mourn.

From his brief stint in Hollywood restaging for film "The Small House of Uncle Thomas" number he choreographed for Broadway's *The King and I,* Robbins absorbed lessons on how to make a dramatic narrative fluid. There would be barely a wasted moment in *West Side Story,* no pockets of the "dead time" that plagued many a Broadway musical of that period, even the best. It grabs you in the *kishkas* (Yiddish slang for "gut") and doesn't let go.

Transitions between scenes weren't executed with the drop of a curtain or an operatic pause. Each episode just seemed to flow effortlessly into the next. When Maria twirls around as she models her new party dress in the bridal shop, her motion and the music whirl us into the dance at the gym, instantly evoked with a fierce shift of music, lighting changes, and a thicket of festive-colored streamers dropping from the rafters.

How Robbins dreamed up the latter effect exemplifies his open-ended ingenuity. "I happened to turn my back as they were flying in the gym set," he remembered, "which had streamers at the corners. By turning my head at the fortunate moment, I saw those streamers come down. I ran to [set designer Oliver Smith] and asked him, 'Can we make a whole curtain of that,' which we did. Without that accident happening . . . I don't think that transition going into the gym would have been half as good. You always have to keep your eyes open for the mistakes, because they can be great."

Robbins's unyielding obsession was to make *every single moment* of the show meaningful, and to make *every stage action* an expression of character. Sondheim recalls Robbins gruffly interrogating him about what Tony would be *doing* while singing the love ballad "Maria." Robbins could not bear the idea of theatrical stasis, so if Tony was going to just stand there and sing, he made sure the scenery danced around him.

Robbins's theatrical acumen came from an exhaustive work ethic and teeming imagination, and from scrupulous craft, observation, and intensive experience. He had hoofed in Broadway choruses and been a featured dancer with the touring Ballet Theatre (later renamed American Ballet Theatre). The brilliant and exacting George Balanchine, one of his primary mentors, saw his potential and encouraged him to branch out into choreography, and invited him to do so with Balanchine's new company, the New York City Ballet. He also fanned Robbins's theatrical aspirations by setting an example: Balanchine was one of the first esteemed classical choreographers to successfully straddle the worlds of classical ballet, Broadway, and Hollywood film. And he pioneered the use of extended story-dance sequences onstage and onscreen in the musicals *On Your Toes* and *The Goldwyn Follies.* Though NYCB would remain a lifelong artistic haven for Robbins, it could not contain him. By 1944 he was also bringing buoyantly accessible modern American dance to Broadway in his and Bernstein's *On the Town,* an outgrowth and expansion of their ballet *Fancy Free.* And by the late 1940s, Robbins had won a Tony Award for choreographing the show *High Button Shoes* and was looked upon as a new-guard wunderkind in musical-theater circles.

Robbins's grounding in popular musical theater, under the tutelage of top producer-director George Abbott and others, groomed him to be one of Broadway's next big hitmakers (and a sought-after behind-the-scenes show doctor).

But he was never content with the conventions of the standard Broadway musical-comedy crowd-pleaser, even though he mastered them handily as director of hits like *Peter Pan* and *The Pajama Game.*

Everything else Robbins believed about what a Broadway musical *could* be at its most daring, everything he wanted to make possible in a commercial stage format, he invested in *West Side Story.* Achieving what he envisioned, he later said, forced him to reach "far beyond myself."

Of course, Robbins wasn't a one-man band. For *West Side Story* he relied on his co-creators and a loyal retinue of trusted, gifted associates, most prominently his assistant director Gerald Freedman and assistant choreographer Peter Gennaro. Laurents has said the double-burdened Robbins also consulted with him on some of the staging and had him work with the cast as needed.

But the rehearsal hall was largely Robbins's fiefdom—a realm where, according to Tony Mordente (the original A-Rab), "He is the commander, he is the president, he is God." And as God (or Big Daddy, as some performers called him in amusement, respect, and fear), Robbins set mile-high standards for his chosen people—and expected from them a total submission to his will.

AUDITIONS AND CASTING

Up to this point, roles in Broadway musicals were usually cast according to individual skill set. A dancing chorus handled the dance numbers. The members of the singing chorus would often be given bit speaking parts and provide background hubbub. The leads tended to be singer-actors who might dance a little—or in rare cases like Fred Astaire and Gene Kelly, great dancers who could also croon a tune.

The formula changed with *West Side Story.* Robbins sought triple threats for the Jets and Sharks roles—highly athletic dancers who could act with conviction, sing a high-ranging score, and move with demonic speed, savvy, and grace. Ideal would be a multiethnic cast of "unknowns" who weren't yet old enough to vote but had the technique and stamina to tough out an exacting regimen.

No wonder the casting process took six months to complete and was, according to Bernstein, "the hardest show to cast I've ever heard of." Along with Freedman and assistant stage manager Kenneth Le Roy, Robbins spread his net wide. He scouted ballet academies and amateur teen haunts, held vast open calls, visited settlement house programs and high schools in search of raw, exceptional, malleable talent.

"[The] characters had to be able to not only sing but dance and act and be taken for teenagers," noted Bernstein. "Ultimately, some of the cast were teenagers, some were twenty-one, some were thirty but looked sixteen. Some were wonderful singers but couldn't dance very well, or vice versa . . . and if they could do both, they couldn't act."

There were other priorities set that added to the difficulties. The dancers should not look or move like ballet dancers, despite the difficulty of the choreography. Why?

Peter Boal, one of Robbins's favorite NYCB lead dancers in the 1990s, who added the *West Side Story Suite* to the repertoire of the Pacific Northwest Ballet when he became its artistic director, pointed out in an interview with the author that ballet and show dancing were miles apart aesthetically at the time.

"I think ballet dancers were a different breed in the 1950s," he suggested. "They were very proper, the movements were different. Like shoulder movements—in ballet your shoulders are down and still, not up and agitated. And there was a type of acting in classical ballet, in a traditional 'Swan Lake' or 'Sleeping Beauty,' that was quite formal. Jerry helped change that."

Bernstein and Robbins faced a similar problem in seeking highly skilled singers for the main roles who didn't sound like they were opera soloists. Opera singers were then like thoroughbreds groomed and prized for one asset: their arduously trained, bedazzling vocal abilities. Their pear-shaped tones and supported high notes were richer, heavier, more studied than the way musical-theater singers sounded, particularly when cast as ghetto teens blurting out their ardor and anguish. The ability to believably act a role was, more or less, optional at the Metropolitan Opera in those days—and it certainly was *not* optional in *West Side Story.*

By the same token, Maria and Tony each had vocal assignments nearly as demanding as those for many opera roles. The vocal range, especially for Tony, was one of the broadest ever required of a Broadway leading man in a non-opera/operetta. And Maria had to reach her sky-high notes naturally, without audible strain. The choral segments were also tricky, with their cross-hatched rhythms, contrapuntal passages, and off-kilter harmonies.

So the hunt was on for diamonds in the rough. "We tried nearly all the young actors you see in television shows about juveniles making them cha-cha and mambo as they read the lines." Robbins told the *New York Times.* "But generally they lacked the kinetic physical energy, the ability to move, that dancers have."

Bernstein's surviving audition notes contain pithy comments on tryouts by such Tony wannabes as Warren Beatty ("Good voice—can't open his jaw—charming as hell") and Jerry Orbach ("Good read. Good loud baritone"), and for Maria candidates including starlet Suzanne Pleshette ("Hoarse").

In the end, there were inevitable compromises as the ideal gave way to the practical and the start of rehearsals loomed. Most of those finally chosen were theater professionals, many with some experience as Broadway choristers, and "gypsies" (show dancers). Despite the best intentions and combined efforts of Robbins and his team, only a few (including two Puerto Rican performers: Chita Rivera, the original Anita, and Sharks member Jamie Sanchez) were Hispanic. (Since there were few training and work opportunities for Latinos in this realm, few had the qualifications.)

Though the emphasis was on securing very young performers, hopefully teenagers, the median age in the original cast was in the mid-to-late twenties. Laurents recalled that during twenty-four-year-old Carol Lawrence's final audition for Maria, "Lenny leaned over and asked me her age. I replied, 'How old is the part?' I mean you just couldn't hold on to that."

Lawrence, a graceful Italian American actor-dancer with the flowing black hair and dark-featured beauty of a classical Madonna, impressed the entire team. (Bernstein's audition note: "Lovely soprano. Not quite Maria. Much realer with accent.") Lawrence reported that she was called back to read and sing for the role *thirteen times*—and tried to look "as young as possible" at every audition. During her first audience with Robbins, she came in heavily made up. He ordered her to go home and return makeup-free. (Lawrence claimed her experience helped trigger a new rule by Actors' Equity Union that specified producers could not audition a performer more than three times without compensating for their time.)

For Tony, the creators sought a tall, blond singer-actor who could pass for a gentile of Polish background. But after auditioning him for Bernardo and Riff, they made the smart decision to ask Lawrence ("Larry") Kert (a veteran Broadway chorus boy and buddy of Chita Rivera (and a dark-haired Jew) to have a go at Tony. After a tense month of auditions and rejections, the handsome pro, a flexible high-baritone who could also dance, was asked to come in once again, this time with Lawrence. Unbeknownst to Kert, Robbins made Lawrence hide in a high alcove in the back of the stage, out of sight, before the actor came in. Robbins asked him to sing "Maria," while hunting around to discover where Lawrence was hiding. (There was some Method to this madness, because in the show Tony "finds" Maria hiding in plain sight at the dance, and he later locates her apartment balcony almost by instinct.)

In a 1987 National Public Radio interview, Kert explained that he was searching around the darkened stage for Lawrence when she whispered to him from her perch, "'Quick come up!' So, I see a spiral staircase and a pole going up the middle—and I figure the quickest way to get up there is to shimmy up that pole." After that athletic feat, remembered Lawrence, "We did [the balcony scene] breathlessly, and sang ["Tonight"]—held each other, kissed. . . . it was pin-drop silence, and then they all stood up and applauded." The coveted leading roles, finally, were theirs.

The highlighted role of Anita went to the dynamic Chita Rivera (born Dolores Conchita Figueroa del Rivero in Washington, D.C.), who, then age twenty-four, had paid her dues with featured dancing roles in *Call Me Madam, Guys and Dolls, Can-Can*, and other big Broadway shows. This would not be the first time Rivera played a Latin firebrand, but it would be her first portrayal of someone of her own heritage.

Mickey Calin (born Calienoff, and in the 1960s changed to Callan) was a good-looking kid of twenty-one who had only been in a couple Broadway shows (most notably, *The Boyfriend*) before scoring the part of Riff. And the dashing role of Bernardo went, rather unexpectedly, to Ken Le Roy. From a family of performers and a veteran of small parts in many musicals (including the Robbins-staged *The Pajama Game*), Le Roy signed on as assistant stage manager for *West Side Story* but was later encouraged to audition for and accept the role of the Sharks leader, when no one else seemed quite right for it.

The audition process could also be extraordinary for those in the smallest parts. Because there were no throwaway choral roles in *West Side Story*, and every second of stage time mattered, every character was cast very scrupulously. Martin Charnin, trying out at the end of the process for one of the Jets parts, had an audition experience that lasted just one day—but an extraordinary day he recalled in detail to this author fifty years later.

In the summer of 1957, Charnin (the future writer-director of the Tony-winning Broadway musical *Annie,* among other shows) spotted a *New York Times* item reporting that Robbins had almost completed casting for *West Side Story* but "was two Jets shy." On a whim, the twenty-two-year-old recent college grad, who had scant acting or theatrical experience and was new to New York, showed up at an open call the next morning on a lark. "I got into my tightest pair of jeans, rolled a pack of Lucky Strikes in my t-shirt sleeve and tried to look as much like James Dean as I could," he recalled. Then he joined an estimated 2,000 other Jets candidates, all of them trying to look cool and punky, waiting in line in a Broadway theater alley. Based only on appearance, the crowd was quickly cut down to 200 men, then 20, with Charnin still in the running.

The hopefuls then had to run through quite a challenge. Charnin described first walking across the lobby so assistant choreographer Peter Gennaro could see how he moved. (The roles in question did not involve much dancing, so he wasn't required to perform any specific steps.) Next Charnin was led into the theater to read lines from the script, for Laurents. (Taking the role of Big Deal, Charnin was pleased to get a chuckle out of the author.)

He was then brought to Sondheim, to sing a show tune he'd prepared, the Richard Rodgers–Lorenz Hart number "I Wish I Were in Love Again." Remembered Charnin, "Steve made me sing it a second time, but faster. He raced me through it, and I later found out he wanted me to sing in 'Gee, Office Krupke,' which has a mile-a-minute lyric. So he wanted to see if I could articulate well."

Another singing audition, for Bernstein, followed. Finally, "at about 11 p.m. at night, there were just a few of us, and we met Jerry [Robbins] for the first time. He asked us to do one thing: snap our fingers. I was a good, loud snapper. I didn't even have to wet my fingers."

And that was it. To Charnin's amazement, he was one of the two out of two thousand to be hired, and "we went upstairs, signed a union contract for $265 a week, which got me into Actors Equity, and I was in 'West Side

Story' for the next two years. I didn't know very much at that point, but I know now that the audition was very unusual. There's never been another like it, before or since."

REHEARSALS

To be in *West Side Story* meant much more than learning and executing songs, steps, and lines proficiently. It meant doing things no chorus boys or gals had been required to do in the past and would later be expected to do as a matter of course on some occasions.

It meant writing a full biography for your character, then continually expanding and elaborating on it (a common Method acting technique). Being in *West Side Story* also meant interviewing Puerto Ricans and studying their accents (if you were a Shark), and researching delinquency. It meant reading the clippings Robbins posted on a bulletin board, to stay aware of the outbreaks of gang violence around New York City.

It also meant opening your eyes to what was right in your own neighborhood. Grover Dale, the original Jets member Snowboy, lived on the Upper West Side, on a block that "was one of the most gang-infested areas in New York," he later explained. "You could recognize the gang members just by the way they would look at you, and if you were smart you looked straight ahead, and just walked past, hoping that you didn't get a kick in the butt or worse."

On August 29, 1959, the extremes of that reality hit very close to home. Within hours after the curtain rang down on a performance of *West Side Story* at the Broadway Theatre, a sixteen-year-old Puerto Rican immigrant and member of the vicious Vampires street gang, named Salvador Agron, went to a nearby Hell's Kitchen playground for a rumble with a rival crew. There he stabbed two white male youths, innocent bystanders who were strolling together in the wrong place at the wrong moment. Agron was dubbed the Capeman by the press, because he was wearing a black, crimson-lined cape that night.

The shocking story of his crime, his lack of repentance and background of crushing poverty and childhood abandonment, was splashed all over the news in the days and weeks to come. (Years later, Agron was the subject of a short-lived Broadway musical by pop star Paul Simon, titled *The Capeman*.) Rivera recalled that on the cast blackboard of the rehearsal hall, Robbins pinned "a full page [news] photo of this handsome young man with a black cape. I believe it was a knife in his hand and a body under his foot."

Robbins scrawled on the press clipping, "This is your life"—a clear instruction to the cast to identify with Agron and boys like him. "It just grabbed us around the throat," according to Rivera. "Me being Puerto Rican—I mean, we were all aware of gangs and things, but we didn't live those lives. It smacked us right between the eyes."

In addition to crawling into the social circumstances and ids of their characters, the performers had to answer to four very engaged bosses and submit to the extreme acting boot camp run by master drill sergeant Robbins. They were the raw clay he molded, in a thorough and often grueling process of discovery and inspiration, trial and error—a regimen that tested everyone mightily but also stretched their talents and endurance skills to the max.

At the beginning, Lawrence remembered, "We broke a lot of [union] rules. A month before rehearsals began, [assistant director] Gerry Freedman took the principals . . . to this tiny little garret, so hot I can't tell you, for no pay at all, eight hours a day, and we would dissect the characters, talk for hours about why they did the things they did."

Reported Tom Abbott, who played Gee-Tar, in a 1984 interview, "None of us knew what we were getting into. Rehearsals were intense—you wouldn't associate with a member of the opposite gang. Our notice board was full of news clippings about street fights, muggings, gangs, rumbles, police."

David Winters, the baby-faced actor who played Baby John, told the tribute website davidwinters.net that Robbins once punished some cast members who were tardy for a rehearsal by making them do rolling moves on a floor with treacherous splinters of wood and exposed nails all over it—knowing full well the pain it would cause them. And others tell a story (which has many variations) about Robbins walking backward onstage during a rehearsal, unaware that he was about to tumble into the orchestra pit—and no one saying a word to alert him before he did.

Experienced and highly disciplined dancers in the show like Rivera were most inclined to idolize Robbins and readily tolerate his exacting standards, perfectionism, and withering criticism—which were less of a shock in the more physically unforgiving, hierarchical dance world than in the Broadway trenches. Robbins spoke their language, he was a fine dancer himself, and at thirty-nine he was still fit and flexible enough to execute his complex choreography right alongside them, which won him additional respect. (In a famous movie-rehearsal photo, he demonstrates a high, tennis shoe–en pointe side kick from "The Prologue" alongside some of the Sharks, a pose that became a visual emblem of *West Side Story*.)

But it was the acting dimension that most excited, and worried, the performers who were primarily dancers. Rivera had never been asked to "be a person" onstage before, rather than a type, and found it "a thrilling thing." It was also terrifying, she told *The Sondheim Review*. "People always ask, 'How did it feel? Did you know that it was going to be such a huge hit?' Well, we knew nothing. None of us realized what was going on because we were so busy. And so every day was another challenge for us."

Those who came in with more of an acting background may have respected their maestro's prodigious talent, but some received a daily battering they did not anticipate and never forgot. "Rehearsals were a very painful experience," Kert recounted. He described Robbins as "a perfectionist, who sees himself in every role, and if you come onstage and don't give him exactly what he's pictured the night before, his tolerance level is too low, so in his own way he kind of destroys you."

Mordente was a Robbins ally and favorite but confirmed that the director put Kert, Calin, and others he picked on often through the wringer. "Jerry not only attacked you, he attacked your family, your background, where you lived, how you lived, who you studied with," Mordente said. "He never stopped." But his decrees and threats (unhappy with Calin, he made sure the actor heard auditions for his possible replacement taking place in a nearby room) spurred people on to give their all. Recalled Dale, "Every dancer in the cast competed for [Robbins's] approval. A few did it well. Most fell flat on their faces. Little did we know how rarely he gave it . . . even to himself."

The much-abused Calin expressed gratitude to Robbins years later. "Even when he yelled at me, I liked the man, because I believed he was doing it for a reason, to make the show the best," he told Robbins biographer Amanda Vaill. "I don't know whether he cared about me or the kids . . . the show was the thing with him."

Only an artist of Robbins's caliber and status could get away with such abusive treatment—and with ordering Prince to supply three rehearsal pianists (he had to settle for two), terrorizing his collaborators on occasion and constantly second-guessing himself to try a dozen or more variations of a few measures of a dance, before torturously settling on one.

Observed Boal, "When you worked with Jerry there was always an A, B, C and D version, and an A-3, a D-4 and so on. For Jerry it was always about the work, how the work looked. It wasn't about you, or your feelings. And he could smell your fear, and use it against you."

Lawrence considered him a tyrant in rehearsal (though "warm, thoughtful and generous" in social situations). In one of her war stories, she recalled that Robbins urged her to hit Kert harder and harder on the chest in the moment when Maria expresses her range at Tony because he murdered her brother Bernardo. Finally, Kert was so battered that a doctor who examined his bruised ribs insisted he take no more punishment. Robbins's reaction? "'Hit him in the head, you can't do any damage there,'" reported Lawrence. "He wasn't joking."

Though horrified by such tactics, Lawrence knew the director's constant admonishments to "literally become our roles" was for the good of the piece. In this vein, he demanded that the gulf and animosity between Sharks and Jets be maintained at all times—on- and offstage. "I thought it was pretentious," noted Sondheim, "but of course it was perfect . . . there was a sense of each gang having its own individuality, so that you had two giant personalities onstage."

Anecdotes abound of Jets and Sharks being ordered to eat lunch separately, to not fraternize socially, to cultivate a foaming animosity that grew more toxic by the week. "It was strange, both 'sides' were working on a common project but from two complete different points of view, and a lot of the hate between Jets and Sharks during rehearsal was authentic," observed Abbott. "We found things out about ourselves: we were prejudiced, bigoted. If you stripped off the civilized veneer, there was a sort of barbaric feeling underneath."

But not everyone carried it to the extremes their director encouraged. According to Charnin, few took the edict to not fraternize with the "enemy" literally, and there was plenty of the usual Broadway-after-hours kibitzing and pub hopping by the Sharks and Jets together. Mordente and Rivera even managed to fall in love and become engaged across turf lines. They married during the show's run, and according to Rivera, "Jerry loved it. He gave us our wedding dinner." But according to Mordente, after he started secretly dating Rivera, "the other Jets didn't speak to me for a week."

Some of the intensity in the process came from Robbins trying out the ideas he was picking up in scene-analysis classes with the commandingly authoritative Method acting teacher Stella Adler. She was, he admitted, one of the rare people who could intimidate him in an artistic context. In a letter to his dear friend, former New York City Ballet dancer Tanaquil Le Clercq, he described the onetime Group Theatre leading lady and longtime acting guru as "crazy and wonderful. She's really madly inspiring or maybe it's just inspired madness, and makes what hair I have stand on end."

But to some his use of the Method verged close to madness. Lawrence has compared Robbins's extreme Method techniques to William Golding's Darwinian allegory *Lord of the Flies,* where young boys left to their own devices descend into barbarism. According to her, "We human, civilized actors were becoming the hate-filled, violent street gangs we were portraying. If you think onstage was exciting, it didn't compare to backstage! Sharks and Jets lived! Violence and sexual intimidations, fights and injuries, you name it."

The sense of realism could push everyone to the edge. When the Jets were encouraged to pull out the stops in the terrorizing attempted rape of Anita, Rivera found the verbal and physical assault "overwhelming" in rehearsal—though her castmates hastened to comfort the beloved performer when she broke down crying.

In another instance, during a rehearsal of "A Boy Like That," in which a venomous Anita urges Maria to give up Tony, Freedman told Rivera to imagine how she'd feel if Tony had killed one of her own brothers. "So I started singing and all of a sudden the song hit me, it hit me right between the eyes and I couldn't stop crying . . . And I kept backing out of the room because I was being exposed. If I had known I was going to be exposed, I wouldn't have minded, but it was such a shock to suddenly connect with my soul, my deep feelings. And when he finally said, 'That's it!,' I was up against the wall, up against the door almost, exiting the room. It was an amazing moment."

The question of whether Robbins took more than his (justifiably large) fair share of credit for the success of *West Side Story* is another point of controversy that arose as the show was being fleshed out in rehearsal. His collaborators were stunned and upset when they learned he'd separately negotiated a line under the title on the program: "Based on a Conception by Jerome Robbins." Though by all accounts Robbins had the initial idea for a contemporary urban musical based on *Romeo and Juliet,* no one disputes that Laurents and Bernstein came up with the Latin-versus-Anglo gang theme during that famous Beverly Hills poolside chat. And without that, *West Side Story* might never have happened.

Another credit line, "Entire Production Directed and Choreographed by Jerome Robbins," raised the pesky question of whether Gennaro, who all agree was put in charge of devising the Latin-style dances in *West Side Story,* was not given his due. Robbins made Gennaro sign a contract with him that explicitly stated all the choreography would "belong to me exclusively, and you hereby assign to me, any and all rights in and to any and all choreographic material created or suggested by you" for the show.

Lawrence later suggested that Robbins "stole from Peter Gennaro, he stole the knowledge that Gerry Freedman had of acting, and then he took credit for it. I'm sorry, for that I do not appreciate him or respect him at all." But Gennaro, when asked about it in interviews, never complained about the arrangement. And others saw the dances he worked on as more of a collaboration, given Robbins's penchant for constantly tinkering with every number and his determination to refine the choreography in future revivals of *West Side Story.*

In the end, every move in the show had Robbins's aesthetic sensibility imprinted on it. Sondheim told Robbins biographer Greg Lawrence that "America" wasn't quite right in rehearsal until "Jerry got his hands on it, and reshaped it and suddenly the number worked." In Laurents's view, "All Peter's work in 'West Side Story' sparkled but it was Jerry who pulled it into the style of the show and made it dazzle. A little change here; a small addition there; an attitude made specific where it had been general; the structuring of a number like a play."

During the Dramatists Guild symposium, Robbins gratefully and publicly acknowledged that Gennaro "did most of 'America' and the Sharks' dances in the dance hall competition and he was very supportive all the way through."

As for Freedman, he felt Robbins's extraordinary billing was well deserved. "Jerry's vision was very, very clear," he told Lawrence. "And I think conceived, choreographed and directed by, is absolutely apt."

This seems to typify Robbins's complicated relations with colleagues. They have described him as cruel to the point of lip-smacking sadism, maddening, egomaniacal, yet they acknowledge he could also be generous, warm, childlike, and above all, inspirational in his tireless drive to draw the best from himself and his colleagues, to create theatrical art of power and beauty.

That's not to downplay such distressing instances like the time, in Washington D.C., when Robbins marched down to the conductor's podium during the dress rehearsal and demanded a change of tempo in a number that was already set by Bernstein and his arrangers—a bruising, humiliating breach of theatrical protocol that sent the conflict-averse Bernstein racing to the nearest bar to drown his anguish, according to Sondheim.

Yet in PBS's *Something to Dance About* documentary on Robbins, Sondheim also termed his colleague "the only genius I ever met. Genius is a word people sling around, but my understanding of that word is endless invention—and Jerry had that." And so did *West Side Story*.

Theatre and Film Designs

Courtesy of Photofest.

WEST SIDE STORY DESIGN MAGIC

The production designs for the original *West Side Story* were inventive, beautifully executed, and integral to the impact of the musical. They also placed the story within a vivid environment, but without stealing focus away from the performers.

Robbins wanted a vision of dilapidated slum realism that wasn't so literal it blotted out the mythic aspect of the piece.

For the settings, he went to leading ballet and theatrical designer Oliver

Smith. Smith had worked frequently with Robbins (on *Billion Dollar Baby, High Button Shoes, On the Town*) and also designed Bernstein's *Candide*. In addition, he created the settings for scores of other Broadway shows, including *My Fair Lady, Brigadoon,* and *The Sound of Music,* as well as designing many ballets (including Robbins's *Fancy Free*) and numerous hit movie musicals, among them *Oklahoma!* and *My Fair Lady.*

Prolific and gentlemanly, Smith received ten Tony Awards (including one of the two bestowed on *West Side Story*) and one Oscar nomination (for his design of *Guys and Dolls*) during his lengthy career and was nominated for twenty-five Tonys altogether.

As Keith Garebian noted in *The Making of West Side Story,* for this assignment Smith had to conjure an urban milieu that was "both a jungle of brick, concrete, and steel and a micro-cosmic paradise of romantic neon and gaudy streamers."

Smith conceived the *West Side Story* sets as a series of sketches as well as paintings, and (unusually for him) with miniature models, in a style Laurents at first disparaged as "polarized between stunning and scabby." (Laurents later came to appreciate and compliment Smith's work on the show.)

For the architectural elements of the show, Smith devised semi-abstract set pieces that moved on and off to music, as fluidly as the dancers did— Maria's suspended fire-escape balcony (which also figured in the show's promotional designs); a humble beauty shop that gave way to a loudly colorful community center gym; a shabby drugstore/soda fountain.

Some of his beautifully rendered designs are preserved in the Leonard Bernstein Collection at the Library of Congress, including painted backdrops for "The Rumble" (a view from under the Manhattan Bridge, with an ominously dark, cloudy sky) and for the "Somewhere" ballet (an idyllic landscape of sea and sky, with a distant view of Manhattan's skyline).

His use of chain-link fence in "The Rumble" (it was a crucial element in Robbins's choreography for the scene) and some of his other striking effects were repeated subsequently in thousands of *West Side Story* productions— including the fire escape, and those bright-colored ribbon streamers that drop down to begin "The Dance at the Gym."

This show eliminated the traditional drop curtain that hid set changes, in favor of using highly mobile structures that could be whisked on and off without any masking. The smooth progression of the piece was furthered by the creative "light-all-around" effects of Jean Rosenthal, an iconoclastic Broadway lighting genius whose designs helped to maintain a whirling, cinematic pace throughout the show while enhancing the sets and costumes.

Rosenthal's use of shadows and multidirectional lighting, and her avoidance of harsh overhead illumination, was so unconventional it at first sparked some skepticism from the *West Side Story* team. But the designer, whose many achievements included a long artistic association with dancer-choreographer Martha Graham, had also worked before with Robbins and was trusted by him.

She was especially sensitive to the lighting needs of dancers. "Dancers live in light as fish live in water," she wrote in her book *The Magic of Light*. "The stage space in which they move is their aquarium, their portion of the sea. Within translucent walls and above the stage floor, the lighting supports their flashing buoyancy or their arrested sculptural bodies. The dance is fluid and never static, as natural light is fluid and never static."

Robbins also had great faith in his choice of costume designer, Irene Sharaff. Admired at the time mainly for her prodigious work in Hollywood, including her Oscar-honored costuming of *An American in Paris* and ornate Oriental apparel for *The King and I*, Sharaff was also a respected theater hand who had been designing Broadway shows since the 1930s. But Harold Prince fretted that she would be too rich for the blood (and budget) of *West Side Story*.

However, the glamorous Sharaff kept to her modest budget of $65,000, outfitting the show with bright, snazzy party dresses, juvenile athletic jackets, and other theatrical versions of trendy teen duds, in a color palette worked out with Robbins of "muted indigo, blues, ochre and musty yellows" for the Jets, and "sharp purple, pink-violet, blood red, and black" for the Sharks. She also insisted on clothing the gang boys in "distressed" jeans made of a specially treated and dyed fabric to accommodate the exertions of their dancing—an expenditure of $75 per pair (about $600 today), which despite Prince's sticker shock was worth every penny.

Prince wrote later that he first tried to substitute made-to-wear Levi's but realized the pants Sharaff designed were dyed and re-dyed "in forty subtly different shades of blue, vibrating, energetic, creating the *effect* of realism."

She was well ahead of her time: gang colors would become increasingly meaningful to tough young crews in the 1980s and 1990s. And ripped, splotched, and otherwise distressed Levi's would eventually become all the rage—marketing retail, at the top-of-the-line, for hundreds of dollars a pair.

JEROME ROBBINS BIO

Jerome Robbins was born Jerome Wilson Rabinowitz on October 11, 1918, in New York City, to Russian Jewish immigrants Herschel ("Harry") Rabinowitz and Lena Rips Rabinowitz. The family soon moved to New Jersey, where young Jerry's father and uncles ran a corset factory.

As a child Robbins demonstrated an aptitude for dance and theater. After high school, his college studies in chemistry were derailed by the Great Depression. He took the chance to study ballet and seek a performing career, and soon found work as a dancer in New York's Yiddish theaters, in revues at Jewish resorts, in summer stock, and in the choruses of several Broadway shows.

In 1940, Robbins was accepted into the newly formed Ballet Theatre (later known as the American Ballet Theatre), where he gained notoriety for his standout appearances in works by Agnes de Mille, George Balanchine, and other major choreographers.

With Balanchine's encouragement, Robbins branched into choreography himself and in 1944 had great success with *Fancy Free,* his entertaining and innovative ballet about a trio of sailors on leave, set to music by Leonard Bernstein. Later that year the piece was expanded into a hit Broadway musical, scored by Bernstein with book and lyrics by Betty Comden and Adolph Green. The dances were again by Robbins, but the show was directed by legendary Broadway hitmaker George Abbott.

With Abbott as mentor and co-director, in 1948 Robbins staged his modestly successful autobiographical musical *Look, Ma, I'm Dancin',* then went on to choreograph and/or direct such 1950s hits as *Call Me Madam, Peter Pan, The Pajama Game,* and *Bells Are Ringing* and to become a coveted behind-the-scenes "show doctor" who could help whip a sagging Broadway tuner into shape.

Robbins maintained his place in the ballet world also. In 1949 he joined Balanchine's New York City Ballet and made dances for the company throughout the rest of his life. He also ran his own touring dance company, Ballets U.S.A., from 1958 to 1962. After staging and choreographing *West Side Story,* Robbins co-directed the film version of his theatrical masterwork with Robert Wise.

Robbins's magic touch as a choreographer/director brought him further acclaim for the musicals *Gypsy* (1959), *Fiddler on the Roof* (1964) and the lauded anthology show based on numbers from his previous Broadway productions, *Jerome Robbins' Broadway* (1989).

After *Fiddler,* Robbins devoted most of his creative energies to the NYCB (where he assumed the title of "ballet master"), for which he created such landmark ballets as *Les Noces, Dances at a Gathering, In the Night*, and *Dybbuk.*

Robbins died at home in New York, as the result of a stroke, on July 29, 1998. His many prestigious prizes include five Tony Awards, two Academy Awards, an Emmy Award, a Kennedy Center Honor, and the title of Chevalier of the French Legion of Honor.

The cast making glorious music with Stephen Sondheim at the piano and Leonard Bernstein conducting. Courtesy of the New York Public Library for the Performing Arts, ©Billy Rose Theatre Division.

5

THE MOST BEAUTIFUL SOUND I EVER HEARD
THE MUSIC AND LYRICS OF *WEST SIDE STORY*

I f the book for *West Side Story* is the show's bone structure, and the dancing is its pulsating heart, the music is the soul of the show.

West Side Story is one of very few American musical scores that has approached the sweep and aspirations of George and Ira Gershwin's landmark Broadway jazz-folk opera *Porgy and Bess.* The latter was a revelation in its exploration of African American musical traditions (blues, gospel, jazz, work songs) in an indigenous dramatic setting (Charleston's Catfish Row), and in its bridging of symphonic, opera, and popular music idioms.

It is difficult to imagine a *West Side Story* had there not been the synthesis of drama and serious music on Broadway in *Porgy and Bess,* a work both Stephen Sondheim and Leonard Bernstein were influenced by and cherished. (Sondheim called it "the most rewarding music ever written for the American musical theater, the best—and it was never a success." And Bernstein commented, in his book *The Joy of Music,* that "with 'Porgy' you suddenly realize Gershwin was a great, great theater composer.")

Yet while Bernstein's musical landscape for *West Side Story* was influenced by Gershwin, Aaron Copland, and other composers, it is not a carbon copy of anything. It has its own thrilling, many-layered uniqueness and was far more musically adventuresome than other Broadway musicals of its day.

The score is distinguished by its dramatic and dance-driven urgency and its broad sonic palette of musical modes (from Wagnerian leitmotifs to Latin dance music to big-band blues and American avant-garde music). It constantly, restlessly shifts rhythms and keys and confounds the then-circumscribed categories of "show music" and "longhair music" with agility. And just as Laurents came up with his own lingo for the Jets rather than overburden them with contemporary slang, Bernstein incorporated some musical trends of the day (mainly Latin American dance rhythms) while bypassing rock-and-roll (which at that pre-Beatles phase was still in its rustic infancy).

The *West Side Story* score sweeps, jolts, and jazzes the story along. Songs open into other songs. The music speaks from the deepest recesses of the characters—from their adolescent fears, vulnerabilities, arrogance, romanticism, hostility, and confusion.

Though not the "goddamn opera" Laurents feared it might become, Bernstein's sophisticated score demands superior vocal and instrumental performances. And for the most part it is all of a piece, in its recurrent motifs and foreshadowing devices, its surges and self-references. Discussing the three-note tritone device that is repeated in "The Jet Song," "Cool," "Maria," and some instrumental passages of *West Side Story,* Scott Miller wrote, "What makes the score so remarkable is that Bernstein can use this interval and this melody fragment so frequently and yet so subtly, giving the score great unity without being boring or monotonous."

For a show that spun off numerous standards, *West Side Story* also shares with *Porgy and Bess* the rare attribute of being a Broadway work beloved and recognizable for some of its orchestral passages, as well as its tunes—starting with the instantly recognizable opening bars of "The Prologue."

The lyrics are also a lasting (and sometimes underrated) achievement. Sondheim has been his own harshest critic of some of the words he set to Bernstein's music (and the scattering that the composer, who began their collaboration as a co-lyricist, supplied). But if he winces at every alleged clinker, much of Sondheim's writing is appreciated by colleagues, fans, and critics for its bite, verve, and romantic expressiveness, and its fidelity to Laurents's supple scenario and Bernstein's intoxicating melodies.

Of course, not every measure of the *West Side Story* score is fresh or masterful. The "Somewhere" Ballet, for instance, is glaringly derivative of

Copland. There are indeed a few clumsy or mawkish lyrics here and there, mostly in the romantic ballads. But overwhelmingly, the score is a treasure—a gift that yields up new pleasures and discoveries on a fifth or fiftieth hearing.

WHEN BERNSTEIN MET SONDHEIM

In 1949, when his friend and *On the Town* cohort Jerome Robbins first came up with an idea for a contemporized *Romeo and Juliet* musical, Bernstein was already riding a first wave of prolific creativity and success as a leading conductor, ambitious composer, and musical educator.

From his early twenties, Bernstein had been on a fast-track path to his goal of becoming a genuine Renaissance man of American music. His flamboyance at the podium excited audiences (and cameramen). His capacious knowledge and appreciation of "serious" and popular music won him the respect of musicians in both camps and contributed to the cultural education of the nation. But Bernstein wanted to be a great composer, too. And some colleagues have remarked that there was often a conflict and tension in his compositional work between emulating the "serious" opera and orchestral music of his canonized forbears (i.e., Wagner, Mahler, Beethoven) and the modern canonical composers he admired (i.e., Copland, Igor Stravinsky, Paul Hindemith), and then mining the zest and pungency of the show tunes, pop songs, blues, and modern jazz sounds he also loved. (As a college student, under the name "Lenny Amber," Bernstein earned money arranging tunes and transcribing jazz solos for the music publisher Harms, Inc.)

"I'm not sure he ever got over those two combating influences in his life," said his daughter Jamie Bernstein in an interview with the author. "Some people would say the tragedy is that he hadn't written four more symphonies. I'd say the opposite—what three other amazing, classic Broadway musicals would he have created?"

Only in *West Side Story* did Bernstein manage to integrate the two halves of his split musical personality, by fully exploiting both. "There are a hundred borrowings in the score," suggested musical-theater scholar Geoffrey Block in an interview with the author. "Bernstein was trying to write very ambitious theater works, and he had absorbed a whole history of contemporary and classical music to draw on."

Another influence on the score (subliminal or conscious), which is pointed out frequently by musicologists, is the Jewish liturgical music Bernstein grew up with as the son of orthodox Russian Jews. The opening three notes of "The Prologue" are particularly striking in this regard, given that those same tones are blown on the ritual shofar (ram's horn) in synagogues, on the High Holy Day of Rosh Hashanah (the Jewish New Year).

When Sondheim came aboard the *West Side Story* team, he was a largely untried Broadway newcomer. Certainly he was the junior partner in the firm. But in a less flashy way, Sondheim was just as creatively and professionally ambitious as his decade-older, far better-known collaborator—and, it appears, a good balance for some of Bernstein's excesses.

Sondheim never considered himself a lyricist alone. And he reiterated in his book *Finishing the Hat* that he always preferred composing music to writing lyrics. He initially worried that if he took on the role of lyricist for *West Side Story,* he'd be trapped in that role. But when the invitation to work with Bernstein, Robbins, and Laurents arrived, his sage advisor Oscar Hammerstein told him to "leap at it."

Sondheim's instincts and technical training as a composer aided his partnership with Bernstein, who told the *New York Times,* "I could explain musical problems to him and he'd understand immediately, which made the collaboration a joy. It was like writing with an alter ego."

Sondheim's adroitness as a wordsmith was the most essential thing he brought to the enterprise, however. In constructing the lyrics, his personal and aesthetic temperament balanced out Bernstein's leanings— just as Bernstein's warm, encouraging tutelage of the cast was an effective counterbalance to Robbins's tough, unyielding, rule-by-fear style.

There were some creative frictions. Sondheim later said he "knew from the start that I was getting into a collaboration with someone whose idea of poetic lyric writing was the antithesis of mine." Bernstein preferred more "noble" sentiments and romantic language, conveyed with the expansive emotionalism commensurate with his own personality. Sondheim by nature was more introverted, cerebral, exacting, and (in the view of Bernstein) a "violently opinioned" person who "suffers all the pains a perfectionist suffers." Sondheim's lyrical style was strictly modern and vernacular. He wanted to avoid all verbal clutter, hyperbole, and cliché, while staying true to story, character, and musical structure.

One can hear the difference between the two men's lyrical approaches in some of the swoonier phrases in "Tonight" ("Tonight there will be no morning star") preferred by Bernstein, versus Sondheim's crisper, more incisive lines in "Cool" ("Boy, boy, crazy boy / Get cool, boy!").

But despite his lasting dissatisfaction with some of what they forged for the show, Sondheim also knew the value of Bernstein's personal generosity and a collaboration he felt was "never for a moment less than exhilarating." (In *Finishing the Hat,* he recalls that at fourteen he got a "rush of excitement" from hearing Bernstein's *On the Town* score for the first time and found it to be "a fresh, individual and complex sound, a new kind of music.")

There were important aesthetic lessons Sondheim would glean from Bernstein, which he would later apply to his own adventuresome theatrical scores. "I had been brought up to think of Broadway songs in terms of four-and-eight bar phrases," he wrote in *Finishing the Hat.*

"Lenny taught me by example to ignore the math. Four bars may be expected, but do you really need them? How about three bars? And why have the same number of beats in every bar? How about varying the meter?"

Bernstein later looked back fondly on their collaboration. "Steve and I worked together in every conceivable way—together, apart, sometimes with the tune first ('Cool' and 'Office Krupke'), sometimes with the words first ('A Boy Like That')."

The two men met in the small, bare studio in Bernstein's otherwise sprawling and glamorous Upper West Side apartment, whenever the overcommitted maestro (who was also composing *Candide* during this period) was able.

While they put in many hours alone together, Sondheim and Bernstein were always members of a four-man team in which everyone had a say about nearly everything. Sondheim particularly appreciated Arthur Laurents's lean and well-plotted book, which he was allowed to freely raid for lyrics. Bernstein noted, "It just would never occur to me write a lyric like, 'A boy like that who'd kill your brother.' That looked like a line of prose to me, but when Steve saw it in Arthur's book, he pulled it immediately."

Sondheim also felt he prospered from Robbins's insistence that every song be rooted in character and stage action. After Robbins barked at him for having no idea what Tony would be *doing* while singing the words to "Maria," Sondheim realized that "to tell a compelling story, there had better be either some stage action or some development in the lyric to keep things moving forward." In the future he would stage every song in a show in his mind before composing the music for it.

Bernstein had a near-mystical creative affinity with Robbins that, had it continued (and had toiling in the theater been less taxing for someone about to lead one of the most prominent symphony orchestras in the world), might have yielded the additional Broadway masterworks his daughter Jamie envisioned. Bernstein frequently recalled to her and others his "tactile feeling" of composing with Robbins standing behind him, hands on his shoulders, saying to him, "'Four more beats there,' or 'No, that's too many,' or 'Yeah, that's it.'" And Robbins spoke in turn about the "enormous excitement" of "the continual flow between us" in their joint creative efforts.

But there was also some artistic frustration on *West Side Story* (possibly exaggerated) on Bernstein's part—and probably some bruised feelings from Laurents's adamant aversion to anything operatic. Reflecting on his "poor little marked up score" in the feverish lead-up to the Washington, D.C., debut, Bernstein lamented in a letter to his wife, "All the things I love most in [the score] are slowly being dropped—too operatic, too this and that. They're all so scared and commercial success means so much to them. To me too, I suppose—but I still insist it can be achieved without a price. I shall keep fighting."

His colleagues have disputed this. Sondheim told Simeone, "Lenny's endless complaint that his score was getting eviscerated because it was too 'operatic'—none of us (Arthur, Jerry, and me) said that, so who made him change things? The record company? Hal [Prince] and Bobby [Griffith]? Never. The songs were changed for the reasons songs should be changed: they were too clumsy, too long-winded, too monotonous, not theatrical, whatever.'" (One can imagine, though, that late in the process frayed nerves may have heightened the sensitivities of Bernstein and everyone else.)

What the performers later recalled about their work with Bernstein was his graciousness, supportive instruction, and openness. "He never lost his temper or his good manners," remembered Carol Lawrence in her memoir. "He didn't drive us: he led us by believing in us. He is one of the gentlest, most thoughtful men I have ever known, and we knocked ourselves out for him because we loved him."

When all elements of the show clicked on opening night in D.C., Bernstein was overjoyed. "I can't believe it," he crowed in his reconstituted *West Side Story* log, "40 kids singing five-part counterpoint who never sang before—and sounding like heaven. I guess we were right not to cast 'singers'; anything that sounded more professional would inevitably sound more experienced and the 'kid' quality would be gone. A perfect example of a disadvantage turned into a virtue."

PUTTING IT TOGETHER

As with all other aspects of *West Side Story,* the score went through many revisions, with numbers added and cut by consensus. When it came to orchestrating the finished work, Bernstein was aided by two highly capable and trusted co-arrangers, Sid Ramin and Irwin Kostal (who would later share an Oscar for orchestrating the film score of *West Side Story*). Though they did an exemplary job, Ramin later stressed that every note in the score was Bernstein's, and if "he'd had the time he wouldn't even need us."

There are some lingering questions as to who wrote which lyrics. But the vast majority were penned by Sondheim—which Bernstein generously acknowledged by giving him a sole lyricist credit for the musical. According to Flora Roberts, Sondheim's agent, "what Lenny did is fairly unheard of in the theater. Too many people get credit for things they don't do, much less remove their names."

Sondheim wrote Bernstein an affectionate note of gratitude for their work together on the day of the Broadway opening—the first Broadway premiere of many ahead for the young man destined to become the Great White Way's most important composer of the next half-century.

"'West Side Story' means more to me than a first show, more even than the privilege of collaborating with you and Arthur and Jerry," penned Sondheim. "It marks the beginning of what I hope will be a long and enduring friendship."

He went on, "I don't think I've ever said to you how fine I think the score is, since I prefer kidding you about the few moments I don't like to praising you for the many I do. 'West Side Story' is a big step, Leonard, for you as it is for Jerry or Arthur or even me, and in an odd way, I feel proud of you. . . . May [it] mean as much to the theater and to people who see it as it has to us."

THE SCORE

Before considering individual components of the score, it is helpful to note certain hallmarks that run throughout it. These include: (1) the frequent use of minor chords; (2) melodies that don't neatly resolve but hang suspended; (3) finger snaps and claps, as prominent percussion elements; (4) driving rhythms from a trove of percussion instruments (including trap drums, xylophone and vibraphone, timbales, and bongos); (5) cross-rhythms that overlap two signatures to create a sense of agitation and unease; (6) swiftly cascading and ascending string lines; (7) jazzy bursts of brass and winds; and (8) Latin accents.

Additionally, there is much foreshadowing and cross-referencing—chord progressions and melodic motifs from one song quoted in another, which help give the score a sense of being cut from whole cloth.

And most remarked upon by musical critics and scholars is the use of the "tritone"—an "unstable" and pungent pair of notes forming an augmented fourth, consisting of two successive notes with three tones between them. In classical harmony, the tritone is a dissonance that demands resolution to a consonant interval. So sharp and unsettling is its dissonant quality that during the Middle Ages it was termed *diabolus in musica,* or the "devil in music," and the sound of a tritone was considered ominous, even heretical, and generally avoided by composers. Modernist composers, however, embraced the device, and in *West Side Story* Bernstein savored the inherent tension of the tritone enough to introduce it into the Broadway musical lexicon.

Bernstein made full and inventive use of his diverse sonic arsenal. The variety of instruments and rhythmic schemes in the score, initially arranged for at least thirty players, is extraordinary for a Broadway pit. And like Robbins did with dancing bodies, Bernstein kept adding and peeling away instruments, changing textures, setting up and interrupting symmetries.

There is no overture in the stage version of *West Side Story* (the film added one). In 1957 that audacious omission was effectively "hanging a sign" to the audience, reading: "*My Fair Lady* This *Ain't.*"

The initial plan was to kick off the show instead with a spoken and sung ensemble number that would take place in a Jets hangout ("The Clubhouse") where gang members would be, as Sondheim described, "simply fooling around, reading comic books, playing games, doing push-ups, waiting for Riff to arrive."

Robbins was not pleased with the first song drafted for the scene, which Bernstein later recalled had "millions of lyrics to insanely fast music." Robbins thought it was better to introduce the Jets and Sharks, and their turf battle, through dance. To that end, a new "militantly aggressive" number for the Jets called "Mix!" (with the repeated, in-your-face rhyming of "Mix" and "Spics") was written to cap an opening dance number. That was junked, too, paving the way for an introduction of *West Side Story* that consisted almost entirely of dance and music—a less conventional, more confrontational way to plunge into the story (and, incidentally, more faithful to the opening, brawling scene in *Romeo and Juliet*).

The Major Musical Segments in the Score

"The Prologue"

Thanks to the perfect fusion of choreography and music in this opening salvo, one gets a potent introduction to the explosive, racially charged turf war between rival gangs, right off the bat—a sense of the youthful *thrill* of having turf, and the *dangerous excitement* of defending it.

The music opens with an edgy blast of notes, the first two forming a thundering C to F-sharp tritone. The staccato chords at the beginning have a raw grittiness, thanks to their jazz/blues harmonies. Moreover, they sound in asymmetrical rhythms that convey a nervous, jumpy feeling.

As the Jets prowl their turf, cocky and tough, the music then switchbacks between resonant individual elements—opening with "blues crush" chords (of major and minor thirds), followed by a solo saxophone riff, tinged with bluesy modernity. The sax phrase is soon repeated at a slightly higher pitch, a gesture that adds more tonal uncertainty. It's as if the musical ground is shifting beneath our feet. Nothing is safe or predictable—on the streets, or in this score.

A burst of hard-driving hand drums, an ominous threat of tom-toms, the Jets' crisp finger snaps, claps, and piercing whistles, some robust orchestral gestures by the strings. All these elements keep the mood veering between adolescent exhilaration and eerie hints of rumbling, gathering menace—which, once the Sharks appear, artfully quicken into a percussive chase, building to the furious storm of a brassy brawl between the gangs that's cut short only by the scream of a police whistle.

In just under four minutes of music, Bernstein establishes the tone and temperature of a mutual vendetta that will end in double murder. The music fuels the discord, propelling the action forward, and introduces devices and motifs that will be reprised cannily and often—particularly the tritone. And the first three notes of "The Prologue," in fact, are also the opening three notes of "Maria" and "Cool."

All of this is in service of plunging you willy-nilly into the epicenter of an urban battleground, where a dust-up of schoolyard jeering and roughhousing will inevitably escalate into more serious violence. With the dancing, and the smattering of verbal insults the Jets and Sharks spit out, the music of "The Prologue" sets the stage and attunes the ear for all that is to come.

"The Jet Song"

This gang anthem was written, then replaced by a different number ("This Turf Is Ours"), then "reinstated" because the replacement was deemed "too harsh," according to Sondheim.

That was as it should be, because the exuberant "Jet Song" fits into the moment like a pair of skin-tight Levis. The jaunty tune emerges organically from the Jets' powwow after the police have broken up the melee with the Sharks.

The number introduces the Jets as individuals, Riff first. After barking orders to his eager, rough-housing "acemen" and "rocketmen" about attending the dance and challenging the Sharks, Riff jacks up morale in song by reminding his troops that the gang is their family ("You're never alone / You're never disconnected / You're home with your own") and a commitment for life ("From your first cigarette / To your last dying day").

After Riff dashes off to find Tony, the song is picked up by Action, Baby John, and Big Deal, soon joined by other Jets as they strut, skip, punch at the air, and otherwise flex their muscles and cheeky machismo. Sondheim's lyrics are laced with bravado, with boasts and images of male prowess suited to the 1950s yet perennial. A Jet is the "top cat in town" and the "gold-medal kid / With a heavyweight crown." He's the "swingin'est thing." And a nifty bit of wordplay advises us that when you're a Jet, "Little boy, you're a man; / Little man, you're a king!" Another verse cleverly exploits car and driver imagery, with the words "gear," "cylinders," "clickin'," "steer." (There's also a short four-measure bridge that begins, "Oh when the Jets fall in at the cornball dance / We'll be the sweetest dressin' gang in pants!," but it was left out of the movie and is sometimes cut from live productions.)

The more puffed-up the Jets get, the more their boasts turn into threats. When they're on the rampage, enemies better "go underground, " better "run," "hide," keep their noses hidden. This gang is hanging a "Visitors Forbidden" sign (aimed especially at the encroaching Puerto Ricans) and will take on any trespassers.

The song climaxes with a promise to beat "Every last buggin' gang" on the "whole, buggin', ever mother lovin'" street. Sondheim was limited here (and later in "Gee, Officer Krupke") by the unwritten but firm rule that profanity was then largely verboten in Broadway musicals (as well as on network TV and in mainstream Hollywood films). By the twenty-first century, the word *fucking* would not only be acceptable but expected, instead of *buggin'* and *ever-lovin'*. The "F-bomb" would be dropped often in such later Broadway youth musicals as *American Idiot* and *Avenue Q,* and it's flung around so frequently in other media it's become defanged and nearly meaningless.

But in 1957 it would have shocked and repelled many Broadway patrons to hear even asocial New York ruffians utter certain "swear" words onstage. And while censorship is abhorrent, it's refreshing to hear some of the colorful, varied, and apparently un-offensive substitutions Sondheim and Laurents were forced to come up with by necessity.

"The Jet Song" melody alone is easily hummable, but the complex rhythmic setting makes it challenging to perform. Such intricate pacing here and elsewhere is another way Bernstein brought modernist musical ploys into his score.

The melody swings along in ¾ time, over a shifty orchestral accompaniment in ⁶⁄₈ time, and it's tricky for the singers to stay on tempo. But it ain't easy being a Jet, either, and the impatient rhythms and wandering bass lines give the number an excitable, precarious quality.

Note: The melody for "The Jet Song" was originally the basis for "My Greatest Day," a song with different lyrics that was intended as an introductory number for Tony.

"Something's Coming"

This solo ode for Tony was the last song added to *West Side Story,* written twelve days before the show's Washington, D.C., world debut. According to Sondheim, the team felt a number was needed to give Tony "some strength at the beginning of the show." Or to butch him up, as Bernstein bluntly suggested in an August 8, 1957, letter to his wife: "[It] gives Tony balls—so that he doesn't emerge as just a euphoric dreamer."

"Something's Coming" also projects Tony's emotional openness, optimism, and impatience (a kinder, gentler sort of restiveness than the Jets exude), which make him so susceptible to falling in love at first glance with Maria. He's on tenterhooks—waiting, longing, anticipating something undefined but imminent to fill the void in his life where the gang once was. Riff senses what it is when he tells Tony, just before the song begins, "Who knows? Maybe what you're lookin' for'll be twitchin' at the dance!"

Inspiration for "Something's Coming" came from "a big long speech that Arthur wrote for Tony," Bernstein told Craig Zadan in *Sondheim & Company,* to introduce the character. "It said how every morning he would wake up and reach out for something around the corner or down the beach. . . .We were looking through this speech and 'Something's Coming' just seemed to leap off the page. In the course of the day we had written that song." In this case Sondheim had direct input into the music, suggesting a rhythm scheme that helped Bernstein make it a "two-four"—theater lingo for "a very driving kind of showbiz song," like Hugh Martin's "The Trolley Song" sung by Judy Garland in the film *Meet Me in St. Louis.*

"Something's Coming" doesn't just rush along—it lifts off. Nigel Simeone calls the melody "a breathless pre-echo of 'Maria'"; there is an emotional and musical throughline that runs from this openhearted entreaty through the unabashed ardor of Tony's upcoming love ballad.

In the "Something's Coming" arrangement favoring strings and woodwinds, a syncopated $^6/_8$ melody line surges over a $^3/_4$ accompaniment, once again exuding a sense of restlessness. (The superimposition of two distant rhythmic patterns is another example of Bernstein's use of modernist complexity, and a gambit he returns to often.) When the bridge arrives (on the line "around the corner and whistling down the river"), the melody soars from a G to a high F. (On the show's final refrain, the "Maybe *tonight*" soars from C to a high G—testing the range of any light baritone, and even some tenors. It's used optionally but is shiver-inducing when the singer pulls it off.)

Sondheim's incandescent lyrics here are beautifully matched to the arc of the music. The second time the bridge comes along, the sensuous verbal image of "humming" air is evoked in a light trembling of strings that positively shimmers. And in the verses, lines are frequently punctuated with emphatic, clipped, single-syllable words—"reach" and "beach," "shock" and "knock," "soon" and "moon." These are contrasted with the luxuriously elongated vowels in phrases like "A- *rooow-ned* the corner" and "the *aaaaaair* is humming." The result is an exultant yet guileless expression of joyous premonition. Sondheim later singled out his lyrics to "Something's Coming" (and "The Jet Song") as his favorites in the show, because they "have character and flavor and I don't hear the writer at work."

"The Dance at the Gym"

This instrumental suite for dancers is a Bernstein tour de force. It draws on the composer's deep knowledge of and affinity for jazz and Latin music. And it is an extension of and catalyst for Robbins's choreography—building on, then surpassing Bernstein's earlier dance music for collaborations with Robbins, in *On the Town* and *Wonderful Town*.

Formally the suite is divided into three sections: Blues, Promenade, and Mambo. But they are bracketed with other brief but integral transition pieces—an entr'acte dervish of strings that spins Maria into the dance, a delicate cha-cha that parallels Romeo and Juliet's masked pas de deux, and the short cool-jazz "jump" at the end of the scene, as Bernardo and Riff agree to a war council.

It is all dance music, but unlike anything you'd have found in a New York community center in 1957. Like the dancing itself, it exaggerates and twists and intensifies the ordinary in extraordinary ways. And like the entire score, it quotes and reworks motifs we've already heard—in "The Prologue," "The Jet Song," "Somewhere"—and previews others (from "Maria").

The opening Blues movement (left off many recordings of the score, sadly) is soulful and sultry with a loose-limbed, drunken feeling in dissonant, akimbo bebop lines for the brass and winds. The Jets have the floor here, strutting their too-cool-for-school stuff, but they're interrupted once again by another loud whistle of authority—this time from a nebbish of an adult youth leader.

A brief, Latin-style Promenade (in "paso doble" time) follows as the Jets and Sharks and their women sulkily go through the motions of a "get together" circle dance proposed by the leader they've been mocking. But when Riff and Bernardo opt out of the circle game and grab back their usual gals instead of partnering with those from the rival gang, the orchestra swerves into the Mambo, a roof-raising challenge dance.

Ushered in with Latin drums, strings, and more brass, the music is *muy caliente,* fast and tumultuous, in a jazz-salsa Tito Puente/Maynard Ferguson mode. As the two gangs go toe to toe on the dance floor, their moves getting more abandoned and acrobatic, the music escalates in tempo, volume, passion, like a mounting fever.

The fever breaks once Tony and Maria spot each other and, oblivious to the frenzy around them, gravitate to the center of the room. The entire mood of the music (and dance) alters with the Cha-Cha, in which the "Maria" melody is previewed by the violins in quiet pizzicato accented by finger snaps. This is music to fall in love by, music of tender astonishment. The tune swells gradually into a full symphonic treatment, then gives way to Tony and Maria's first words to one another. (Tony: "You're not thinking I'm someone else?" / Maria: "I know you are not.")

During their gentle first kiss, the spell breaks as Bernardo angrily intervenes, and Riff joins in. Underneath their short swatch of dialogue is the Jump, a catchy, nervous little scamp of a jazz tune, spiked with muted brass and plucked strings. As Tony leaves the dance, the music follows and gathers into the opening bars of "Maria."

"Maria"

Unlike Romeo, the Hell's Kitchen kid Tony can hardly extol the virtues of his new sweetheart in high-flown poetic stanzas. He can only sing his ardor as he stumbles, thunderstruck, out of the gym into a shadowy slum street—which under the spell of infatuation is now a paradise to him.

Bernstein already had the title and a draft lyric for "Maria" when he began working on the tune with Sondheim. But the final version took longer to complete than any other number in the score. "I had a dummy lyric, a terrible lyric," he confessed to Mel Gussow of the *New York Times.* "'Lips like wine…divine. Very bad. Like a translation of a Neapolitan street song." (The Italian folkloric influence on the song was, initially, deliberate.)

He later realized the opening notes "had the kernel of the piece, in the sense that the three notes of 'Maria' pervade the whole [show]—inverted, done backward. I didn't do all this on purpose. It seemed to come out in 'Cool' and the gang whistle. The same three notes." Significantly, the first two of the notes form a tritone. (One can hardly overstate the audacity of beginning a Broadway love anthem with the most harmonically ambiguous interval available.)

Sondheim had no quarrel with the melody. "The problem here," he recounted, "was how to write a love song for two people who have just met. They have exchanged exactly ten lines, but they have encountered each other in a surreal, dreamlike dance sequence, so the audience believes that they have an intimate, even mystical connection."

In an echo of *Romeo and Juliet,* Tony knows just two hard facts about his new love: (1) that she is from the enemy camp (as Shakespeare's Juliet put it, "My only love sprung from my only hate!"); and (2) that her name is Maria.

So he sings of just meeting "a girl named Maria," and as the song unfolds, her name is repeated more than two dozen times (by Tony, and in the original show, by otherworldly offstage voices). The melody unspools in triplets against a ¾ beat. And the elemental lyric has an amazed Tony telling himself what has happened ("I just met a girl named Maria") because he can't quite believe it.

The sincere words are accompanied by a sweeping orchestral arrangement (with a graceful tango underpinning), achieved without entirely burying the ballad in sentimental goo. The song begins with a spoken "Maria," a hushed marveling over "the most beautiful sound I ever heard," then soars into a rapturous, full-voiced aria, with the strings and brass paralleling the singer.

Then as the orchestra reiterates the melody, Bernstein's music again ascends, as it did in "Something's Coming." Tony savors the name Maria again and again, taking it higher and higher with different inflections, climaxing in a sustained, skyward "Ma-*riiiiii*-a" before landing back on earth with the reverential "Say it soft and it's almost like praying." As the strings recede to a whisper, Tony seals his adoration by singing the final reiteration of her name on a high G—sometimes lowered to accommodate the range of the singer. But when the note is reached, and sustained, it gives the song a breathtaking climax.

Though Sondheim has always disparaged a certain "wetness" in the lyrics for "Maria," he understood their powers of enchantment when he first played the song for Oscar Hammerstein and his wife, Dorothy. He recalled that when he finished, Dorothy "came across the room and kissed me on the behalf of both of them."

"Tonight"

When Tony and Maria first pledge their love on her fire escape/balcony, the show required a euphoric duet—its own version of the iconic balcony rendezvous in *Romeo and Juliet*.

The first song Bernstein and Sondheim came up with for the spot was "One Hand, One Heart," originally composed for *Candide*. But "as the score developed," explained Sondheim later, the tune "seemed too settled and stately for a first declaration of passion." (It found a more suitable home in a later scene where Tony and Maria exchange vows in the bridal shop.)

The alternative, "Tonight," borrowed the melody from a duet already written for Tony and Maria, as their part of the ensemble number, the "Tonight Quintet." That tune was developed, according to Sondheim, into "a more turbulent and spontaneous" fire escape moment than "One Hand, One Heart" had conjured.

"Tonight" now emerges directly from Laurents's dialogue for the couple, as they embrace and share their overwhelming feelings for each other. Maria says to Tony (with unconscious irony), "Imagine being afraid of you!" And when Tony soon urges her to "See only me," from there flows Maria's lovely intro verse: "Only you, you're the only thing I'll see forever . . . "

After a trading of pledges, the strings pick up the tempo and Maria sweetly asserts the main theme, "Tonight, tonight, it all began tonight / I saw you and the world went away . . . " The lilting but fervent melody gives her a chance to express the same dazed ardor that Tony projected in "Maria."

The "Tonight" lyrics have a mystical quality that is apropos but that, in some lesser performances, can be cloying. The couple sing of a world "wild and bright" with "suns and moons all over the place" and stars that "stop where they are." Such phrases dissatisfied Sondheim, who explained he had a "language problem" of "how to combine the artificial jive talk Arthur had invented for Tony and the Jets with the style he had adopted for Maria and the Sharks—elegant and polite, rather like a literal translation from the Spanish . . . Hence the formality of the lyric, and its lapses into 'poetry.'"

But in "Tonight, "as with the other romantic ballads in *West Side Story,* the fulsome and sonorous music overpowers any literary missteps. The song nearly bursts with an ecstatic rush of first love. And if it is sung with the right emphasis and intensity, one can imagine that these bedazzled kids are giddily reaching for metaphors, even far-fetched ones, to articulate unfamiliar emotions they can barely contain.

Musicologists point to "love motifs" and "death motifs" that resurface throughout the score of *West Side Story.* "Tonight" certainly offers a love motif. Prescient hints of the more somber "Somewhere" (symbolizing hope, but also death) are seeded in "Tonight," noted musicals scholar Geoffrey Block, and "as with Wagner's 'Tristan und Isolde,' another 'Romeo and Juliet' prototype, love and death, like love and hate," as the fleetingly overjoyed Tony and Maria will soon learn, "are inextricably entwined."

At the song's conclusion, suggested Block, "the idealistic lovers show their oneness by singing in unison and the celestial heights of youthful optimistic love by singing and holding high A-flats. Meanwhile, back on the earth, the omniscient orchestra warns audiences of their imminent doom."

Like Shakespeare's paramours, Tony and Maria say good night but she calls him back again and again, and they finally sing their own hushed, limpid equivalent of "parting is such sweet sorrow," with the lines "Good night, good night / Sleep well and when you dream, dream of me / Tonight." As their voices rise in octave-apart unison on the climactic note, the melody of "Somewhere" is quoted instrumentally—and a hint of the pain their newfound joy will later bring is presaged.

"America"

The genesis of this rousing showstopper was a tune Bernstein already had in his drawer—or as they say on Broadway, his "trunk." Bernstein loved Latin culture and frequently sampled it in his travels and via the culture of his South American wife, Felicia. He initially told Sondheim that he'd returned from a vacation in Puerto Rico, "fired up . . . by a dance rhythm he had heard called *huapango,* which seemed a perfect choice for the song, and was. What I didn't know at the time was that he had written the tune years earlier for an unproduced ballet called 'Conch Town.'"

According to Sondheim, "America" was first designed as a sung and danced debate between Bernardo and Anita. It would bolster their characters and comment humorously on the downsides of the U.S. immigrant experience for Puerto Ricans. However, Robbins felt it should be changed into a number for the Shark women alone, to balance out the male-dominated parts of the show.

So a rather ditzy Shark girl, Rosalia, was substituted for Bernardo as Anita's comic foil, and Sondheim rewrote the lyrics from a different perspective: instead of Anita declaring her affection for her adopted country, and Bernardo sardonically challenging her rosy image of the United States with some home truths about being a dark-skinned foreigner there, it was Rosalia pining for Puerto Rico while Anita sardonically challenged her romantic view of their native land—and sang the praises of U.S. affluence and modern conveniences.

The movie returned to the male–female configuration in the number and reclaimed Sondheim's original lyrics. Many of us can join Sondheim in believing it is the sharper of the two versions (and still the timelier, fifty years later). The Anita–Rosalia sparring is more of a repudiation of living in a poor Third World nation (and thereby a rationale for leaving it). The Bernardo–Anita dialogue is a stinging critique of life in America for new residents of color who find "lots of doors slamming" in their faces and are free only to "wait tables and shine shoes." (Both versions, however, make a point some listeners miss: "Puerto Rico's *in* America.")

Though the Broadway redo was a more benign, less ironic defense of America's virtues, one phrase stirred controversy: the line that referred to Puerto Rico as an "island of tropical diseases." Dr. Howard A. Rusk (founder of the famed Rusk Institute) took the phrase literally and reacted with a September 27, 1957, *New York Times* op-ed piece, "The Facts Don't Rhyme: An Analysis of Irony in Lyrics Linking Puerto Rico's Breezes to Tropical Diseases." Rusk wanted to reassure the public that the island was now rid of such maladies. The line was left in the stage show, but it was not in the lyrics used in the film.

Apart from that spot of bother, it was obvious from the first preview of *West Side Story* that "America" was an audience favorite. Though conventional in structure, the lyrics were unusual in their willingness to puncture a near-sacrosanct illusion that the United States is a land of plenty and abundant opportunity for every new arrival. Such a poke at the American dream was most uncommon in Broadway musicals of the time—almost as rare as the inclusion of Puerto Rican characters in a show. The number was also a respite from the tragic story's mounting tension and foreboding, which would crank up soon after in the seething war council between the Jets and Sharks and explode in the fateful rumble.

"America" tapped into the vivacity and brio of pan–Latin American culture (not entirely Puerto Rican culture, as some have objected). And it made audiences more familiar and comfortable with the Sharks, particularly the immensely likable and worldly-wise gang queen bee, Anita.

Music scholar Elizabeth Wells has pointed out in her detailed analysis of "America" that the *huapango* dance form Bernstein was enamored of was actually a form indigenous to Mexico, not Puerto Rico, and traditionally taken at a quick tempo with the cross-rhythms *West Side Story* favors. It is combined in this number with a kind of Puerto Rican folkloric dance music, called *seis.*

The music simmers down during the verses and erupts when the women are dancing, as marimba, bongos, castanets, tambourines, and the claps and foot stamps and cries ("Ai! Ai! Ai!") of the dancers drive home the *picante* rhythms. Again, the staccato punctuations in Sondheim's clever internal rhyming scheme ("I like to *be* in America, OK by *me* . . . Everything *free* . . . For a small *fee* . . .") helps the number to stamp and build until the final, tempestuous dance segment, capped with a lusty choral "Olé!"

Musically, "America" could arguably have been inserted as "the Latin number" into many a more generic Broadway show. But the sardonic, heretical lyrics are specific to *West Side Story,* especially those heard in the movie, which Sondheim described as "rooted in real character conflict rather than in an artificial argument consisting of punch lines set up by an ad hoc straight man (woman in this case)."

"Cool"

As the Jets hang out at Doc's drugstore, waiting for the Sharks to arrive for the war council, they get a bad case of the heebie-jeebies. They are spoiling for a fight, and this jazzy twelve-tone fugue, erected on the same opening tritone as "Maria," is a cautionary command from Riff to save their fire for the street battle ahead. (Introducing the twelve-tone writing associated with daring composers like Schoenberg and Stravinsky in this number was another modernist coup for Bernstein.)

The song and combustible dance give us another kind of war—one waged internally, between anarchic and controlled fury. The conversational lyrics cut stiletto-sharp. Riff tells the "crazy boy" Action, and the other Jets, to "stay coolly cool," to "stay loose" and "turn off the juice," to not go off like a "yo-yo schoolboy" (a pithy image of adolescent loss of control). There are more nods to aeronautics as a Jets brand ("got a rocket, in your pocket" and "breeze it, buzz it"). And everything that needs saying is spat out in a trenchant sixteen lines.

Bernstein's music, however, is some of his most complex in the entire score. The temperature is at first cool in the West Coast jazz sense, with Cal Tjader–like xylophone riffs reiterating the melody.

As the tune heats up, Simeone points out, previous motifs return and give the number a "gloriously flamboyant big-band treatment" with a thundering herd of brass spurring on the athletic and controlled/manic dancing. When the breathless Jets finally reprise the lyric, "fragments of the dotted counter-melody from the fugue return and gradually disintegrate, ending with a nihilistic descent in octaves . . . using the song's opening interval in reverse to bring the number to a close." Again, this kind of fugal counterpoint, like the twelve-tone writing, was virtually unprecedented in Broadway show tunes or mainstream pop music in this period.

Though "Cool" befits its pre-rumble position in the stage version of *West Side Story,* as a kind of perverse twist on a coach's pregame exhortation to his team, it switched places with the comic number "Gee, Officer Krupke" in the movie adaptation. The bursting-at-the-seams lyrics were deemed even more apt when sung by the new Jets leader Ice (a role invented for the film), as the gang members hunger for the chance to "get even" with the Sharks after Riff's slaying.

But the main reason the numbers were rearranged by the filmmakers was that they felt the vaudeville antics of "Krupke" were out of kilter with the Jets' grief over the death of their leader. The notion of comic relief, à la Shakespeare and sociopathology, didn't wash for Hollywood.

"One Hand, One Heart"

This soulful love duet was shuffled around twice. It was first composed for *Candide,* then slated for the *West Side Story* balcony/fire escape scene. But it wound up fitting more naturally into the scene in the Puerto Rican bridal shop after-hours, when Tony and Maria imagine their marriage ceremony— at first lightheartedly in jest, then solemnly in song. The lyrics are wedding vows—"Make of our hands, one hand / Make of our hearts, one heart," with a shiver of foreshadowing ("Only death can part us now").

Sondheim has said he felt hemmed in by the short-verse structure of the Bernstein melody, and it forced him to write simply—"a little too simply." The song was not a favorite for Laurents, either, who recalled that whenever it started in run-throughs, he, Sondheim, and Robbins headed out of the theater for a coffee break, while Bernstein stayed behind and was invariably moved by the tune.

Though it is certainly less harmonically sophisticated than most of the score, the clarity and meaning of the promises exchanged, and the beauty of Maria's voice entwined with and floating over Tony's, give "One Hand, One Heart" a sense of timelessness and artless purity. After the frenetic "Cool," and before the convulsive "Tonight Quintet," here is a moment of calm before the hurricane breaks. But it is also the moment when the gravity of their situation and depth of their bond really come home to Tony and Maria, in words that recall those of Romeo, as he tells Friar Laurence in the marriage scene with Juliet: "Do thou but close our hands with holy words, / Then love-devouring death do what he dare."

"Tonight Quintet"

In this tumultuous prelude to the rumble, Bernstein gives all the youthful *West Side Story* figures a magnificent outlet for their mutual anticipation. From different corners of the neighborhood come the sounds of ferocity, bigotry, adoration, lust—a contrapuntal chorus of clashing hopes and fears. What in the balcony scene was a rhapsody becomes something else entirely here—a call to arms, a prayer, an erotic promise.

Once again Bernstein overlays two conflicting meters (the singers in double time, the accompaniment in triple time) to rev up the intensity. First the Jets crow their war cry ("The Jets are gonna have their way tonight!") and are echoed by the equally adamant Sharks ("We're gonna hand 'em a surprise, / Tonight!"). They then battle it out in traded measures and accusations ("Well, they began it!" "Well, they began it!").

The jabbing brass make way for another "blues crush" saxophone figure as Anita sings of her planned post-rumble tryst with Bernardo: "Anita's gonna get her kicks tonight / We'll have a private little mix tonight."

That motif is eclipsed by Tony's robust, sped-up reprise of the earlier "Tonight" verse from his fire escape duet with Maria, expressing his longing for that old devil moon to grow bright and "make this endless day / endless night." His reverie is interrupted by Riff, who presses Tony in song to come to the rumble, which provides the undercurrent for Maria's own reprise of the earlier "Tonight" melody. (Sondheim considers the ensemble to be technically a quartet rather than quintet, because Maria and Tony echo the same melodic line.)

The piece grows increasingly heated and layered as the Jets and Sharks return to the mix, then Anita joins as well, and all the disparate vocal parts merge into a reverberating ensemble "tonight!" with Maria soaring an octave above everyone else on a high C. Though the quintet is sometimes likened to ensemble passages in grand operas by Verdi and Mozart, critic Frank Rich viewed it in more cinematic terms. "It's the fulcrum of the show, dramatically, when everything has become like a train rushing forward, in a tragedy," he suggested. "And you have this cinematic cross-cutting, done without cinema; done by the art of the theatre."

Sondheim explained that he and Bernstein first intended the "Quintet" to be performed *before* the mock wedding in the bridal shop, believing that "Tony would never agree to rumble after he'd 'married' Maria." But Robbins insisted it come just prior to the rumble, even if he couldn't articulate why to his colleagues. It was agreed the number would be tried in both positions to see which worked better, and Sondheim told NPR, "as you might guess, Jerry turned out to be right. The plot logic may not have made much sense, but the show flowed better. That was when I learned that there is a significant difference between logical truth and theatrical truth."

The theatrical veracity that prevailed made the sense of apprehension that much keener and the imminent defeat of love by hatred that much more agonizing.

"The Rumble"

Triggered by Tony's cry, "Don't push me!" as he is goaded into a knife fight with Bernardo, this instrumental segment is form-fitted to Robbins's fight choreography for the battle royal between the Sharks and Jets.

A condensed mini-drama in itself, in two and a half minutes it provides a blow-by-blow soundtrack of the gang fight under the highway and its bloody aftermath as a police siren wails and chimes ominously toll for the fallen warriors Bernardo and Riff.

Aggressively strident and muscular, the composition is foreground rather than background music, and every movement the performers made in the scene was plotted and timed to it, beat by beat. Motifs from "The Prologue" are echoed, but here the hard-charging strings and brass build and build, broken briefly by Tony's cry, "Keep out of this!" after Bernardo pulls a knife on him, then climbing again with the murders of Riff, then Bernardo. A dissonantly malevolent multi-octave arpeggio then ushers in the cacophony of a full-out riot—similar to the one that caps off "The Prologue," but this time deadly. Varying the tension levels are a few measures of quietly skittering strings, which after the fight ends follow Anybody's rescue of the battered and horrified Tony as he is kneeling and weeping over the corpses. (While it references other parts of the score, the "Rumble" music also is tonally and texturally similar to passages in Bernstein's film score for the 1954 dockside strife drama *On the Waterfront,* particularly the percussive and dissonant "Presto barbaro" passages that are preludes to violence.)

"I Feel Pretty"

Although they have admitted this song plays like gangbusters (so to speak), Laurents and Sondheim were united in their distaste for "I Feel Pretty," which opens act 2 in (ironically) high spirits. (In the film it is moved, with lessening effect, to a spot before the rumble.) But this comic bagatelle has a valid theatrical purpose, and most audiences find it beguiling—or, at least, irresistibly campy.

Maria doesn't yet know that her brother and Riff were slain at the rumble. In fact, at this point she naively believes that Tony has managed to prevent the battle. And like any teenager in the throes of a first love, she's brimming over with happiness she can't hide from her peers.

Bernstein set a task to create his own Strauss waltz for the scene. But his melody is also right in the Broadway zone, with a Rodgers and Hammerstein "I'm In Love with a Wonderful Guy" zing to it. The number allows Maria and her girlfriends to cut up and cavort in time-honored romantic-comedy fashion: she's deliriously infatuated, they're skeptical. With its clowning and giddiness, the number also grants Maria her last, blissful gasp of innocence. Soon we will see a different Maria emerge, no longer the larking sprite but life-scarred and bereft.

"I Feel Pretty" recalls yet softens the Latin flavor of the "Mambo" in the gym dance suite, and the "olé!" high jinks of "America." As the lyric implies, it is indeed "pretty and witty and bright," with short brass fanfares, horn whoops, and whimsical rhythmic accents that include strategic handclaps and a tingle of chimes.

Sondheim has frequently singled out for self-abuse the lyrics to "I Feel Pretty." He took to heart the observation of a colleague (*Fiddler on the Roof* lyricist Sheldon Harnick) that lines like "It's alarming how charming I feel" and "I feel stunning and entrancing" seemed beyond the linguistic reach of an unschooled girl with a rudimentary grasp of English. He duly rewrote the lyrics to make the wording simpler and less cosmopolitan but explained later, "My collaborators would have none of it—they liked it the way it was. And is. I have blushed ever since."

But this reprises the question of theatrical logic versus nontheatrical reason. What comes across in "I Feel Pretty" is not Maria's overreaching vocabulary, but her playful and guileless delight and the easy-on-the-ear sparkle and pop of the rhymes—dizzy / sunny, fizzy / funny, stunning / entrancing, running / dancing, alarming / charming.

The mocking call-and-response chorus ("Have you met my good friend Maria?") is deliciously sassy. When Maria looks in the mirror to sing rhetorically, "Who can that attractive girl be?" she is snappily answered by Rosalia and Consuelo: "Which?" "What?" "Where?" "Who?"

And in the stage show, there is another pinch of irony: her friends really do not know "who" and "what" Maria's lover is, or how he has just turned Maria's life and their own world upside down—until moments later, when Chino appears with the bad tidings.

"Somewhere"

Capturing the anguish and yearnings of the ill-fated Tony and Maria at this point in the tragedy was a lofty task for the *West Side Story* team. The vehicle they chose was a fantasy ballet similar in a fundamental way to Agnes de Mille's watershed dream story ballets for *Carousel* and *Oklahoma!*

The "Somewhere" sequence interweaves with the dance a ballad introduced by Tony and Maria, then performed solo by a singer offstage, then echoed by the ensemble. The music and choreography have a simple resonance that has made "Somewhere" reverberant for many, in many different cultures. It is a universal impulse, is it not, to in crisis seek a place of "peace and quiet and open air" and yearn to believe such a haven exists "somehow, some way, somewhere"? (One indelible example: when the Motown pop group the Supremes sang "Somewhere" on Ed Sullivan's TV variety show, following the assassination of civil rights leader the Rev. Dr. Martin Luther King Jr.)

The number begins in Maria's small tenement bedroom, at a dramatic juncture, with a flurry of rushed strings and the bloodied, sorrowful, on-the-lam Tony promising the distraught Maria that he will take her "far, far away out of here."

She chimes in, as the song becomes more anguished. As it breaks apart, and as some high, sustained string chords shift the piece into a Coplandesque Scherzo, Tony and Maria are scenically transported out of the oppressive city into an idyllic open space. Joining them are the Jets and Sharks—all garbed in "pure" white garments as they dance and frolic like innocents in a pastoral utopian playground.

Eventually, a disembodied soprano voice (identified in the program only as "A Girl") drifts in from the wings, introducing the melody of the song—"There's a place for us / Somewhere a place for us"—as the ethereal music transports the dancers into an otherworldly realm of collective grace and compassion.

Musical scholars have suggested various classical models for the melody of "Somewhere"—most often, Beethoven's Piano Concerto No. 5, Op. 73 ("Emperor"). (The first four notes of "Somewhere" match the opening notes of the concerto's middle movement.) But whatever its deliberate or unconscious origin, the song has a hymnlike quality that stays with you.

And the deep-rooted yearning it expresses taps an international nerve: "Somewhere" has probably been recorded more often, by more diverse singers and musical groups, than any other song in the score. (It doesn't reach everyone: hard-nosed British director Jonathan Miller drily singled out "Somewhere" as so egregiously sentimental, you "find yourself wanting to say: 'No, Lenny, there isn't such a place.'")

As the song recedes, Tony and Maria and company gather in a bridal procession and the orchestral music grows sober, with those tolling bells and a choral repetition of the phrase "There's a place for us" (juxtaposed presciently over the opening notes of "I Have a Love"). Then the music darkens and breaks into jagged discord in a nightmare movement, as Sharks and Jets reenact the mayhem of the rumble. Gradually, with plaintive figures from the clarinet and flute, we are returned to the grim reality Maria and Tony face. As the lovers reprise the final measures of the song ("Someday, somehow, somewhere . . .") the dream of a transcendent communality fades, eclipsed by the dystopian present.

"Gee, Officer Krupke"

To lighten up the descending darkness of *West Side Story* a bit, here is some razzmatazz and mordant comic relief.

After the rumble, the Jets regroup. They are still stunned by the mayhem of the fight, and they're trying to evade the cops. But they blot out the agony temporarily and blow off steam with a bouncy and gag-laden, vaudeville-style novelty tune in which they rambunctiously send up their delinquent ways and the squadron of "helping professionals" bent on reforming them.

To Bernstein's oompah backing, Sondheim's sly lyrics cut two ways. On the one hand, the gang members display their bitter, alienated stance against authority. On the other, it's no wonder the youthful objects of social consternation reject the stereotyping of their kind as "punks" and "hoodlums"—a resentment echoed throughout the show (and in most American teen literature and drama of the period). These kids may be aimless and dangerous, but they'll be damned if headshrinkers, social workers, and the criminal justice system get to define them and argue over which one-size-fits-all remedy will whip them into shape.

Sondheim must have sensed what was just on the horizon: generations of troubled youths being shunted from social agency to shrink's office to courtroom, in a frustrating bureaucratic maze that often did more harm than good.

For the melody, Bernstein reappropriated a tune he'd first written for *Candide* under the title "Where Does It Get You in the End." The number thumps along in march time, each verse followed by a jaunty brass tattoo.

With the physical pratfalls and clever lyrics, "Krupke" becomes a zany vaudeville skit spliced in after Baby John and A-Rab elude the flummoxed Officer Krupke. Joined by Snowboy, Action, and other Jets, they make fun of the lumpish cop ("A big fat nuthin!") and protest their treatment by the adult establishment, but also brag about conforming to the media image of hooligans—because it's expected of them. (Action: "To them we ain't human. We're cruddy juvenile delinquents. So that's what we give 'em.")

In this raucous parody of adult oppressors, Action plays the kid who is pleading his case while running the gauntlet. The other Jets, impromptu, mug it up as caricatured versions of Krupke: a judge, a German-accented psychiatrist, and a social worker—all of whom give up on Action and pass him on to the next authority figure. Action offers a tongue-in-cheek brief to each of them, filled with standard-issue justifications for his waywardness—until he and the gang tell the adult world to, essentially, shove it and get off their backs.

For every nugget of truth about genuine deprivations and maltreatment, there's a punchline. Action's parents treat him rough—how? "With all their marijuana/They won't give me a puff." He's a mess because his father's a "bastard," his mom's an "S.O.B.," his sister "wears a moustache" and "brother wears a dress." He's "not anti-social," just "anti-work." So to make like a lowly "soda jerker" would mean "like be a schmuck."

The Jets chime in on the rowdy chorus and impersonate their elders with much gleeful grimacing and head whacking. They're like a street gang suddenly transformed into an improv comedy troupe.

Sondheim's rhymes are cunning and nimble, sprinkled with cartoon expressions (i.e., "gloriosky" and "leapin' lizards"). And the put-downs by the authorities are punchy and cruelly dismissive. ("This boy don't need a job, he needs a year in the pen.")

The number ends with a recap of the adult decrees, punched up with rim-shot bonks on Action's noggin. The trouble is "he's crazy," "he drinks," "he's lazy," "he stinks," "he's growing," "he's grown"—it's a no-win, lose–lose situation. But the Al Jolson–like climax turns the tables and has the Jets telling off the establishment—closing with their last salvo, "Krup you!"

"Krup you" was not, of course, the tag line Sondheim originally wrote, but the specter of self-censorship reared its head again within the company. Emboldened by a character in the recent Tennessee Williams drama *Cat on a Hot Tin Roof* saying "Bullshit!" on a Broadway stage and getting away with it, Sondheim thought he might slip through the Jets shouting "Fuck you!" at the world. The show's producers, and the honchos at Columbia Records, quickly informed him otherwise. They felt the epithet would restrict the commercial prospects of the show and the cast album considerably.

So it was not used, and perhaps it turned out all for the best, reflected Sondheim later. "Lenny came up with 'Krup you!,' which may be the best lyric line in the show and which was actually an improvement over it, since it fitted the kidlike nature of the Jets better than the harsher and more realistic expletive."

Columbia Records also had a problem with the use of *schmuck,* a Yiddish slang word for "penis"—equivalent to calling someone a stupid jerk. Though it stayed in the musical, on record the verse was rewritten to end with the insult *schmo* (another Yiddish mock) instead. And in the film Sondheim changed it again, to the rhyming (with *job*) *slob.*

There was also an internal conflict in the *West Side Story* ranks over where "Krupke" belonged in the show. "It was hard for me to believe that a gang on the run from being accessories to a double murder would stop on the street to indulge in a sustained comic sneer," Sondheim reported. But again, it went to a vote and he was overruled—Laurents's point that Shakespeare frequently injected ribald comic relief into his tragedies (Mercutio's Queen Mab speech in *Romeo and Juliet,* a soused-servant bit in *Macbeth*) carried the day. Ultimately, Sondheim conceded to putting "Krupke" in the second act, "on the old Shakespearean drunken-porter principle. In the middle of a melodrama, you cut in with comedy."

The more literal-minded movie of *West Side Story* followed Sondheim's first instinct and switched "Krupke" with "Cool." But this made sense, too: with Riff still alive, actor Russ Tamblyn got to take Action's part and goof off with handstands and backflips, and moving "Cool" to after the rumble exploited the white-hot emotions of the Jets. Surprisingly, these songs have such elasticity that they work in either place within Laurents's dramatic framework.

A final note: "Krupke" is one of the longest and wordiest songs in the entire musical. Several additional verses cut from the song are published in *Finishing the Hat,* and all are as amusing and sly as those used.

"A Boy Like That / I Have a Love"

There's no jocularity in these two conjoined songs, arias for Maria and Anita in the aftermath of the murders of Riff and Bernardo. Or for that matter, in the rest of the show.

Tony leaves Maria's room by the window after their first, and only, night of lovemaking, to hide at Doc's. The bereft Anita comes in and with one look at the open window and rumpled bed realizes what has happened. With a characteristic Bernstein opening of dissonant thrusts of brass and percussion, the minor-key "A Boy Like That" becomes a vehicle for Anita's fury and disgust—hurled at Maria in no uncertain terms. Anita's words paint Tony as a monster, the kind of boy who would (and did) "kill your brother." Dump him, she demands, get another boy, but this time "stick to your own kind, only your own kind."

She goes further, insisting a boy who kills "cannot love" and "has no heart." He "wants one thing only" (sex) and will "leave you lonely." Then Anita prophesies, "He'll murder your love" like "he murdered mine"—a denial that Tony *is* Maria's love.

The force of "A Boy Like That" hits you with its stabbing melodic line, its twitchy time changes (3/2 to 3/4 to 4/4 to 6/4), its dark echoes of the familiar tritones heard in "The Prologue" and elsewhere. The aria represents the crashing and burning of the dream of multicultural harmony that Tony and Maria had shared and Anita had at least accepted as a remote possibility.

But Maria cannot let this stand. No longer a malleable child, she rebuts her friend's assertions in counterpoint, then sings her down with the cry, "Oh no, Anita, no!" Anita's words, Maria insists, are "true for you, not for me." Then she pleads for mutual understanding and defends her bond with Tony in the poignant ballad "I Have a Love."

Reminiscent in sentiment (if not musical style) to Rodgers and Hammerstein's "What's the Use of Wondering?" (in *Carousel*), Maria's answering aria argues for a purist, eternal, and universal kind of love, a bond that transcends conventional morality: "I have a love, and it's all that I have / Right or wrong, what else can I do?" One can't simply abandon real love. It is immutable, and in tragic times there's simply "nothing to be done," nothing but "hold him forever, / Be with him now, tomorrow and all of my life!"—a foreshadowing of the grief she will carry for Tony once his short life ends. (The first bars of "I Have a Love" also are echoed at the show's finale, as Maria effectively leaves the stage a widow.)

In the end, the two women join voices, alto and soprano, to sing the final measures of "I Have a Love:" "When love comes, so strong, there is no right or wrong." They finish an octave apart on the stirring climactic line "Your love is your life!"

Yes, in psychological terms, Anita's anger at Maria has deflated absurdly quickly, followed by a near-saintly gesture of sisterly solidarity. But this is, after all, melodrama, with the emotions now pitched high. Soon enough the feelings of sisterhood between the women are subverted by the Jets' bigoted taunting and physical attack on Anita at Doc's drugstore—which, in tragic order, provokes the bitter lie that will catalyze Tony's demise.

"A Boy Like That / I Have a Love" is the score's most overtly operatic number (or a near-second to the "Tonight Quintet"). It is also the only song in the show for which Sondheim completed the lyrics and they were then set to music by Bernstein without any changes in the wording. Sondheim considered this a sign of his own growth as a lyricist over his time working on the show, and he viewed the last songs he wrote for *West Side Story*—including this one, "Something's Coming," and "Krupke"—as more confident, "less self-conscious" than his earlier contributions. "Perhaps that was the most important thing the show did for me," he mused. "Despite my mixed feelings about what I contributed to it, [*West Side Story*] was—along with 'Allegro'—the show which shaped my professional life."

Taunting Scene and Finale

There are two other pieces of music, short instrumental passages, that serve essential dramatic purposes.

When Anita comes to Doc's drugstore to deliver a message from Maria to Tony, only to be reviled and threatened by the vengeful Jets, a bit of the feverish, brassy instrumental music from the Mambo segment of the "Dance at the Gym" is grotesquely reprised. As Scott Miller points out, "The Jets have taken the sexually charged music of the Puerto Ricans and twisted it"—thereby unwittingly provoking Anita's fatal betrayal of their friend Tony.

Finally, after Tony is shot by Chino, he and Maria sing a last, a cappella refrain of "Somewhere" as he expires. That was not the original plan: the creators agreed that Maria should sing out her rage and anguish after comforting her dying lover. But as Bernstein later confessed, "I can't tell you how many tries I made on that aria. I tried once to make it cynical and swift. Another time like a Puccini aria. In every case, after five or six bars, I gave up. It was phony."

Instead, after a brief instrumental reprise of "Somewhere," a "dummy lyric" that Arthur Laurents had written into the script to describe the dramatic action was again purloined and used as Maria's final speech. It was followed by a processional of somber bells over a mournful refrain of "I Have a Love," as the characters file offstage—a procession led by members of both gangs bearing Tony's body aloft and ending with Maria, head bowed in her Madonna-like mantilla.

Carol Lawrence, the original Maria, said Bernstein never even played her any of the arias he'd drafted for the finale. The decision to use Laurents's text instead was sealed during a pre-opening run-through, when Lawrence recited the speech to "pin-drop quiet," followed by a big ovation. For Lawrence, it was the perfect ending. "Maria is alone and she has to deliver the message of the entire play: 'Are there enough bullets for all of us? Do we either cleanse ourselves or do we all die?' It's my favorite moment in the entire play."

It was indeed a perfect end to Bernstein's brilliant score, which begins with thunderous bravado and ends with hushed desolation.

ORIGINAL WEST SIDE STORY INSTRUMENTATION

Reed I: piccolo, flute, alto saxophone, clarinet in B$^\flat$, bass clarinet

Reed II: clarinet in E$^\flat$, clarinet in B$^\flat$, bass clarinet

Reed III: piccolo, flute, oboe, English horn, tenor saxophone, baritone saxophone, clarinet in B$^\flat$, bass clarinet

Reed IV: piccolo, flute, soprano saxophone, bass saxophone, clarinet in B$^\flat$, bass clarinet

Reed V: bassoon

2 horns in F

3 trumpets in B$^\flat$ (2nd doubling trumpet in D)

2 trombones

Timpani

Percussion (four players) *

Piano/celesta

Electric guitar/Spanish guitar/mandolin

Violin I–VII

Cello I–IV

Contrabass

* Traps, vibraphone, 4 pitched drums, xylophone, 3 bongos, 3 cowbells, conga, timbales, snare drum, police whistle, gourd, 2 suspended cymbals, castanets, maracas, finger cymbals, tambourines, small maracas, glockenspiel, woodblock, claves, triangle, temple blocks, chimes, tam-tam, ratchet, slide whistle

LEONARD BERNSTEIN BIO

Leonard Bernstein was born Louis Bernstein in Lawrence, Massachusetts, on August 25, 1918, to Ukrainian Jewish immigrants Samuel Joseph Bernstein, a businessman , and housewife Jennie (Resnick) Bernstein.

Young Leonard (as he was always called) showed an early aptitude for music and was given piano lessons. When the Bernsteins moved to Boston, he excelled academically and went on to Harvard University to major in business. But he continued to study and perform as a pianist, and his abiding passion was music.

After graduation, Bernstein found an avid mentor in conductor Serge Koussevitzky, maestro of the respected Berkshire Music Festival. With Koussevitzky's encouragement, Bernstein studied at Philadelphia's Curtis Institute of Music, and in 1943 Bernstein obtained the assistant conductor post at the New York Philharmonic. After filling in with distinction at the podium one night for ailing maestro Bruno Walter, Bernstein became a media darling and a popular guest conductor for major orchestras in the United States and abroad. In 1958, he was appointed the principal conductor and music director of the New York Philharmonic—a great coup for a musician his age.

Bernstein's charisma and gift for pedagogy made him a national figure when he began educating the masses about classical and popular music in his *Omnibus* musical series and televised Young People's Concerts.

Bernstein was equally ambitious as a composer. His first symphony, *Jeremiah,* premiered in 1944, followed by a second symphony, *The Age of Anxiety,* in 1949. (He debuted a third, *Kaddish,* in 1963.) He wrote many more orchestral works, but his most critically and commercially successful compositions were his scores for Broadway musicals—the hits *On the Town* (1944) and *Wonderful Town* (1953) and the shorter-lived *Peter Pan.* (1950). Though it flopped at the box office, the 1956 show *Candide* sports one of his most dazzling scores. And the follow-up a year later was *West Side Story,* often ranked as Bernstein's finest creative achievement.

Bernstein composed one more Broadway show (*1600 Pennsylvania Avenue*), as well as two operas (*Trouble in Tahiti* and *A Quiet Place*), a mass, and other works that found a place in the modern canon.

He became one of the world's best-known, most-travelled conductors, headed up Tanglewood Music Festival, supported liberal political causes, and appeared on TV before millions around the world as he conducted Beethoven's Ninth Symphony in Berlin on Christmas Day 1989, in honor of the fall of the Berlin Wall.

Bernstein married Felicia Montealegre in 1951, and they had three children: Jamie, Nina, and Alexander. He died of a heart attack and complications of emphysema on October 14, 1990. Among Bernstein's many honors: more than twenty Grammy Awards, including a Lifetime Achievement Award; ten Emmy Awards; a Tony Award; and a Kennedy Center Honor.

STEPHEN SONDHEIM BIO

Stephen Joshua Sondheim was born on March 22, 1930, in New York City to parents Herbert Sondheim, a dress manufacturer, and Janet Fox, a fashion designer. Musically and intellectually precocious, Sondheim was ten when he moved to Bucks County, Pennsylvania, with his mother, after his parents divorced. Through new schoolmate James Hammerstein, he met James's illustrious father, Broadway lyricist-author Oscar Hammerstein II, who became a mentor to and major influence on Sondheim. Sondheim attended Williams College, where he wrote several student musicals, then did postgraduate studies with another mentor, avant-garde composer Milton Babbitt.

After some freelance writing for television and theater, Sondheim crafted the lyrics for *West Side Story* and his career on Broadway took off, as a composer-lyricist for *A Funny Thing Happened on the Way to the Forum* and lyricist for *Gypsy,* both directed by Jerome Robbins.

In 1971, he wrote both lyrics and music for the boldly contemporary show *Company,* and he went on to create a long string of other innovative, influential, and widely hailed Broadway musicals, many in collaboration with director-producer Harold Prince, including *Follies, A Little Night Music, Sweeney Todd, Sunday in the Park with George,* and *Into the Woods.*

Sondheim's work as the most lauded, dominant Broadway composer of his generation brought him eight Tony Awards (including one for lifetime achievement), seven Grammy Awards, an Academy Award, and many other tributes. Sondheim founded Young Playwrights, an organization that nurtures young dramatists, and on the occasion of his eightieth birthday a Broadway venue, Henry Miller's Theatre, was renamed the Stephen Sondheim Theatre in his honor.

The Jets soar, in the original Broadway choreography for *West Side Story*. Courtesy of Photofest.

6

SHOOTING SPARKS INTO SPACE
THE DANCES OF
WEST SIDE STORY

Dance in *West Side Story* is not just for show. Dance is danger and braggadocio, sex and rebellion. It is love, and death, and life—furious, delicate, combustible, undeniable.

Robbins's choreographic achievements in *West Side Story*—the seamless welding of gesture and movement to the Bernstein score, the primacy of dance as an expression of narrative and character—still stand unequaled, unrivaled in Broadway musicals.

Joey McKneely, who performed in the anthology musical *Jerome Robbins' Broadway* and was among the choreographers anointed by Robbins to preserve his theatrical work into the twenty-first century, told the *New York Times*, "If you remove Jerome Robbins's choreography you lose significant plot, storytelling moments, and you lose characterization elements that are set in the dance. It's the emotional glue."

One of the qualities esteemed dance critic Edwin Denby praised highly in the Robbins dances for *On the Town* is also evident in his *West Side Story* numbers: "They generally emerge from the stage action," he wrote, "and melt into it again so as to give value to a scene rather than a hand to the dance."

Robbins's work was so different from the usual theatrical choreography up to that point, it had a jarringly profound effect on those performing it. Noted Grover Dale (the original Snowboy in *West Side Story*, who would stage future revivals of the musical), "Once you work with Jerry Robbins you never look at dance the same way again. You become acutely aware that dance goes beyond movement and has the power to convey ideas and emotions."

McKneely seconded that: "The emotions I felt doing the choreography of *West Side Story* was something I had never experienced before. The pure challenge of just getting through it pushed my limits." Karen Olivo, who won a Tony for her turn as Anita under McKneely's choreographic supervision in the 2009 Broadway revival, put it this way: "When I do [Robbins's dances] right, I feel like I'm flying." It feels that way to the audience, too.

For the initial production, Dale and his castmates were prodded, bullied, sometimes hoodwinked by Robbins into fully occupying the emotional states of their *West Side Story* characters—before, during, and between performances. But while emoting they also had to master challenging moves drawn from ballet, jazz, Latin, jitterbug, acrobatics, gymnastics— sometimes in lightning-fast combinations, often to tricky and mercurial Bernstein rhythms. And like Riff's exhortation to "Walk tall!," they were pressed to confirm who their alter egos were in every posture, every toss of the head and snap of the fingers, and whether standing still, strolling across the stage, or leaping and soaring. "It wasn't just dancing, it was *physicality* as well," explained Tony Mordente.

The sheer volume of dance in *West Side Story* (a dozen major choreographed sequences) was a daring aesthetic choice, but also one entirely in tune with the subject matter. Dance was the perfect psycho-sexual outlet for hormonally driven, pent-up, barely educated adolescents. Some were not native English speakers, and others were American-born but not facile in their native tongue. All found it hard to verbalize what they were thinking and feeling.

"You saw how they dance: like they have to get rid of something, quick," observes Anita, of the gang boys. "That's how they fight." When Maria asks what they need to get rid of, Anita answers, "Too much feeling."

Robbins outlined his dances on paper, plotting them like playlets. But he liked best to choreograph on his feet, in the studio, finding and then experimenting with movement, demonstrating the steps and attitudes and emotions with his customary adroitness, trying them out alongside the dancers and then reworking and reworking them. (To choreograph Mary Martin in flight in *Peter Pan,* he got himself hoisted up in the air, on a wire alongside her.)

He also researched contemporary social dances for *West Side Story.* As his biographer Deborah Jowitt recounted, he attended a high school dance in Spanish Harlem and in a letter to Tanaquil Le Clercq vividly described not just the moves, but the attitude: "They do dances that I've never seen before, evolving their own style and approach. In one dance, after starting with your partner for about 1 bar, you leave and separate and never touch or make any contact again for the whole rest of the dance. . . . each person seems to be having a ball on their own but I'm told that the partners know damn well who they're dancing with."

Dance making was for Robbins about driving, searching, soul-scouring invention. But it was also about engineering. In an interview with Rosamond Bernier he compared the satisfactions of making a dance to those of designing and erecting a bridge from scratch: "You build a step, and then you build another step, and another step," an arc "over nothing," until "it meets at the end of the ballet."

An arc stretches over the full range of the modern Shakespearean drama of *West Side Story.* Though he had associates who made important contributions to the choreography, it was Robbins who shaped and finalized the physicality of every scene. Even portions of the show that were not technically "dances" were tightly choreographed—like the flouncing comic shtick of the giddy Maria in "I Feel Pretty," which was devised by Gennaro, then re-improvised by Carol Lawrence, and finally "frozen" by Robbins.

There is dance and stylized movement throughout the show—in the buffoonery of "Gee, Officer Krupke," in the unnerving taunting and near-rape of Anita, and in the slouches and saunters and collapses and roughhousing, the running and leaping and shoving and kicking that arise organically out of the dramatic action.

The primary dance numbers in the show, as choreographed by Robbins (in stage versions and on film):

"The Prologue"

The original production of *West Side Story* began in silence as the stage curtain lifted, then smacked down its calling card in a dance that ran just under four minutes (doubled in size for the movie version), with no lyrics and little talk—an eternity, in Broadway musicals at that time.

Laurents's text describes the opening segment as "half-danced, half-mimed, with occasional bursts of dialogue." To Bernstein's early bars of spacious, soaring, syncopated music, the Jets start out "owning, enjoying, loving" their turf, until members of the Sharks get in their faces to express their own pride of ownership, and a "growing rivalry" between the gangs erupts—"mild at first: a boy being tripped up, or being sandbagged with a flour sack or even spit on," then increasingly violent, until a "free-for-all" ensues.

"It's an entire history, a prelude to the events. It's a true prologue—a Shakespearean prologue," Sondheim suggested. "You know who these gangs are, you know their rivals, that's all you need to know. It's all done in a style that says, 'You're going to see an evening of a kind of choreographed movement that's neither ballet nor traditional musical comedy dance, but you're going to see action in movement.' It was in a zone of choreographed movement that had never been done before."

The number begins with crisp staccato finger snaps by the Jets. And with high kicks, raised arms, tight pirouettes, and meaningful glares, these boys celebrate a kingdom of a few crummy Manhattan blocks as they posture like scruffy bobcats. They move with abandon yet precision, in and out of unison, enter the dance state gradually, organically. A walk becomes a strut, a strut turns into a swagger, gliding into jumping, skipping into running. Loose-hanging arms are half raised and curved in a balletic "sailing" step, then tensed into fisted thrusts. Loose turns tighten into coiled spins. The kinetic *West Side Story* dynamic of tension and release, artless everyday movement and extraordinary dancing, adolescent shenanigans and lethal force, is established.

Former dancer and Robbins colleague Peter Boal noted that in the very first moments of "The Prologue," Robbins introduces several quintessential moves that will reappear throughout the show. One is the "snap"—not just the snap of fingers clicking, but the snap as "a tight, angry, chopping" motion of the arms, the torso, the entire body, "the reduction of a punch or a stab or a kick" that becomes physical shorthand for both the Jets and Sharks.

George Chakiris (Riff in London, and Bernardo on film) pointed out in an NPR interview that in "The Prologue" the Jets "don't start dancing right off the bat. They build up to it. And again, that building up allows it to 'explode' in the way they feel about their turf and the way they own the street, and how the street feels to them . . . it's theirs."

"By the time you notice that the two groups of boys are dancing," observed Jowitt, "you've understood the restless animosity that powers the movement, and it becomes as interesting as the steps."

Something else that is subliminally established in "The Prologue" is the seductive allure of these hoodlums. Unlike vicious muggers menacing you on a dark street, they don't immediately instill fear or outrage, but fascination. They're limber, attractive youths—more about posing and swagger than serious business.

By police-blotter standards, objected critic Kenneth Tynan, "The boys are too kempt; their clothes are too pretty; they dope not, neither do they drink. This makes them unreal, and gives the show an air of sociological slumming."

So does that mean they're imposters? Not in the world *West Side Story* conjures. Just as Shakespeare charmed us in early scenes with Romeo's band of high-spirited, Verona town-square slackers and party crashers, led by the brawling ringleader Mercutio, Robbins's choreography gives Riff, Bernardo, and company a high-voltage and ingratiating introduction. These are, after all, lads full of attitude and wariness, but not at this juncture stone-cold killers eager to murder one another—even if Laurents and others think they *should* be. If the prologue helps us identify with or invest in them, Sharks and Jets alike, isn't that more useful theatrically than quickly demonizing them? Or confining them to the sociological pigeonholes Sondheim so deftly mocks in "Gee, Officer Krupke"? Time enough for us to discover how bad "the worst of us" can be, and what the jabs and jeers juiced up with bigotry can lead to.

"The Jet Song"

This dance and song, after the cops break up the street fracas, is a rollicking celebration of gang as brotherhood, as surrogate family for street castaways in need of protection and kinship. As the lyric announces, "You got brothers around, you're a family man!"

The rousing paean to gang fidelity is also a sort of mock military drill with horsing around. The Jet troops hoist their general Riff up by his legs. (In the film, he hoists himself up on a bar and does a hanging backflip off it.) When Riff heads off in search of Tony, the Jets continue the song, shadowboxing and mock-punching straight at the audience as they declare their allegiance, and continuing the pattern established in "The Prologue" of unison lines of dance continually broken up by individual offshoots of movement. All is camaraderie and cockiness, before the real, looming battle changes everything.

"The Dance at the Gym"

This splendid suite is as dramatically revelatory as the engagement party in *Romeo and Juliet,* but with dancing doing the heavy lifting instead of spoken verse.

As a bonus, it isn't one single, sustained number but several different dances in varying moods and modes, smoothly interlinked by musical transitions, all contributing to the narrative. The number bursts through from the previous scene in the dress shop: as Maria pirouettes excitedly in her new party dress, the music circles with her, and the community center magically materializes as lines of gang boys and their girls race onstage to party.

In the opening blues movement of the gym dance, there is a brief stretch of ebullient terpsichorean harmony. The Jets and their girls, looking, as Riff commanded, "sweet and sharp" in colorful suits and splashy party dresses, raise their arms and shout and take to the dance floor en masse to the raucous, infectiously delirious music, as do the Sharks, garbed in suave black suits, and their gals, in hot pastel, full-skirted frocks.

The rival groups, in a rare show of separate-but-equal unity, are sharing the same virtuoso partner-dance vocabulary at first. The choreography shrewdly and humorously combines social-dancing basics with jazz-dance athleticism, Latin accents, and jitterbug moves. There are deep knee bends, raised-high arms, quick pivots, and grinding thigh-to-thigh couplings (similar to the "fish," the dance move Robbins observed at a barrio gang dance). Again there's Robbins's trademark of short individual movement riffs that shake up the ensemble patterns, including an en pointe sequence in loafers for several Jets and (in the movie, at least) a body-twisting back handstand that was a precursor to break dancing.

The short second movement, a Promenade with a Latin fanfare, begins as tensions surface and there's new division on the dance floor. When the doltish social worker cuts in between the groups, pitifully trying to involve everyone in a "get together" dance, it's a square joke. He orders the "boys and girls" to promenade in two concentric circles. But when the music stops, the game breaks up quickly as the Jets and Sharks spurn each other's dance partners. Bernardo immediately grabs Anita, and Riff gets back with his Velma (Graziella in the film), and let the dance-off begin!

In his own version of a teen social dance, Robbins demonstrated first that the two rival groups are part of a broader American adolescent culture and actually knew and executed the same dance steps. But when forced together to "make nice," the melting pot was no more. And there were things to like and bemoan about that state of affairs.

In the thrilling third part of the number, the Mambo challenge dance, the Jets and Sharks assert themselves and bring on what each has to offer. The number is of course predominately Latin in flavor: musical scholar Elizabeth Wells likens it to the tradition of the "Cuadro Flamenco" music and dance of Spanish Gypsy derivation, "in which groups form a semicircle and take turns performing as soloists. In fact, this is exactly what Robbins's dancers do; each gang forms a semi-circle around its own dance performers who try to outdo the other 'team.' Certainly the average amateur dance enthusiast would not be able to execute Robbins's choreography, but the dance moves are based on conventions of Latin social dancing."

To intensify the rivalry, and instill more spontaneity, Robbins insisted on initially rehearsing the two would-be gangs separately for this sequence. (Gennaro worked with the Sharks; Robbins commandeered the Jets.) To the hard beat of the conga drums, the partner moves accelerate and diversify—there are spins, kicks, lifts, throws. And in one dazzling and iconic display, a dramatic diagonal line of Sharks, led by Anita, raise and arc their arms, and stomp sideways flamenco-style as they cry "Mambo!" in time with the music, in the manner one would shout "Olé!" The Jets then take over with lunging dashes across the floor, bobble-head neck jerks, and their own acrobatic, jitterbug-style pairings, escalating to exciting lifts and throws and high kicks as the music and choreography reach a pinnacle of erotic, ecstatic delirium.

The intensity is at its peak when Tony and Maria lock eyes across the room and drift slowly toward each other like enchanted sleepwalkers. This is the segue into the next dance: the cha-cha (which is, according to Wells, closer to a Puerto Rican seis couple dance). It is as chaste and serene, minuet-like, as the previous sequence was frenetic and carnal. As the Jets break back into racing lines and shout "Mambo!," scattered couples remain to take up the gentle leans forward and side steps, swiveling pliés and finger clicks of the delicate cha-cha.

Tony and Maria converse for the first time, share a gentle kiss, then the circle-dance music returns, more empathically, quickening and quickening to break the romantic spell. Finally, against a hip little musical motif of California cool jazz (the Jump), fraught words are exchanged as Bernardo upbraids Tony, and Riff demands a Sharks-and-Jets war council. And the dancing? The thrilling dynamism has dissipated, and the couples are no longer on fire but simply going through the low-key motions of pedestrian two-stepping. A new, bloodier battleground awaits to replace the boisterous and pleasurable warring of the dance floor.

"Cool"

There is so much memorable dancing in *West Side Story,* it is almost impossible to single out one Robbins number as a favorite. But "Cool" is the most volatile and, arguably, original number in its gloriously ambivalent commotion. As does the music, the dance represents a visceral kinetic struggle between chaos and order, repression and expression.

Eagerly anticipating the rumble, the Jets have "rockets in their pockets"—an image in the lyric in sync with the barely contained erotic impulses mirrored in the dancing. The Jets and their girls seethe and crumple and pop under the pressure of the pent-up rage and anxiety mounting inside them. Riff urges them to simmer down, to play it cool but also to channel their frustrations into the coming fight. They try to do so but keep erupting, separately and together, in fitful, angular spasms of movement, hysterical laughter, shouted cries of "Crazy!" "Go!" "Pow!" "Cool!"

Added to Jets moves already well established—finger snaps, corkscrew spins, pivots, skyward arms, glancing references to conventional social partner dancing—there is a battalion of new motifs here. At various points, the dancers clutch their stomachs, slide and swivel on their knees, leap into half splits, roll like logs across the floor. At one dramatic juncture, the hunched-over women, arms curved into wings, prance forward like menacing, hovering, flapping birds of prey.

To the mercurial music, which like the temperature of the dance freezes and burns, there are lightning displays of gymnastic bravura. And in a dance image that encapsulates *West Side Story* like no other, the crouching Jets ensemble coalesces into one surging organism that makes a running, jumping progression forward—then abruptly pivots and makes the same iconic journey in the opposite direction, backs to the audience.

The "Cool" dance was, recalled cast member Grover Dale, "the most difficult choreography I've ever experienced. It was six minutes long, and we had seven versions of it that we had to remember . . . Each movement was unpredictable because even if you were a trained ballet dancer, and you knew what an attitude turn was, and you knew what a relevé was, you'd never had to infuse it with such extreme emotion. [It was about] getting out of your skin, and punching out your rage against the world."

What's most remarkable about "Cool" is how completely the combinations and acrobatic fireworks embody the seething, conflicted passions of the characters at this point. The number leaves you not only admiring the prowess and endurance of the movers, but also fearing for their lives—and the harm they could inflict on others. The dance is both cathartic exorcism and battle cry. And it's an illustration of "cool" as the precarious state of emotional contents under extreme pressure.

"America"

This rooftop rave-up (which in the stage show features Anita and her sister Shark gals, and in the movie is a dance colloquy between the women and their guys) is to an extent more typical of conventional Latin-flavored show dances of the era than what comes before, or after, in *West Side Story*. But the wit and élan of the Gennaro–Robbins choreography and staging make it such a singular treat that the not-easily-impressed British director Jonathan Miller hailed it as "one of the great musical episodes of the twentieth century."

In the stage version, Anita and company teasingly bid *adios* to their men (who are going to the war council with the Jets) and strike up a debate about the merits of living in the United States versus their native Puerto Rico. Between verses of Rosalia's homesick plaint for San Juan and Anita's mockery of her provincialism and praise of U.S. prosperity, the women lustily prance, hike up and swish their skirts flamenco style, and arch into deep backbends to execute high kicks.

These grandiose moves are spiced with comic pantomimes of driving a new car, with familiar Latin cries of "Ai! Ai! Ai!" and with artfully placed and accented isolated moves—a thrust hip here, a circling raised knee there, strategic hand claps. This is an opportunity for the Puerto Rican women to show off their tantalizing verve and humor (much more of a chance, let it be said, than the more jaded Jets gals get).

In the movie, the debate-dance is brilliantly developed and expanded. Now Anita and the other women are touting life in the United States while Bernardo leads the men in sardonically pointing out its failings. It's another competition dance, with the flamenco theme adopted by the sleek, fleet men, whose suave moves are interspersed with wacky clowning—waltzing around with one another, kicking and slapping, pratfalls. Robbins has preserved the best of the women's number, but doubled the effect by unleashing the prowess of their paramours on the rooftop, as well.

"The Rumble"

"No one else," said Laurents of Robbins, "could have or would have taken a murderous knife fight and [later] an attempted gang rape and choreographed them so vividly and theatrically that the impact was emotionally devastating."

Though not officially a dance, the suspenseful and incendiary rumble scene was not simply blocked but exactingly performed to specific beats, even in the silent passages. Graceful and devoid of the phony grunts and fake slaps and punches so frequently seen in staged combat, the epic battle proceeds in thrusts, jumps, rushes, lunges, and collapses, building with the adrenaline of the music, cresting as Riff's solar plexus meets Bernardo's knife—followed immediately by Tony's impulsive stabbing of Bernardo. Then follows a shocked hush before a ferocious brawl, a police siren, and the acrobatic spectacle of gang boys scaling, vaulting, tumbling over tall fences for a quick getaway, like so many clones of Spiderman. The rumble is basically a dance of death, with nary a wasted or easeful motion.

"Somewhere" Ballet

Due to its classical ballet idiom and abstract dreaminess, the dance and vocal components of this stage number were left out of the film—though they are still staples of live productions of *West Side Story*. It is a descendent of

Agnes de Mille's famed psychological ballet "Laurie Makes Up Her Mind" from *Oklahoma!* And in the context of *West Side Story,* it is the number most representative of Bernstein's vision of the show as "an out and out plea for racial tolerance." Subsequently, it's been especially moving for those performing it and for many in the audience—though less often for critics and others who find it too didactic, obvious, and/or sentimental compared to the grittier dance passages in the show.

Dance critic Allan Ulrich acknowledged both responses by opining that "for all the naiveté and studied informality of the [ballet], its sincerity is never in doubt. Here, you feel, was the genesis of Robbins's masterwork, "Dances at a Gathering.'"

Robbins's written notes break down the ballet from the "chaotic turbulence" of the opening movements, to images of harmony emerging from dissonance as the two enemy camps come together in a "growth of [the] harmonic whole" that segues into a procession with "large open movement in enjoyment of space" in "an open area."

The primary motifs of the "Somewhere" fantasia are the separations and joinings of groups and individuals—and a vision of mutual tranquility triumphing over the all-too-real horrors of the darker aspects of existence (a theme that fascinated Robbins and was explored in other dances he made).

Tony has secretly reunited with Maria after killing her brother at the rumble, and the distraught couple sing about longing for a place "far far away" where they could escape the urban jungle and be together. The ballet then ensues, as Jets and Sharks enter, the tenement settings fly away, and Tony and Maria perform a sensitive pas de deux in front of Smith's airy, white-and-blue backdrop of sky and sea, with Manhattan in the distant background. (Sondheim has joked that the "somewhere" is actually New Jersey.) At this point both gangs, garbed in white, participate in a joyful sequence of simulated child's play and what Robbins described as a "forming of a whole—joining of groups, acceptance of groups." Meanwhile, an offstage soprano sings the plaintive ballad "Somewhere" as the others softly join in.

The dancers coalesce in a wedding procession for Tony and Maria (foreshadowing the tragic procession with Tony's corpse in the show's finale scene). But then the ghosts of Riff and Bernardo, bearing knives, enter to increasingly belligerent music, the rumble is reenacted, the movement (say Robbins's notes) "tightens" and gets "jazzier," more violent, and after the murders are reenacted, the scene fades back, cinematically, into Maria's ghetto bedroom, where the ill-fated young couple are clutching one another and yearning for a "somewhere" they can be together and safe.

For David Winters, a Jet on Broadway and in the movie, the ballet "is one of the true highlights of the show and I always feel somehow cheated when I watch the film and it is not a part of it. It says so much about the feelings, emotions and aspirations of all of the characters . . . It is Jerry at his best, and a brilliant piece of staging."

"This is what the ballet means to me," recalled Robert Arditti, Baby John in the original London company, as reported on the website wssonstage. com. "People who come from different worlds who, given the chance, will make it together. A Shark girl and a Jet boy in perfect harmony the way life should be in Tony and Maria's dream."

This is the final major dance in the show, and the most poignant. After "Somewhere," there's some expertly timed goof-around slapstick on "Gee, Officer Krupke," and the harrowing stylized movement of the "taunting" scene, in which the Jets terrorize Anita. But there is no time, no reason, to dance full-out again, as the gears of tragedy grind the story to its sad conclusion.

WEST SIDE STORY SUITE

In 1995, a stand-alone ballet titled *West Side Story Suite* was premiered by the New York City Ballet at Lincoln Center's State Theater. The piece was made by Robbins at the urging of NYCB ballet master in chief Peter Martins, a former star dancer and a fervent fan of the musical. According to Amanda Vaill, Martins and NYCB co-founder Lincoln Kerstein pressed a somewhat resistant Robbins to make "a choral ballet" of the piece—because, Kerstein wrote him, the company needed "a new 'Sleeping Beauty' . . . If we had 'West Side Story,' I would not feel so deeply worried about our repertory, and the ageing of our audience."

Robbins was persuaded, and the resultant dance was described by NYCB as a "distillation" of the original major dance sequences from *West Side Story,* separated by momentary pauses—essentially an encapsulation of the show in song and dance.

To slightly reworked arrangements of the Leonard Bernstein score, Robbins revisited and did some tweaking of "The Prologue," "The Dance at the Gym," "Cool," the "Rumble," "America," and "Somewhere" sequences, and he created a new solo for the character of Tony to "Something's Coming."

He also asked the thoroughbred NYCB dancers who appeared in the suite to do something few had ever done: sing in public. (Professional singers, positioned offstage, were also used as soloists.) Former NYCB dancer Peter Boal recalled that dancers had to audition for Robbins with a song, and some were tied up in knots with nervousness. One went in with one of the few tunes she felt comfortable with: the children's singsong rhyme "I'm a Little Teapot"–to the great amusement of Robbins and others in the room.

Singing aside, Robbins told the *New York Times* that he probably couldn't have used ballet dancers in the original *West Side Story* but found that in the 1990s they had little difficulty mastering the jazzy choreography in the suite.

"Today's popular dancing, every kid knows, all the ballet dancers know," Robbins explained. "They can jive as well as anybody else can jive, so they can move their bodies in all those different ways. They just have to push the right buttons and release them."

West Side Story Suite has indeed been a box office winner for NYCB, which held the rights closely for a decade. But in 2007, the National Ballet of Canada was able to perform the piece. And since then, the San Francisco Ballet and other companies have added it to their repertoires as a crowd-pleasing staple.

"It has been a boon to all of us," acknowledged Boal, who brought the suite into the repertoire of Seattle's Pacific Northwest Ballet, which he assumed artistic leadership of in 2005. "I feel that Jerry gave American ballet companies around the country this huge gift, and we should be very grateful for it."

"Parting is such sweet sorrow" for Norma Shearer and Leslie Howard, in the 1936 film adaptation of *Romeo and Juliet*. Courtesy of Photofest.

7

~~~~~~~~~~

I HAVE A LOVE
ROMEO AND JULIET AND
WEST SIDE STORY

Before there were the Jets and the Sharks, there were the Capulets and the Montagues. Before Maria and Tony pledged their fond devotion, so Romeo and Juliet did.

A gulf of more than three centuries separates the warring and wooing rival clans in *Romeo and Juliet* and the gangs mixing it up in *West Side Story*. But a great many conscious, canny correspondences link the musical to its Elizabethan model—a play written sometime in the 1590s by a young actor and aspiring scribe named William Shakespeare.

Both the parallels with and departures from *Romeo and Juliet* are intriguing in *West Side Story*. The show was designed by Laurents and his cohorts to transfer the Renaissance romantic tragedy to modern Manhattan. But they also wanted to keep faith with the spirit and essence and, to some extent, the form of the Bard of Avon's work—one of the most beloved and most performed English-language plays ever written.

People who know nothing much else about Shakespeare know who Romeo and Juliet are. Their names alone epitomize youth, untimely death, epic love, even when crooned in a pop ditty like the 1964 doo-wop tune "Just Like Romeo and Juliet" ("Our love's going to end in tragedy / Just like Romeo and Juliet") or the 2008 Taylor Swift country hit "Love Story" ("You were Romeo / You were throwing pebbles / And my daddy said, 'Stay away from Juliet'").

Fables of enraptured but doomed lovers, torn asunder by social oppression and ancient grudges, are rooted in the lore of most cultures through the epochs. Prominent variations on the archetype range from ancient Britain's Tristan and Isolde, to China's "Butterfly Lovers," to Tidus and Yuna in the popular Japanese video game Final Fantasy X.

Scholars speculate that Shakespeare himself pinched the basics of his plot from contemporaneous works penned by other authors—a narrative poem by Arthur Brooke ("The Tragicall Historye of Romeus and Juliet," from 1562), a version of the story from a book of legends by William Painter (*The Palace of Pleasure,* circa 1580). And those works were likely patterned on Italian tales Shakespeare may also have read—including the oft-cited *Giulietta e Romeo,* a 1554 Italian novella by Matteo Bandello.

Such is the soup pot of myth, as it bubbles, is stirred, absorbs new ingredients and flavors while others are skimmed away. As Jung expounded, the great legends cling to our collective consciousness, transcending time and geographical borders. Thus Shakespeare's *Romeo and Juliet* has been adapted countless times, in countless ways. And attempting to get literature-resistant youths excited about Shakespeare, many a modern American English-lit teacher has primed the pump with a screening of *West Side Story.*

But unlike Shakespeare's masterpiece, which is a treasure on the page with a text steeped in allusion, wit, and profundity, the Broadway musical is not in the main an act of literature. To be experienced, it must be seen and heard, witnessed and engaged. As theater director Norris Houghton noted in his preface to the joint paperback edition of Shakespeare's script and the text of *West Side Story,* just reading the musical's libretto is not enough to "lift it toward the heights of poetic rhapsody that Shakespeare's verse accomplishes unaided."

"My ears have not yet drunk a hundred words / of thy tongue's uttering / Yet I know the sound," Romeo tells Juliet in their balcony rendezvous. In *West Side Story,* song and dance must convey much of what Shakespeare's lovers say to each other in poetry and the Montagues and Capulets argue in prose and iambic pentameter.

"Maria" and "One Hand, One Heart," in their combination of simple but affecting lyrics and entrancing melodies, must serve as courtly verse. The cocky, crowing banter of Mercutio and his buddy-boys in the Verona town piazza finds its equivalent in the incendiary bravado of "The Prologue" and

"Cool" dances. And some of the comic relief supplied by Romeo's "gang" and Juliet's fussbudgety nurse is taken up in the romping antics of "Gee, Officer Krupke" and saucy dancing in "America."

Laurents and his colleagues were cognizant that a pair of poorly educated American adolescents (one a recent immigrant, who barely spoke English) could not convincingly woo in intricate couplets. It's unlikely a pair of Elizabethan-era kids would, either, for that matter—but no one expects or demands realism from Shakespeare. Nor should they from Broadway musicals.

Romeo and Juliet, had by the mid-twentieth century, already been the basis of many operas, from a 1776 German *singspiel* by Georg Benda, to still-revived works by Gounod and Bellini. (It also had been adapted into more than a dozen movies, beginning in the silent cinema era.)

Though the *West Side Story* approach to the Shakespeare text was like none other, it couldn't help but get entangled in one of the more contentious theatrical–philosophical debates of the post–World War II era. Critics and scholars were sparring at the time over such questions as: Can modern drama ever rise to the vaunted level of tragedy, in the classical Aristotelian sense, in stories about mere peons rather than lofty kings and queens? Was there sufficient sorrow and pity to be gleaned from the short tumble from grace of a Willy Loman or a Blanche DuBois, as opposed to the steep fall of a King Lear or a Phaedra?

Some prominent dramatists of the day were answering in the affirmative, hoping to find and explore something elevated, perhaps even noble, in humanity in the wake of the carnage of World War II and under the new threat of nuclear apocalypse. Wrote Albert Camus in 1945, "A great modern form of the tragic must and will be born."

More often than not, the form for tragedy chosen by leading playwrights was to update and adapt ancient classical works, as did Jean Anouilh in his antifascist resetting of *Antigone,* T. S. Eliot in *The Cocktail Party* (patterned on Euripides' *Alcestis*), and Eugene O'Neill in his epic cycle *Mourning Becomes Electra* (inspired by the *Oresteia* of Aeschylus, transplanted to 1860s America).

Drawing more attention in America were the distillations of the Greek tragedies of such figures as Clytemnestra and Medea, transformed into spellbinding compositions by pioneering modern dancer-choreographer Martha Graham. These were performed, live and on television, to broad acclaim.

Larry Kert and Carol Lawrence rehearsing the balcony scene in *West Side Story*. Courtesy of Photofest.

Graham's brand of tragedy was nonverbal, designed to be abstract, refined, starkly eloquent. She didn't plunk Greek drama queens into Hell's Kitchen. Playwright Arthur Miller, however, drew flak for daring to frame the decline of a lowly Brooklyn salesman (in *Death of a Salesman*) and the implosion of a New Jersey dock-worker (in *A View from the Bridge*) as shattering tragedies.

While a majority of critics accepted and validated the notion of beaming Shakespeare's star-crossed lovers down to the slums of Manhattan in *West Side Story,* a few found it irreconcilably incongruous and accused the musical's creators of overreaching. Consider that the two previous Broadway musical hits based on Shakespeare plays were upbeat, romantic romps which, while polished and entertaining and memorably scored, did not significantly divert from an established musical-comedy formula. *The Boys from Syracuse,* adapted from *Comedy of Errors* with a scintillating score by Richard Rodgers and Lorenz Hart, came first, in 1938. And Cole Porter's snazzy *Kiss Me, Kate,* which adroitly played a backstage show-biz romance (and Jack Cole's jazzy and inventive choreography) off a snappy musical-within-a musical based on *The Taming of the Shrew*, won raves when it arrived in 1948.

West Side Story had another agenda, more akin to high-minded poetic modern drama yet aimed at mainstream showgoers. And it was torquing a serious, almost piously revered classic, which posed additional risk for the adaptors.

An analogy can be made here with Shakespeare's own enterprise. In *Romeo and Juliet* he went against the popular grain by furthering the development of *romantic* tragedy—which departed from Greco-Roman tragedy by disobeying the unities, by showing violence onstage (rather than suggesting it had happened offstage), and by making the protagonists lovelorn kids who were well born but less than royalty, and victims of the hubris of elders rather than their own. The play was also a departure from *medieval* tragedies, which spun on the concept of fate as a wheel of fortune that can lift you high or lay you low at whim, without rhyme or reason (like a longstanding feud between two great houses).

To an (uncredited) reviewer who covered the premiere of *West Side Story* for *Time* magazine, the show's blending of realism and romanticism, grittiness and loftiness seemed forced and melodramatic. The critic argued that the "drugstore Friar Laurence" and the fire-escape balcony scene were not only distracting and anachronistic, but "tinged with bathos."

In a more thoughtful analysis, Keith Garebian suggested that *West Side Story* is more "melodrama than tragedy or even good drama: there isn't enough of a balance of contrary experiences—a balance between the malevolent gangs and a patterned world (society)" to make it really credible. He also agreed with a common objection that the hint of a rapprochement between the Jets and Sharks as they carry out Tony's body together in the end was too unmotivated to be convincing. For Garebian, "the play is finally social propaganda rather than true tragedy."

In *Romeo and Juliet,* on the other hand, Prince Escalus restores order in Verona at the play's end with a stern decree that the feuding must stop between Capulets and Montagues, but as the curtain comes down the jury's still out on whether a cease-fire is possible. Of course, there's no guarantee in *West Side Story* that the gangs will make a truce—just that they're moved and shamed enough by Maria's denunciation of hatred and violence to step forward and make a civil gesture together.

Another critical distinction between *Romeo and Juliet* and the musical, in the mind of departing producer Cheryl Crawford, was that *West Side Story* was more consistently downbeat and "humorless." Certainly the show lacks the pervasive sense of irony that flares throughout the Bard's text, partly because Romeo's buddy Mercutio was a more voluble, scathingly humorous commentator on the scene than Riff, particularly in his astonishing Queen Mab soliloquy about the evils of women. (Riff is more like an amalgam of Mercutio with Romeo's loyal, genial cousin Benvolio, whose Italian name means, ironically, "peacemaker.")

In another point of departure, *West Side Story* can be linked to a broader twentieth-century movement that emboldened Shakespeare interpreters to retreat from the so-called Elizabethan style of performance and reset the classic plays in other historical contexts and aesthetic frameworks. Edward Craig caused a stir when he created a modernist-looking *Hamlet* for the Moscow Art Theatre. And in America, by the time Orson Welles was regaling Broadway with his 1930s "voodoo" version of *Macbeth,* transplanted from Scotland to Haiti and featuring an African American cast, nontraditional productions of Shakespeare were becoming both acceptable and trendy.

West Side Story merits special commendation for its canny, streamlined reworking of a very familiar tale, and the inclusion of some resonant parallels between the two works. Some of these correspondences are easy to spot. And there are some, less obvious borrowings from the Bard also—like the Riff–Tony friendship vow "womb to tomb" lightly echoing Shakespeare's lines "The earth that's nature's mother is her tomb / What is her burying grave that is her womb." And the way Tony's song "Maria" bounces off Juliet's "What's in a name?" speech.

Character Parallels in *West Side Story* and *Romeo and Juliet:*

	Romeo and Juliet	***West Side Story***
Lovers from warring groups:	Romeo and Juliet	Tony and Maria
Pack leader/brotherly friend:	Mercutio/Benvolio	Riff
Adult advisor/apothecary:	Friar Laurence	Doc
Other gang's leader:	Tybalt	Bernardo
Spurned suitor:	Paris	Chino
Older woman confidante:	Nurse	Anita
The law:	Prince Escalus	Schrank
Hotheaded gang member:	Sampson	Action, A-Rab

Plot Parallels in *West Side Story* and *Romeo and Juliet*:

1 The story opens with taunts and a street fight between rival groups of youths, which is quickly broken up by adult authorities.

2. A pretty and sheltered young girl, whose family has selected her future husband, prepares to attend a special party where she meets a young man from a rival clan; they dance together, and fall instantly in love, to the chagrin and censure of their kinsmen.

3. The infatuated boy wanders the streets to find his beloved's home and calls up to her room. She appears on her "balcony," and they exchange names and declare feelings for each other in defiance of social norms.

4. The young couple has a secret rendezvous, with the help of older allies.

5. During a violent clash between gangs/clans, the boy's closest friend is stabbed to death by a relative of the girl's, whom the boy then impulsively murders in revenge.

6. After the killings, the lovers unite in secret, reaffirm their love, and sexually consummate their union.

7. Due to a missed message, the couple does not reunite and embark on a life together, and their affair ends with death.

8. The authorities appear, and the senseless warring and loss of young life is publicly bemoaned.

In collusion with Bernstein and Robbins, Laurents copied Shakespeare's template to great advantage, but not slavishly so. When it served the musical's purposes, he took the license to detour from the *Romeo and Juliet* narrative, as Robbins encouraged. In a couple of cases, he claims to have improved on it.

Fully explaining and motivating every aspect of the story, at the expense of its organic emotional core, would be as wrong as if Shakespeare had literally justified everything in his tale—including the strange actions of Juliet's nurse and the unusually tolerant priest who "enables" the lovers.

Answering Cheryl Crawford's contention that Tony's murder did not seem "inevitable," in a classical-tragedy sense, Laurents countered by letter, "Neither is Romeo's or Juliet's. And I don't think it matters. What does matter to me is that the audience is convinced of [Tony's] desire to be killed. That is character and this is more important than all the sociological, crotch-scratching facts in the naturalistic world."

Key Differences Between *West Side Story* and *Romeo and Juliet:*

1. *Motivation for the Jets-versus-Sharks feud:* The Capulets and the Montagues shared a longstanding enmity not uncommon to clannish societies in the Renaissance and medieval eras. What incident or curse their mutual hatred was initially based on is unexplained and immaterial to *Romeo and Juliet.*

   In *West Side Story* there is an immediate, urgent, and comprehensible reason for the gangs' rivalry. It is an enmity born of poverty, ignorance, and cultural prejudice. The white Jets believe they are protecting what is theirs—indeed, it is all they "own"—by keeping the immigrant Puerto Rican Sharks off their turf. Says Riff, "We fought hard for this territory and it's ours. But with those cops servin' as cover, the PRs can move in right under our noses and take it away. *Unless* we speed fast and clean 'em up in one all-out fight!"

   By the same token, the Sharks react to this hostile reception with disdain and violence of their own. Their hatred of "white boys" is born of experience, as is their need to defend themselves and establish a safety zone, a home turf.

2. *No parents, no former loves:* Laurents "threw out Rosalind," the former girlfriend of Romeo whom he pines for before meeting Juliet. Romeo is teased by his friends for carrying the torch, and later for his fickleness in swiftly banishing from his heart one love and replacing her with another. As Laurents put it, Shakespeare made Romeo "lovesick for Rosalind, but two minutes later, one look at Juliet and he is lovesick again."

   By editing out this aspect of the tale, Laurents streamlines the action and makes the Tony/Maria romance all the more special. He loses

Shakespeare's ironic commentary on the fickleness of young love, and Romeo's romantic immaturity prior to his fateful union with Juliet.

As the musical opens, Tony is already entering adulthood by shedding the gang colors and working at Doc's. Part of this is a difference of class: the Capulets and Montagues are "great houses," which implies wealth and elevated social stature. Tony is the son of immigrants, a working stiff with little time to moon around.

Eliminating the parents of the lovers was a more significant shift. In the fire-escape scene we do *hear* Maria's parents briefly. They urge her in Spanish to come inside and go to bed, while she is on the balcony secretly meeting with Tony. (The lines are spoken offstage by actors from the ensemble.)

Otherwise, the only representation of parents occurs when Tony and Maria affectionately impersonate them, during the scene in the bridal shop. The parents were not in the show, explained Laurents, "because the play no longer centered on a family feud but on a tribal feud: ethnic warfare between juvenile gangs. "

Back when the project was titled "East Side Story," Laurents and company imagined an older relative, a "tante" (auntie) in the nurse role. But by cutting out all blood-related elders, Laurents and company kept the story tightly focused on the milieu and experience of young people. The three remaining adults (Doc, Schrank, and Krupke) are alien life forms to these kids: their warnings and threats are either scorned or ignored by youths alienated from standardized morality, from the law, from any sort of grown-up hierarchy.

The youths answer only to each other, which conveys a sense of their autonomy and their detachment from society at large, or any traditional family structure. And whether this was a choice born of theatrical expediency or sociological awareness (or some of both), it did reflect the erosion of the nuclear family that was already beginning in the late 1950s. Particularly within communities where both parents had to work long hours to make ends meet, adolescents were increasingly tempted out of the family circle into a youth culture with such benign enticements as sock hops and drive-in movies, and such darker bait as crime and violence.

3. *Not getting the messages:* In Laurents's book, the most ingenious detour from Shakespeare (and one that he remarked upon with pride) was another switching of a plot device into a justified action in keeping with the overall narrative.

In Shakespeare, Romeo is sent word of Juliet's plan to feign death, so the two can unite and make a new start together incognito, outside of Verona. But due to a plague, the messenger is delayed in delivering this news. And by the time he does, Romeo has heard that Juliet has died and is rushing back to commune with her in the crypt and join her in the afterlife.

Laurents discarded the device in the musical. Rather than a "convenient plague" screwing up the message, "it's prejudice—the factor basic to the story and the theme."

Such bigotry is forcefully, brutally played out in the scene where Anita goes to deliver a message from Maria to Tony. Juliet's nurse is teased but not physically threatened on her mission to the Montague gang, but Anita is racially taunted and physically attacked by the Jets. After Doc intervenes on her behalf, she is so traumatized and repulsed she shouts out the lie that triggers the final tragedy, telling the Jets that Maria was gunned down by Chino and is dead.

This falsehood quickly leads to Tony's death, a virtual suicide, after he wanders out into the dark street and shouts for Chino to kill him, too. Like Romeo, he does not want to live in a world without his beloved—though it's unclear whether he or Maria shares the Renaissance belief in a heavenly afterlife.

4. *Who dies in the story:* In the musical, Tony stabs to death Bernardo, the brother of his sweetheart. That is a meaningful shift from Romeo's murder of Juliet's cousin Tybalt. Not only is Bernardo a closer relation to Maria, he's also a more developed (and sympathetic) character than Tybalt. His slaying shocks more and heightens the sense of loss, partly because of Anita's grief. (Tybalt has no equivalent of an Anita.)

But the most glaring difference between the two tragic dramas is the final sequence and final murder. In Shakespeare's text, an accident of fate results in a double suicide: Juliet feigns death with the friar's potion; Romeo believes she has perished and kills himself. Then Juliet, awakened in the arms of her dead lover, mortally wounds herself with his dagger to follow him to the afterlife.

The *West Side Story* team seriously considered killing off Maria and debated how it might be done. In a 1955 draft outline, it is *Maria* who learns falsely that *Tony* (then called Romeo) is dead. In reaction she obtains a bottle of poison and drinks it, and it is Tony who survives to mourn. In other drafts they both die, or both survive—which demonstrates the creators' difficulty in forging the right ending, the finale to make the audience (as Laurents put it) "swoon."

According to Robbins, it was composer Richard Rodgers who helped them decide Maria's fate. "We had a death scene for Maria—she was going to commit suicide or something, as in Shakespeare. [Rodgers] said, 'She's dead already, after this all happens to her.'" Indeed, her slow, mournful exit in the show's waning moments speaks volumes about the burden of sorrow this very young woman will shoulder the rest of life.

The ending also gave the show's final words of condemnation and woe to a new, changed, matured Maria—rather than to a more formal authority figure like Prince Escalus (or Schrank). Maria can now articulate how both Jets and Sharks shared responsibility for her beloved's death and deliver (in essence) his eulogy. She's no longer the adorable sprite excited about attending her first dance, but a widow and an oracle. She's become the living embodiment of society's failings.

At the close of *Romeo and Juliet,* Prince Escalus admonishes, "Where be these enemies? Capulet! Montague! / See, what a scourge is laid upon your hate / That heaven finds means to kill your joys with love." But for Maria this is a more personal cataclysm—it is happening to *her.* As she brandishes the gun, she implicates the entire community in Tony's death: "We all killed him; and my brother and Riff." But her very next line pierces the heart, because it is about her own transformation: "I can kill now because I can hate now."

Romeo and Juliet faced criticism from some literary purists over the centuries for not being a classic tragedy for lack of a "tragic flaw" that causes the "tragic necessity" of the hero's demise and the other mayhem in the play. It is *chance t*hat ultimately does the newlyweds in—but the ancient grudges of Verona are what land them in harm's way. Theirs is ultimately a social tragedy, not one triggered by individual misdeeds and hubris. This Verona pair are a couple of crazy kids who are mad for each other, and in a less violently polarized environment they might have just married and been content.

While borrowing many aspects of the narrative and characterizations Shakespeare so indelibly inked, *West Side Story* provides more of a context for the societal failings that result in the denial and death of young, fresh, healing love. Judging by how emotionally gripped and moved audiences can be by the musical's sobering finale, it weaves a spell even Shakespeare himself might recognize as palpably, genuinely tragic.

Inner city high school teacher Glenn Ford menaced by scary teen boys, in the 1955 movie, *Blackboard Jungle.* Courtesy of Photofest.

8

WE AIN'T NO DELINQUENTS
WEST SIDE STORY
AND THE RISE OF JUVENILE
DELINQUENCY

West Side Story did not exist in an artistic vacuum, nor did it emerge from a social vacuum. It emerged from an American society in the midst of reinventing itself and its popular culture. And the show contributed to a flood of popular images of troubled teens promulgated by the news media, the political and social-welfare establishment, the entertainment industry—images of a new adolescent archetype both abhorrent and alluring to the general public.

In 1957, the nation at large was tuned in to the worsening phenomenon of juvenile delinquency—a problem both authentically worrisome and readily sensationalized. The issue of rising numbers of wayward youth was reflected and debated in tabloids and respected newspapers, in cheesy B movies and glossy studio features, in comic books and the burgeoning musical craze of rock-and-roll. There were research studies on this problem, as well as prominent congressional hearings chaired by U.S. Senator Estes Kefauver (D-Tennessee)— including one in 1954 on the threat of comic books as demoralizing influences on the nation's teenagers.

As stories of defiant, troubled teens became more prevalent and lurid, the news reports and studies more worrisome, the bad boys/bad girls syndrome was also closely scrutinized by a battery of experts who came to the fore to give their verdicts on the trend—criminologists, sociologists, welfare workers, psychiatrists. (Sondheim mirthfully and astutely parodied them in the song "Gee, Officer Krupke"—a lampoon that didn't have to exaggerate much to be funny.

Public anxiety in America over hooliganism and immigrant street gangs was not new, of course. It had been part of the country's urban dynamic long before the *West Side Story* era—in fact, since the republic began. As Thomas Hine pointed out in *The Rise and Fall of the American Teenager,* such waywardness "is a subject of constant concern and intermittent panic in the society"—often in relation to immigration, as dramatized in Martin Scorsese's historical film drama *Gangs of New York,* about mid-nineteenth-century Dutch and English New Yorkers carrying out vendettas against newer arrivals to America, and in countless 1930s gangster pics like *Scarface* and *Little Caesar,* focused on antihero criminal bosses who were first-generation Americans of European (Italian, Irish, etc.) background.

In the more squalid sectors of America's Wild West during the California Gold Rush, and especially in the late nineteenth and early twentieth centuries, periods of massive foreign migrations to the United States, violent youth gangs created havoc.

Clashes of race, religion, and ethnicity, not just nationality, precipitated waves of criminal delinquency. Observed Hine, "It's a recurring theme of American life that the generations are ethnically different from one another, and that the rising generation appears less 'American' than the one doing the perceiving."

If it was sometimes treated for dramatic or journalistic purposes as a tawdry sideshow, the upswing of youth crime from the late 1940s through the 1950s is a well-documented fact. According to the U.S. Census, between 1950 and 1959, U.S. citizens aged twelve to seventeen rose from 12.9 to 17.9 million, including a growing influx of newcomers to the mainland from Puerto Rico. According to FBI statistics reported in a 1957 *Life* magazine issue devoted to the nationwide crime surge, criminal acts overall rose 40 percent in the country between 1946 and 1956. (The story is dated September 9, two weeks before the *West Side Story* premiere, and features artwork of a hoodlum in a "Sharks" jacket on the cover).

Chronic truancy was also rising during this period. So were school dropout rates, just as a high school diploma was starting to become a requirement for a decent job and the community college movement was putting higher education within reach of millions more Americans than before. An underlying factor was, not surprisingly, high-density urban poverty. People were trapped in "degrading" living conditions, as Senator Kefauver termed them in his committee report, which bred "hunger and despair" and a belief among young people that "society is their enemy."

In the mid-1950s, New York City began to address teen delinquency with a smattering of special schools, a new Youth Bureau, and some special law enforcement patrols. But without enough well-funded, well-run programs to raise the income of cash-strapped families, keep their kids in school, and improve their housing, such measures were very small Band-Aids on a growing, festering wound.

Newspapers widely reported the findings of the Uniform Crime Report, a 1957 law enforcement study, which charted a whopping increase in the arrest of minors in New York City between 1952 and 1957. The vast majority of arrests were for petty, victimless offenses (underage drinking, breaking a curfew, driving without a license), but the trend was disturbing nonetheless.

The same year, the *New York Herald Tribune* reported that law-abiding citizens felt "a sickening sense of shock" about the numbers and viciousness of such incidents as the fatal knife attack on an innocent young polio victim by one of his peers. "If this alarming growth isn't checked at the beginning," the story warned, "the result may well be that there won't be enough prisons to hold all the criminals."

The constant drumbeat of news coverage of delinquency and gang crime (in Los Angeles and New York newspapers, mainly but not exclusively) was a major factor in the *West Side Story* team's decision to shift the focus and ethnic makeup of their initial "East Side Story" concept. Transporting the story from the Lower East Side, nearer to where so-called Spanish and white gangs were staking out turf and defending it with real switchblades and real blood, was a timely move mirroring New York City's changing demographics.

Robbins, Sondheim, Laurents, and Bernstein were all prosperous and urbane show folk, with no direct experience and limited previous knowledge of New York's gang life. So, as most artists do, they relied on both imagination and research to give *West Side Story* some sense of realism and credulity. Gang members, then and now, have apparently found the musical's plot and characters very credible—or perhaps they just think it validates them. (Youthful offenders over the decades have also identified with somewhat romanticized treatments of antihero urban outlaws in movies ranging from the 1930s James Cagney flick *Angels with Dirty Faces* to the 1983 update of *Scarface* starring Al Pacino.)

An inveterate researcher, Robbins explored gang haunts up to the far reaches of the Upper East Side, in Spanish Harlem, in his quest to give the show immediacy and authenticity. "Just 20 blocks away from my NY office, I found there was a world entirely new to me," he told *Dance Magazine*. "The streets are darker, the signs are in Spanish, and the people lead their lives on the sidewalks."

"I went to the territory of the delinquents when I was developing the show—went to their social directors, talked to gang members and leaders, visited their dances, and came away with the impression that the kids have a feeling of being born into one of the worst possible worlds, and that they think they have to live their lives now—without delay."

To educate his cast, Robbins, as previously discussed, scoured magazines and newspapers for stories about gang-related incidents, which he posted on the rehearsal hall bulletin board. But Robbins also looked to popular culture, past and current—to Dead End Kids movies he grew up watching and to contemporary depictions of delinquency in popular films like *Blackboard Jungle*—for dramatic inspiration.

REAL HOODLUMS

Robbins and company were not the only ones investigating the human dramas behind the statistics. For a project never completed, playwright Arthur Miller tagged along with a youth worker in the poor, mostly Irish American Red Hook section of Brooklyn. (Miller later wrote in his memoir, *Timebends,* about the fights and alienation he observed among those teens.)

And in 1958, a multipart series in the *New York Times,* "The Shook-Up Generation" by veteran reporter Harrison Salisbury, shocked many readers with its in-depth look at the inner workings of gangs like the ones the Jets and Sharks were based on. Salisbury estimated that 75 to 100 street gangs existed in New York City at the time, predominantly in the poorest sections, with up to 20 members in each crew. (Other estimates placed the total number of gangs and gang members much higher.) Black gangs were the most numerous, in his estimation, alongside white crews (mainly Irish and Italian) and "Spanish" outfits (mostly Puerto Rican, with some other Latin and South Americans). There were some racially integrated clans, as well.

Like urban street posses everywhere, the groups offered their members physical protection from rivals and a "pseudo family" to replace the impoverished and/or dysfunctional biological clans they felt emotionally estranged from—and sometimes, due to abandonment or other forced separation, lived apart from them.

In a 2009 *New York Times* story, former gang veterans and other witnesses confirmed that most of the street battles in the 1950s were over turf. Retired police detective Vincent J. Hefferen recalled that the gang credo of the period was "'Don't bother my territory, don't get in my way. . . . This is my territory, stay out of it, and so forth.'" Some gangs had a paramilitary bent, patrolling and defending their borders like occupying armies. "They feel they have to band together to 'own' a piece of a terrible block in a miserable slum area," Robbins noted. "Alone they are nothing, but together, as a gang, they gain a fantastic sense of security."

The gang boys Salisbury reported on got plastered on "sneaky pete" (cheap wine) and flaunted their sexual exploits with neighborhood girls— the "loose" girls, who escaped their own dreary circumstances by latching on to testosterone-fueled punks. When push came to shove, trash talk between gangs and perceived infringements could escalate into a rumble, a kind of battle described by *Time* magazine as "bloody combat with knives, machetes, guns . . . garrison belts" and "skin-slashing with automobile-radio aerials stolen from any handy car."

Some of the assaults were unspeakably brutal. But not all gangs were so bloodthirsty, and some stuck to a code of duking it out only with bare fists (as Tony proposes to Bernardo and Riff), to prove one's dominance the old-fashioned, *mano-a-mano* way. And most scraps were about threats and posturing, sputtering out before anyone got hurt.

But lethal mayhem could flare up suddenly, as it does in the *West Side Story* rumble. with adolescent caprice. For a famous series of photographs shot in the summer of 1959, art photographer Bruce Davidson took candid portraits of a gaggle of stylishly cool but tough-as-nails Irish Catholic kids in poor sections of Brooklyn. He spent days hanging out with these misfits and their girlfriends on their home turf. Decades later, at a reunion with some of those who survived into middle age, Davidson confessed to the *New York Times* that while with his volatile subjects, "'I was very scared. . . . They were very unpredictable. I was never sure if their anger was going to focus on me.''

Robbins reported that he got along well with the troubled kids he met at the time, and he sincerely rooted for their survival into adulthood. It moved him when some of them attended, at his invitation, a *West Side Story* performance on Broadway and they mistakenly prepared to leave at intermission, thinking the show had ended with the murders of Riff and Bernardo. For them, Robbins recalled, "the rumble that left two dead bodies on stage at the Act One curtain seemed like a natural conclusion."

THE YOUTH MARKET

Though taken for granted later, the idea of the "teenager" as a distinct demographic and developmental category was in the early 1950s still a fairly new concept. America's shift from an agrarian to an urban/suburban culture, the prolonging of adolescence due to compulsory education, and the relative peace and prosperity of the Cold War years meant that many teens who did *not* live in slum conditions had leisure time and their own pocket money to spend.

The advertising and mass-media establishments took note. *Mad Men*–style Madison Avenue ad agencies pushed a flood of new products—from soft drinks to acne cream to blue jeans—developed especially for the teen market. And along with the authorized "role models" of clean-cut youths in magazine ads and on wholesome TV sitcoms (*Leave It to Beaver, Ozzie and Harriet*) came the depictions of youth violence, lust, alienation, crime, out-of-wedlock pregnancy, and rebellion against the adult establishment—sometimes on serious-minded live TV dramas, but more often in B-movies, comic books, pulp novels, and rock songs blaring on radios and from soda fountain jukeboxes (like the one in Doc's drugstore in *West Side Story*).

A 1956 article in the showbiz bible *Variety* reported that "in recent months exhibitors have clamored for film fare that would appeal to teenage customers whom they regard as their best audiences." In response to the trend, FBI director J. Edgar Hoover, ever on the lookout for domestic subversion, railed at youth-oriented entertainments that "flout indecency and applaud lawlessness," and he blamed the movie craze on an alleged "undercover army" of traitors who "seek to disrupt our institution of government."

West Side Story was clearly no *Jailhouse Rock* or *High School Confidential,* artistically or commercially. The musical's target audience on Broadway was not disenfranchised teens but fairly prosperous, cultured, theatergoing adults. Indeed, some parents considered the show too dark and seamy for their own impressionable adolescents to attend along with them. (The absence of parental figures in the show reflects a larger trend in representing a teenage sphere that is a world unto itself, where adults are largely viewed as suspicious, oppressive, and unwelcome.) And while the movie *West Side Story* attracted a vast youth audience, it appealed across a broader age spectrum.

Also, unlike the dozens of fairly cheesy and cheaply produced teen flicks, *West Side Story* took its subject matter seriously and was generally taken seriously in return. In *The Saturday Review,* Henry Hewes wrote that author Laurents "penetrates the problem of juvenile delinquency in a way that should give all of us pause. From the beginning he faces the hard fact that today's teen-ager, who alternates between purposeless violence and sullen detachment, cannot really be explained by use of specific phrases like 'insufficient housing' and 'broken homes.' Rather, he implies that adult sins of omission on the highest level of national and international policy create the vacuum which these teenagers feel obliged to fill with their fierce and cool bravado."

 West Side Story is a work of fictional entertainment, not a curative of adolescent misdeeds. But it has been, and continues to be, a catalyst for more awareness and understanding of youth crime and conflict. And it's been applied as such in a variety of situations.

In 2007, in conjunction with its fiftieth-anniversary production of the show, Seattle's 5th Avenue Theatre joined forces with the Seattle Police Department in a well-regarded model educational program involving hundreds of high school and middle school students.

In workshops and "youth summits," the participants considered their own generation's gang activities. The program produced a "modern version" of the musical, performed by students and created with their input. "It's us teenagers that need to talk to our kind of people instead of adults," sixteen-year-old participant Roxie Torres told the *Seattle Times.* "Teenagers can be kind of stubborn. If we can get to one kid, we can get to a lot."

The street punk John Cassavetes threatens Peter Votrian in the 1956 movie, *Crime in the Streets.* Courtesy of Photofest.

TEENS ONSCREEN

Scores of teens-in-crisis films and dramas around the time of *West Side Story* may have influenced the musical or at least whetted the public's appetite for it.

The majority of films in the genre were titillating B melodramas or spoofy comedies—from cheapie dramas like *Reform School Girl,* *Juvenile Jungle,* and *The Fast and the Furious,* to the popular Jerry Lewis romp *The Delicate Delinquent.* There were also numerous horror knock-offs that equated adolescence with monstrousness, like *I Was a Teenage Werewolf* and *Teenage Zombies.*

That's not to discredit the TV, theatrical, and movie dramas on the topic that were intelligent, well-produced, and thoughtful attempts to portray a worrisome social phenomenon and probe the concerns the news media were also highlighting: What do these kids really want? Why? And how do we tame them into law-abiding future adults?

Here is a sampling of some of the more noteworthy and iconic attractions. Along with the wildly successful 1961 film of *West Side Story,* they helped to define the modern "youth problem" for the general public:

> *The Wild One* (1953)—A surly, seductive young Marlon Brando, wearing a leather jacket and a smirk, immortalizes the modern teen antihero in his magnetic performance as Johnny Strabler, the leader of a motorcycle gang terrorizing a small California town. Made on the cheap, the movie benefited at the box office from its kids-take-over-the-world scenario, and even

more from Brando's mesmerizing performance. The script is workmanlike but has one of the all-time great alienated-punk lines. When asked, "What are you rebelling against?" Johnny responds: "Whaddya got?"

Blackboard Jungle (1955)—More genuinely shocking at the time, this film, based on a well-read Evan Hunter novel, sparked a nationwide discussion of youth delinquency in public schools. It depicts the attempts of an earnest teacher (Glenn Ford) to get through to his hostile, unruly, disinterested students, including snarling top thug Vic Morrow and a young and riveting Sidney Poitier. The picture was ahead of its time in shedding light on racial tensions in city schools and posing the moral dilemma of whether an idealistic educator, whose own safety and his family are at risk by his inner-city job, should flee to a suburban school—a corollary to the "white flight" already in progress among white city-dwellers in enclaves being "overtaken" by new influxes of poor and minority residents.

The alternative for the Glenn Ford character was a more heroic stance: stand his ground, risking life and limb, and redouble his efforts to reach and reform his threatening, scary charges.

Blackboard Jungle was also the first Hollywood film to prominently use rock music in the score. The title sequence was backed up by the seminal rock-and-roll tune "Rock Around the Clock" by Bill Haley and the Comets, which shot up the Billboard charts after the movie's successful release.

Rebel Without a Cause (1955)—James Dean's exquisitely sensitive, jammed-up suburban kid was not a gang member per se, though he did act out with drag racing, public drunkenness, and anti-parental torment. But Dean cast the cinematic mold for the beautiful, disillusioned lost boy searching for an alternative family to replace his clueless parents. He formed his own little clan with Natalie Wood (yes, the future cinematic Maria) and budding teen star Sal Mineo. *Rebel* cast member Dennis Hopper described Dean's portrayal of Jim Stark as an amalgam of two alienated-teen archetypes: "Marlon Brando in one hand screaming, 'Screw you!' and Montgomery Clift in the other saying, 'Help me!'"

Crime in the Streets (1956)   Ripped from the same kind of headlines that led to *West Side Story*, this unusually graphic Hollywood feature portrays the escalating war between two white New York street gangs, the Hornets (led by a blazing young John Cassavetes) and the Dukes (including Mark Rydell and the ubiquitous Sal Mineo). When a neighbor "rats" on a gang member involved in a brutal beating, a revenge murder is planned by Cassavetes's hotheaded Frankie. But here adults are very much on the scene, too—including a youth center social worker (James Whitmore) trying to prevent more bloodshed, and some well-meaning but ineffectual, care-worn parents. It's considered a minor teen-noir masterpiece and a frightening portrait of the ruthless young sociopath of America's worst nightmares.

The Delinquents (1957)—Of interest now mainly because it was an early work by director Robert Altman, later a celebrated screen auteur, this independent feature (which Altman also wrote and produced, on a bare-bones budget of $63,000) used Method-style acting techniques to achieve an improvisational flavor that would become a hallmark of the director's idiosyncratic cinematic work.

The plot is moralistic, in the same bag as many early "j.d." dramas. It concerns a suburban teenage boy (played by future *Billy Jack* star Tom Laughlin) who, to his eventual regret, becomes embroiled with a crew of wild teen thugs and implicated in an armed burglary they commit.

After some tense and ugly misadventures, he is able to escape their clutches. But the message was typically mixed: Stay away from bad company—but wow, can hanging out with the wrong kids ever make your life more exciting. The trailer for the film promised a date with "The kids that live today like there's no tomorrow!" (Presumably, their transgressions were far more appealing to many teen viewers than the story's moral epiphany.)

Take a Giant Step (1959). "Here is the real rage behind today's tormented 'Blue Jeans' Generation!" screamed the trailer for this movie. "Here's what makes them tick. What makes them tough. What makes them tremble . . ."

Though the ads were tawdry, the film itself was based on a meaningful 1953 stage play by African American writer Louis Peterson. In the semi-autobiographical story, a black teenager comes into manhood in a white New England community, while tangling with a bigoted teacher at his high school and dealing with ostracism by his white peers.

The film, which starred the handsome young pop singer Johnny Nash, was panned by the *New York Times* for filming the well-received play in a "clumsy, shoddy fashion."

But onstage and even on film, Peterson's work was noteworthy and influential for its psychological and largely realistic portrait of adolescence in a country still riven by racial division. As Harold Clurman wrote in his review of the play in *The Nation,* "the particular color, immediacy and urgency of its feeling—a kind of emotional frankness, a wry naiveté and a rough goodness of heart that smack of something truly native, original in tone and unmistakably lived."

The Jets, led by the airborne Russ Tamblyn as Riff, mark their turf, in the 1961 movie adaptation of *West Side Story*. Courtesy of Photofest.

9

WHAT WAS JUST
A WORLD IS A STAR
WEST SIDE STORY THE MOVIE

H ow did *West Side Story* become a worldwide hit and perennial cultural icon? That is no mystery. We have the Oscar-showered blockbuster movie version to thank for that.

Made for roughly $6.7 million (or about $48 million in 2010 dollars, a steep budget for Hollywood at the time), the cinematic *West Side Story* was released in October 1961, not long after the return Broadway premiere engagement of *West Side Story* closed in New York, and while the debut London production was still running.

A much-touted and instantaneous smash, the movie grossed an estimated $43 million onscreen in the United States alone (the equivalent of $300 million in 2010), won ten 1961 Academy Awards, including best motion picture (making it one of the top Oscar winners of all time), and is rated by the American Film Institute as one of the two best movie musicals ever made, second only to *Singin' in the Rain*. *West Side Story* has also made an estimated $20 million in rentals and sold an unknown (but certainly substantial) number of DVDs and videotapes. It has been deemed "culturally significant" by the U.S. Library of Congress and in 1997 was added to the National Film Registry for preservation.

The movie and the best-selling recording of the movie score enriched the coffers of the show's creators and backers, in amounts far greater than they could have anticipated. "Our investors are the beneficiaries of that movie sale, which was very small [about $350,000] but with a substantial piece of the gross," Harold Prince noted. "When we sold [the rights] nobody wanted it. No one cared and then it turned out to be this monumental success . . . but not because of its life on Broadway."

Prince may be overstating the case here: it's hard to imagine a high pitch of public excitement and anticipation for the movie, without the hoopla and international coverage *West Side Story* had generated on Broadway— attention that belied the relatively modest box office receipts. Another reason the movie was so eagerly awaited, surely, was the popularity of the Broadway cast album of the show.

But it's true that the Broadway reception of *West Side Story* was a pale shadow of what greeted the film. A majority of critics gushed over the latter, prior to its much-hyped first release in deluxe movie palaces (with reserved seating at premium prices). Pronouncing it a "cinematic masterpiece," *New York Times* reviewer Bosley Crowther led the full-throated chorus of praise. "In every respect," he decreed, "the recreation of the Arthur Laurents– Leonard Bernstein musical in the dynamic forms of motion pictures is superbly and appropriately achieved." The *New York Herald Tribune* went further, calling it the "film that must not be missed this year" and promising that "the pure animal energy at times overflows the screen."

Concern arose early on that the youth-gang subject matter might stir up some trouble. At one California showing in a poor, crime-riddled district, a crush of young people turned out and officials feared they might have a riot on their hands. But it turned out to be just an excited bunch of kids eager to see *West Side Story*.

Among the mostly bowled-over reviewers there were some adamant naysayers. A disdainful Dwight MacDonald slammed the movie in his *Esquire* magazine column. The uncredited reviewer for *Time* pronounced the film morally repugnant, declaring hyperbolically that "it goes wildly, insufficiently wrong when it insists that society is entirely guilty, that the teen-age hoodlums are ultimately innocent." But most damning was Pauline Kael's thorough trashing of the movie in her *New Yorker* review. She did acknowledge the depth of fan ardor for the movie years later, by mentioning in a *Modern Maturity* magazine interview that she "broke up with somebody after I wrote about 'West Side Story.' It's very difficult to disagree on a date."

Though it brought renewed attention to their labor of love, the co-creators of *West Side Story* were ambivalent about the film at the least, and at the worst openly reviled it. Laurents, a veteran screenwriter who did not pen the screenplay (Ernest Lehman, who earlier scripted *The King and I,* did the honors and received an Oscar nomination), was the most openly dismissive, pronouncing it "appalling."

"In the movie, gangs became boys with dyed hair doing ballet steps down city streets and clothes became costumes. Even the deaths were overblown in rotating color as was the acting," he complained. "Only the vitality of the music survived."

Bernstein, who composed some additional passages of music for the film, was reportedly disappointed that the sound mix on the musical track was overbearing and lacking in texture and subtlety. Sondheim, obliged to tweak some "objectionable" lyrics at the request of the producers, was pleased about certain changes—the substitution of his original version of "America" and the shifting of the "Gee, Office Krupke" and "Cool" numbers. Still, he, too, has expressed dissatisfaction with the overall product.

And Robbins, who threw himself into the making of the movie and prospered greatly by it? He did not mince words in assessing its shortcomings. After seeing the final cut for the first time, he wrote to a friend, dance critic Richard Buckle: "Some of it is wonderful and exciting (and I don't mean just everything I did), but some of it gets bogged down in the lack of understanding of what the scenes or the musical numbers were about. And occasionally 'Hollywood' rears its ugly head and splatters the screen with the soft lights streaming from Heaven or garish Technicolor or STEREOPHONIC SOUND."

However, the movie was, all in all, a personal victory for Robbins, if a very conflicted one. He was awarded an Oscar for directing the feature, as was his co-director Robert Wise. And he received an additional, honorary Academy Award for, as the statuette read, "Brilliant achievements in the art of choreography on film." But Robbins lost control of the filming process, and the experience clipped short a movie career he had long aspired to. (He was probably the most successful first-time Hollywood director to never work again in the medium.)

Legitimate complaints against the *West Side Story* film were registered (and still are) about the casting of a pair of Hollywood actors who were (to be kind) hardly ideal for Tony and Maria in ability or interpretation. The obvious dubbing of their singing voices and the uninspired editing of some of the musical numbers were also problematic. So were the exaggerated look and accents of the Puerto Rican characters and their makeup, which costar Rita Moreno later complained made them look as if they'd fallen into "a bucket of mud." (The makeup in general, following Hollywood practices of the day, was ghastly—everyone looked oil-painted and lacquered.)

But one can be thankful for the ways the celluloid *West Side Story did* succeed. It preserved Robbins's magnificent choreography (which he ingeniously adapted and in some cases refined and expanded for the screen). It allowed the world to drink in Bernstein's nonpareil score in its true dramatic context, and nearly intact (unusual in a Hollywood film: hardly any of Bernstein's music, sadly, was included in the movie of *On the Town*).

And, despite its minor and larger lapses, the production set a high bar for what a movie musical based on a trailblazing Broadway show could and might be, how storytelling, dance, and music could effectively be synthesized into a visually exciting, semi-abstract framework, and how a tragic tale could (and should) remain tragic for a mass audience, instead of being defiled and defused by a pasted-on happy ending.

Since the 1961 release, the movie has maintained its status as an omnipresent classic and a cross-cultural, universal crowd pleaser. It's a real munch-your-popcorn, pass-the-Kleenex saga, both camp and cool. Devotees tend to revisit it repeatedly via their home entertainment centers. In the second decade of the twenty-first century, it's still frequently screened at film festivals and at rep cinemas specializing in classic movies. And it is periodically subjected to musical, political, theatrical, and media-studies analyses by critics and scholars.

Members of the rap/hip-hop generation of musicians and listeners embraced the DVD and computer-streamed screenings of the film nearly as enthusiastically as young viewers seduced by its first release in giant Super Panavision–equipped auditoriums. The long list of notable artists who have proclaimed their love for the film, and its influence on their own work, range from opera diva Kiri Te Kanawa and ballet stars Rudolf Nureyev and Peter Martins, to "king of pop" Michael Jackson and Puerto Rican–American pop star Jennifer Lopez. (In 2009, Lopez told *Vanity Fair* she'd watched the movie thirty-seven times.)

As we will explore in a later chapter, the film has been referenced, copied, and paid tribute to innumerable times in mainstream media—by celebrities ranging from Carol Burnett and Cher in the 1970s, to rock and hip-hop superstars in a *West Side Story*–themed promotion on MTV in 2009.

Of course, the vast majority of fans of the movie have never experienced the glorious immediacy of the Laurents/Shakespeare love story, Robbins's galvanic dances, and the Bernstein–Sondheim songs in a live performance. They have no way to compare the stage show and the film, and no interest in being talked out of their enjoyment of the glossy epic. In fact, a less-than-ideal production of the show only convinces them that the movie is far superior to the theatrical version.

THE HOLLYWOOD BACK STORY

If today it sounds like a no-brainer, transforming *West Side Story* into a motion picture in the late 1950s was a costly, risky, nerve-racking venture for its lead producers, Robert Wise, Saul Chaplin, and Walter Mirisch—and a trial by fire for Robbins.

Though *West Side Story* had achieved a high level of notoriety in its well-publicized Broadway run, the Bernstein–Sondheim tunes were not familiar to the public at large before the film arrived—except to those who purchased the original cast album. This was an era when radio play was the best sales tool for recordings, and best-selling singers of the day readily covered show tunes from Broadway hits as singles. But there was no stampede by pop artists to cover "Maria" or "Tonight" or "Somewhere" themselves, until *after* the film came out.

The score as a whole was nearly as daring for the film as it had been for the stage. The late 1950s and early 1960s yielded some extremely hip, sophisticated movie scores by such jazz composers as Lalo Schifrin, Miles Davis, Duke Ellington and, yes, the quasi-jazzy Bernstein (for *On the Waterfront*). But no American movie had such an adventurous wall-to-wall sound palette as *West Side Story*—every song and nearly every instrumental segment of which (with the obvious exception of the "Somewhere" ballet music) was reprised in the film.

Also, at this juncture, the fate of the Great Hollywood Movie Musical as a popular genre was uncertain. The famous Arthur Freed unit at MGM, which generated such classic tuners as *Singin' in the Rain* and *Funny Face*, would turn out its last big hit (the Oscar-winning *Gigi*) in 1958 and then disband. The field was surrendered to the new wave of low-budget teen movie musicals that were being churned out, spurred on by Elvis Presley's highly profitable movies, including the 1957 smash *Jailhouse Rock.* And before *West Side Story,* the last previous attempt to transfer a serious Broadway musical drama to celluloid was Otto Preminger's 1959 adaptation of the Gershwins' *Porgy and Bess,* which drew tepid notices and was a financial dud, earning back only half of its $7 million cost.

Also, lest we forget, some of the social ills both *Porgy and Bess* and *West Side Story* addressed were still considered controversial topics for entertainment at the time. The theme of urban poverty was not exactly box office gold. The African American civil rights movement was still gathering momentum and was resisted and reviled in much of the South. The drive for the equal rights of Hispanic Americans was not yet even on the national radar. And the issue of youth violence was more often sensationalized and trivialized by Hollywood than portrayed thoughtfully and truthfully.

Given all these factors, producing a very expensive, artistically faithful *West Side Story* film was something of a gamble for all concerned—just as mounting the stage show on Broadway had been.

THE MAKING OF THE MOVIE

Robbins considered the live version of *West Side Story* to be his baby and intended the film to be also. Though Robbins was then known in the film world only for his choreography of *The King and I* and his restaging of *Peter Pan* for a 1955 kinescope telecast that enthralled legions of little baby boomers, he was eager to work more in the medium and had exercised his prescient contractual option to direct *West Side Story* for the screen. Characteristically, he wanted (and expected) full artistic control of the production, the last word on the way it would be cast, staged, performed, shot, and edited—a luxury reserved for few filmmakers of that time.

Robbins's holistic perfectionism was the movie's salvation—but his own Achilles' heel. Could a first-time director blessed with such outsized gifts and imaginative reach, an often impolitic control freak with a dictatorial manner, find a place in profit-driven, producer-dominated Hollywood? Not for long. But for a while, at least, he wrote his own ticket. And *West Side Story* would certainly have been a completely different movie without him.

Robbins was signed to choreograph the movie and allowed to direct on the condition that he team up with a much more experienced helmer— Robert Wise, a well-regarded and gracious movie veteran who'd turned out such admired features as *Somebody Up There Likes Me*, starring Paul Newman, and *Odds Against Tomorrow,* featuring other Method actors, including Shelley Winters and Harry Belafonte. Wise also had edited that most revered of all prestige pictures, Orson Welles's *Citizen Kane,* the same director's less fortunate *The Magnificent Ambersons* (drastically recut by Wise, at the producers' command), and he was the sound-effects editor on such classic Fred Astaire movie musicals as *Top Hat* and *The Gay Divorcee.*

The co-directors worked out a mutually agreeable division of labor. Robbins would direct all the film's musical segments, with Wise closely consulting, and Wise would handle the dramatic sequences with input from Robbins. Robbins also served as point man with his original *West Side Story* collaborators, keeping them apprised of the movie's progress and seeking their assistance when needed. The musical numbers would be shot mostly on Hollywood soundstages with settings designed by Boris Leven, a respected Russian-born art director whose visual scheme was as arresting and painterly in cinematic terms as designer Oliver Smith's sets had been for Broadway. But Wise was also determined to shoot an expanded version of the opening Prologue on location in Manhattan, on Jets turf.

Robbins embarked on the project having thought long and hard about how best to commit *West Side Story* to film. Before the production was under way, he elaborated his vision in customarily opinionated, detailed, prescriptive memos. As usual, his creative strategies and impulses were spot-on.

West Side Story, Robbins wrote, "was a believable and touching work because of the special poetic conventions which were inherently theatrical. The problem is now to find a new set of conventions, inherently cinematic, which will also convey the essence of a show whose essence is not in any of its separate elements . . . but in their organic unity."

Discovering how to make the movie both visually thrilling and emotionally stirring, was the flip side of figuring out how to make the theatrical production urgently immediate yet cinematic. But being a Broadway rebel is hard enough. Standing up to the Hollywood dream factory was far more difficult, even for a force as formidable as Robbins.

He got his way on many things. When it came to casting, Robbins knew some of the heaviest lifters in *West Side Story* were the actor-singer-dancers who played the Sharks and Jets. At his insistence, the majority of those hired for the screen had already appeared in his New York or London casts of the stage musical. The alums knew the dances, the music, knew how to work under Robbins. More crucially, he knew them and what they could endure and were capable of. Though largely unsung, the contribution these actor-dancers brought to the finished product was enormous.

Additional Jets and Sharks members were added to the movie cast, and some performers were reshuffled into different roles than the ones they played onstage. Tucker Smith (a switch-hitter in four stage parts) was tapped to handle the new role of Ice (based on the original Diesel in the live show). As noted, in the film, Ice, rather than Action, succeeds Riff as the Jets' captain, and he leads the rearranged "Cool" number after Riff's death.

One of the youngest cast members, Eliot Feld (later a renowned choreographer with his own dance company), had performed in the show on Broadway at just sixteen and was awarded the film role of Baby John. Robbins loyalist Tony Mordente, A-Rab on Broadway, became Action; David Winters switched from Baby John to A-Rab and Jose De Vega from Juano to Chino. The two showcased Jets girlfriends, Velma and Garziella, were portrayed again, respectively, by stage veterans Carole D'Andrea and Gina Trikonis.

Apart from Bill Bramley encoring the role of Officer Krupke, the adult characters were handled by Hollywood character veterans Ned Glass (Doc), Simon Oakland (Schrank), and promising newcomer John Astin (who doubled as the nerdy social worker at the gym dance and as Jets member Glad Hand).

Assigning "bankable" stars to the leads in a big-budget movie epic was then, and will probably always be, as critical to producers as taking out a gold-plated insurance policy on their hefty investment. Though Rivera and Le Roy were now considered too old for Bernardo and Anita, Robbins was able to choose counterparts who were not household names (yet) but perfectly cast. They enriched the film and were well rewarded in return (with an Oscar apiece, and a huge career push).

The pale-skinned Greek American performer George Chakiris, an acclaimed Riff in London, did a 180-degree turn to become a suavely brooding (and preternaturally tanned) Bernardo. The juicy part of his lover Anita went to one of the few actual Hispanics in the film cast: the fetching young Rita Moreno, a Puerto Rican–born actress who caught Robbins's attention when she appeared as Tuptim in *The King and I* movie. Moreno's memory of meeting Robbins on that set: "In comes this ferocious person. I'd never seen anything like him in my life. People in Hollywood weren't that way."

Moreno later recalled she was "desperate, desperate to do [Anita]." Fearing that her dance skills were inadequate, she asked a friend who had performed in *West Side Story* onstage to teach her the difficult Robbins choreography for the "America" number, step by step. Moreno rehearsed it faithfully. But she pretended she was "winging it" at the dance audition, and "they were so impressed that I learned it so fast! Sometimes it pays to be sly."

The casting of Riff was also fortuitous. Though from the sidelines Laurents thought he was too clean-cut for the Jets leader, Russ Tamblyn did have a raffish, boyish appeal and real dancing prowess. He'd torn up the screen doing Michael Kidd's athletic choreography in the Old West movie musical *Seven Brides for Seven Brothers.* And he had some impressive gymnastic moves (backflips, cartwheels, hanging from a bar by his knees) that the *West Side Story* made great use of.

In a Turner Classic Movies (TCM) mini-documentary about the film, Tamblyn revealed that he'd been a top contender to portray Tony and playing the Jets leader wasn't appealing at first. "I didn't want to do it," he said. "I thought the dancing was much too hard for me. I wasn't a classically trained dancer . . . But once I got the part of Riff, I was thrilled."

The search for the right cinematic Maria and Tony was more complicated and fraught. Larry Kert and Carol Lawrence had been wonderful together in the theatrical production, exhibiting a rapport that made their romance feel true. But then, and now, Broadway matinee idols rarely get the chance to repeat their performances on film, even those who've been lavishly praised in the same roles. (A prime example was Tony honoree Julie Andrews, passed over in favor of the more bankable Audrey Hepburn to star in the Hollywood redo of *My Fair Lady.*)

Lawrence remembered, with regret, that she was never seriously considered for the film. (Nor was Kert.) The producers wanted a younger movie starlet (singing not required), and the long list of the interested and/or auditioned reportedly included Barbara Luna, Ina Balin, Elizabeth Ashley, Pier Angeli, Suzanne Pleshette, Jill St. John, Anna Maria Alberghetti, and even the future Eliza Doolittle, Audrey Hepburn (whose pregnancy knocked her out of the running for Maria).

Ultimately, and quite late in the process, the part of Maria went to one of the biggest stars in the race: Natalie Wood. She had a solid fan base and lobbied hard for the job. Robbins was immediately charmed by her and convinced she would make a very credible Maria. (Despite all the difficulties both encountered while making *West Side Story,* Wood and Robbins remained good friends until Wood's untimely death in a drowning accident twenty years later.)

Then twenty-two, Wood was a raven-haired beauty who had been in the movies since she was four years old. She was plenty sophisticated but on-camera could still project the dewy innocence and vulnerability of a cloistered adolescent like Maria. She'd worked well previously with Method-style directors—with Nicholas Ray on *Rebel Without a Cause* and Elia Kazan on *Splendor in the Grass* (completed just before *West Side Story* filming began). And she was eager to tackle such a musical role with the much-esteemed Robbins.

Settling on a Tony was harder. The *New York Times* reported that Marlon Brando was very interested, but he backed off in fear he was too old. (He was then in his mid-thirties; Tony is a teenager.) The producers put out feelers to rock god Elvis, by far the most commercial choice and a budding actor, but that went nowhere—thanks, probably, to the wise disinterest of the singer's manager, Colonel Tom Parker.

Many "sensitive" young screen hunks like Warren Beatty, George Peppard, Bobby Darin, Anthony Perkins, Gary Lockwood, and even the blander Tab Hunter and Troy Donahue were candidates. And the part finally went to one of the blandest and least experienced in the bunch: Richard Beymer.

Like Wood and Tamblyn, Beymer was a former child actor, but far less experienced and equipped than they were to handle a demanding romantic lead. However, he was a looker, and a teen heartthrob thanks to his recent appearance as the dreamy love interest Peter in the film of *The*

Richard Beymer and Natalie Wood in the cinematic "Tonight" duet. Courtesy of Photofest.

Diary of Anne Frank. Snaring the Tony assignment was a coup, but he was in for a real trial by fire.

Once all the gang casting was set, Robbins's boot camp cranked up. As in the Broadway show, every character, down to the least significant Jet and Shark, had to invent a complete psycho-biography for their role. Again, Robbins decreed (with mixed success) that the Sharks and Jets not fraternize during the lengthier-than-usual rehearsal process and while filming. They were to maintain the hostile vibes between the gangs even when off-set. This was familiar territory for those who had worked with Robbins before, but perplexing and uncomfortable for some of those new to the material and to the Method—especially Beymer. In the documentary film *West Side Memories,* he spoke of his discomfort with Robbins's penchant for "playing tricks to make sure people had an emotional reaction."

Probably because he was committing his dances to film posterity, Robbins was an even more doubt-wracked, iron-fisted perfectionist than ever. Rehearsing and filming the difficult "Cool" number (which was shot, at his insistence, on the hard concrete floor of an Los Angeles parking garage) was so arduous, for instance, that the dancers ultimately burned their worn-out kneepads in a ritual exorcism and left the charred remains in a pile in front of Robbins's office. And in an oft-reported incident, Robbins told his cast (ironically and wrongly, as it turned out) that he was not expendable on the film, but they all were.

Moreno, whose career was made by *West Side Story,* later put her experience with the film into perspective. "I will be eternally grateful that I had Jerome Robbins in my life," she said. "As cruel as he could be, he really brought out the best in everyone. We were all scared to death of him, and it's not fun to work when you're that frightened. I had the most reason to fear him because I was the one with the least dancing experience, but he just made you do things you didn't know were possible."

Meanwhile, the two people on-set who should have been most eagerly fraternizing with each other, Method-wise, were barely communicating. According to Beymer, Wood would greet him coolly each morning and then, apart from playing scenes with him, ignore him for the rest of the day. There they were, playing the modern-day Romeo and Juliet, and Beymer got the repeated impression Wood could not stand the sight of him. (One possible grievance with Beymer is that she had suggested her actor husband Robert Wagner for the part.)

Though Wise reportedly treated everyone with his customary courteous civility, Robbins adored Wood and lavished much individual coaching time on her—while demeaning Beymer's abilities. "I was from Iowa, I was 21, and I just got dumped into this whole world I knew nothing about," Beymer told the *Los Angeles Daily News* many years later. "It created an entree for me for the rest of my life. But it was strange." And yet, in retrospect he expressed gratitude for Robbins's astute suggestions on how to portray Tony—since Wise gave him so little acting direction.

THE MANHATTAN SHOOT

"The Prologue" of *West Side Story* was filmed on location in New York City on several blocks in the West 60s, cleared of inhabitants to make way for the construction of Lincoln Center for the Performing Arts. There were no longer any tenants in the grimy, dilapidated tenement apartment buildings, but the exteriors and the trash-heaped vacant lots in the area would not be bulldozed until the shooting was over. (A playground sequence in "The Prologue" was shot farther north, at a site on West 110th Street).

"I fought from the beginning to open the film in New York in its setting, in its background, because we couldn't put stylized sets on movie stages like they had on the theater stage—they didn't work on films," Wise explained in an American Film Institute interview. "So I fought to have the whole early part, down through 'Something's Coming,' in New York."

Robbins was initially worried about this sort of cinematic verisimilitude. Wise recalled Robbins telling him, "You've given me the most difficult task right off the bat: to take my most stylized dancing in the piece and put it against the most real backgrounds."

Robbins, Wise, and crew shoot "The Prologue" on the streets of Manhattan. Courtesy of Photofest.

Wise likely eased his co-director's anxieties by approximating and trying out the New York lighting and terrain in test shots made in downtown Los Angeles during the daytime, with a camera (and a pianist) mounted on trolleys and the dancers "rehearsing as Jerry studied, developed and adapted the dance steps to the outdoors and the sunlight." Harvey Evans, who played one of the Jets, told NPR, "We did [the choreography] in front of a Salvador Dalí kind of surrealistic drop once. Then we would go down to the slum section and we would test stuff down there. And we did it with a lot of dancing, and then we did it with no dancing."

After ten weeks of hard-driving rehearsals that began in Los Angeles on May 31, 1960, the company of twenty-two dancer-actors descended on Manhattan's Upper West Side for a miserably muggy shoot that began on August 10. It was slated to last two weeks. It stretched into five weeks, due to Robbins's endless inventiveness and chronic insecurities, and his reluctance to ever say "Print!" Commented Frank Rich in *West Side Memories,* "He wouldn't take yes for an answer—but that's what great artists do."

The performers became exhausted, frustrated, angry. The producers were admiring but impatient and worried about huge cost overruns. The final product, however, would be an eight-minute opening scene of astonishing and unforgettable virtuosity, unique in movie musical history.

As usual, some of the more veteran and trained members of the cast found it easiest to tough out the rugged physical conditions and the constant tracking of what Robbins meant when he barked a command to do the 16B or 12F version of a short take. They also knew the grueling work was probably well worth the final product.

Chakiris has repeatedly stated through the years his delight in working with Robbins, calling it "the greatest experience I've ever had, because it was Jerry who first showed me how a dancer could express himself in dancing rhythms and how an actor could intensify his dramatic performance with the graceful, expressive body movements of a dancer."

But the shooting conditions eventually got to even the most seasoned *West Side Story* alums and Robbins favorites. Compared to executing the dances on-stage, the film choreography, explained Mordente (who served as dance captain for the movie), featured "similar steps, but a lot of the formulations had changed." And as the dancers endured painful shin splints and other injuries, and unforgiving heat (and in Eliot Feld's case, when they got back to Los Angeles, a bout with pneumonia), tempers flared and stamina waned.

Tamblyn despised the grueling regime. Noting it was "extremely hot and painful to be dancing on cement all day," he claimed Robbins wasn't satisfied until the dancers' "feet were bleeding."

Even when Robbins and Wise finally agreed to print one of the many takes, Tamblyn recounted, "Jerry would say, 'I'd like to do it one more time, only this time I'd like the dancers to do it on the other foot.' What difference did it make, it was the same step except, you know, it was nuts. That's the kind of sadistic director he was."

Co-producer Saul Chaplin commented in his memoir *The Golden Age of Movie Musicals and Me* that "Jerry was by far the most exciting choreographer I had ever watched. He seemed to have an endless stream of exciting ideas . . . At the same time, he was such an insane perfectionist that it was impossible for any of the dancers to achieve the standards he demanded immediately. To make matters worse, he had a very low tolerance point. When he was displeased, he heaped such verbal abuse on the dancers that the place took on the atmosphere of a concentration camp. They didn't dance out of joy, they danced out of fear."

According to David Winters, he and Mordente organized impromptu rain dances in sweltering Manhattan, in hopes a downpour would arrive and a day's shoot would be canceled. (Occasionally it worked.) There were also security problems on location. The neighborhood was still dangerous, despite the urban renewal project under way for Lincoln Center, and rocks were thrown at the cast from rooftops of abandoned buildings. Finally, art imitated life and a genuine street gang was hired as a security squad to keep the "turf" of the fake gang safe.

The reward for all this anguish, and for Robbins's obdurate commands to try a segment again and again, every which way? An artistic bonanza of vivid, arresting shots from a kaleidoscopic array of angles. A trench was dug to shoot the performers at ground level. Cameras perched on cranes captured the action from a bird's-eye perspective. Close-ups and long and medium shots of the dancers showed off the propulsive choreography, the swaggering physicality in different ways—at foot level, knee level, from high above, up close, at a tilt. Robbins let his visual imagination roam free as more seasoned (and fiscally responsible) big-studio movie directors rarely could. When it came to assembling the pieces in a cohesive whole, there was a wealth of images for editing veteran Wise (in consultation with Robbins) to choose from—which helped the film to, as critic Stanley Kauffmann described it, "[burst] into life, not merely into action, from its opening split-second."

"The dailies were the most exciting of any film I have ever seen," co-producer Mirisch remembered. But they cost the production and Robbins dearly. In the theater, running into overtime is pricey. In the film world, it can bankrupt you. By the time the company jetted back to Los Angeles, *West Side Story* was bleeding money and a month behind schedule. In September, Robbins directed the shooting of the "America" and "Cool" numbers, in his usual fashion. Then in October, before the "Dance at the Gym" number could be completed, Robbins was (to the shock and amazement of the cast and crew) fired from the project and barred from the set.

The reason given by Mirisch: "too many cooks" on the project, taking too much time. So Wise would go solo as director, finishing the remainder of the film (somewhere between 30 and 60 percent, by varied estimates) on his own. But Wise, too, took his time, and when shooting ended in 1961 the film was over budget by more than $2 million. (The total shooting budget was roughly $6 million.)

SINGING THE SONGS

Dubbing singing voices (replacing an actor's own voice with that of a different performer) was a common Hollywood practice at the time *West Side Story* was made. If Fred Astaire had been a young player in the 1960s, his light, distinctive tenor would probably have been jettisoned for a fuller, deeper (and less interesting) baritone. But back in Astaire's heyday, movie musicals were cast with multifaceted talents who'd mostly come up through the ranks of vaudeville and Broadway. By the early 1960s, the Hollywood star machine was focused on grooming young movie actors prized for their looks and potential screen charisma, not their skill sets.

That didn't mean some stars didn't *want* to sing and dance. Wood, in fact, initially believed the voice coming out of Maria during the "Tonight" and "I Feel Pretty" numbers would be her own. Perhaps to humor her, the producers encouraged that belief. And the nervous actress was recorded singing the score in her thin, determined, but far from pitch-perfect voice. (A sample of her vocal tracks can be heard in *West Side Memories*.)

Wood's untrained voice was clearly inadequate for the taxing Bernstein score. So the producers engaged Marni Nixon, the classically trained and extremely versatile soprano who dubbed Deborah Kerr's songs in *The King and I* (and later, Audrey Hepburn's for *My Fair Lady*). But Nixon told NPR's Terry Gross that the producers were "afraid to upset" Wood and "created a monster" by leading the actress on to believe she'd be singing all but the very high notes herself.

To humor their star, they let her lip-sync five of Maria's six songs to her own, unusable vocal tracks. That just complicated the inevitable redubbing process later. According to Nixon, Wood "was really furious when, at the end, they told her that I had to really come back and redub the whole thing."

Betty Wand (who dubbed for Leslie Caron's songs in *Gigi*) was also brought in on an "emergency" basis to dub some of Moreno's vocals. Wand and Nixon were employed day to day without contracts and used as "vocal insurance" for the final print. Weirdly enough, Nixon also filled in for the ailing Wand, on the final version of the "Tonight Quintet." She noted in her memoir *I Could Have Sung All Night* that when Anita sings about "getting her kicks tonight, that's me." (Nixon even dubbed Maria's final words to the expiring Tony, "*Te adoro,* Anton," after a giggling Wood flubbed them.)

Nixon understandably felt her day-laborer pay scale had been exploitive, given how much her voice was used. She sued for a share of the movie's royalties but settled when Bernstein, characteristically, resolved the matter by giving Nixon (who had performed as a soloist for him at the New York Philharmonic) a half percentage of his own royalties from the film. With that "generous gesture," wrote Nixon, Bernstein "helped to set a precedent that would assist me and other ghosts in being recognized." (Wand also pressed her case for additional remuneration and settled out of court.)

Wood faced other challenges, beyond singing—her lack of chemistry with Beymer, her difficulty with Maria's Puerto Rican accent, her discontent with Irene Sharaff's girlish costumes for her character. "I remember that she was aloof and I think she was uncomfortable with all of us," Moreno opined. "I think that at some point . . . she thought that she was way out of her league and, indeed, she was. I think she regretted taking the role. So, she wasn't terribly comfortable with any of us." But Wood also blossomed in several scenes, particularly the charmingly re-choreographed "I Feel Pretty," which was a delightful showcase for her frisky, clowning side.

Richard Beymer's songs were dubbed also (by practiced singer-musician Jim Bryant), without his objection. Russ Tamblyn was dubbed (by castmate Tucker Smith) for "The Jet Song"—yet not for "Gee, Officer Krupke," which he sang perfectly well.

Overall, some of the dubbing was accomplished smoothly, with no obvious mismatch between screen actor and offscreen singer. But sometimes there is a disconcerting disconnect, particularly when Nixon's semi-operatic soprano pours out of Wood's pretty mouth.

ROBBINS: DEPARTED, NOT GONE

Though he had been a holy terror in some respects, the firing of Robbins shortly after the New York shoot ended was a stunner for the cast. Wood was, by all accounts, furious and complained vigorously to the producing team. Other performers were also upset. The timing was efficient, however, according to Jets member Harvey Evans: "They didn't let Jerry go until he had choreographed and rehearsed the dance numbers. So everything was ready. And the best parts of the movie are what Jerry [directed]: 'America' and the 'The Prologue' and 'Cool.'"

But if he had been effectively banished from the film set, Robbins would not let go of his "baby" so easily—and Wise very much wanted his input. Three Robbins assistants— Mordente, Tom Abbott, and Margaret Banks—stayed on the film and ensured its faithfulness to his choreography and vision.

Robbins was also able to screen all the musical and rumble sequences, and according to Jowitt he made "detailed, pointed notes on how to improve them." Examples: He advised Wise that there were too many finger snaps in the opening number. The rumble (which he'd mapped out in detail for screenwriter Lehman) looked "too dancey." The moment when Tony and Maria first lock eyes at the dance, across a crowded room, should be a sustained long shot, he urged, with some "softening optical to enhance it."

He also advised reediting the balcony scene because it felt like "you're back in an old MGM musical and you have Jane Powell and Howard Keel singing *at* each other." Wood missed that special Robbins creative touch and noted later that he "didn't give technical advice. He would say, 'Cut to the emotion, cut to the people, cut to the movement.' I also found he was a fantastic actors' director. . . . And the way he moved the camera with the dancers was truly innovative."

Wise valued and used some of his postproduction directives, and Robbins's aides were a great help with the musical numbers. The project also brought out Wise's own perfectionism: without Robbins present, for instance, he shot sixty takes of the brief cha-cha duet of Tony and Maria during the "Dance at the Gym" before getting what he wanted.

THE FINAL CUT

And the finished product? Wise assured the press that he was very happy with it and that Robbins was pleased also—enough to keep his name on it, at least. "It's all movie, we hope," Lehman told *The Saturday Review,* "and it is also 'West Side Story.'" And for all its imperfections, the picture can still cast a unique spell a half-century later.

First, over an overture that had very deliberately *not* been part of the stage version, the movie begins with a memorable opening sequence designed by Saul Bass. The ultrawide Panavasion screen is suffused with a changing background of intense colors (hot orange, cool blue, purple, lime green), bearing lightly sketched black marks as in a pen-and-ink drawing. As the colors bleed away, the markings darken and transform into the famous panoramic camera shot of the Manhattan skyline. We are then treated to a breathtaking bird's-eye-view tour of the island (silent except for the buzz of the helicopter it was shot from)—bridge, harbor, Empire State Building, maze of freeways, the old Yankee Stadium—before the film zooms us down into to the belly of the beast: an Upper West Side playground where Riff and his comrades are sitting, snapping, surveying their territory.

We get a more detailed sense here of how they patrol that turf than we do onstage, as they strut, dance, leap, disrupt a basketball game, own the streets, mark their boundaries, and with swagger and glare let everyone they encounter know who's boss in this neighborhood. But then the Sharks appear, disturbing the Jets' sense of dominance. The Puerto Rican boys mark out their own terrain with dancing. Egged on by Bernstein's rollicking, rampaging music, tensions bristle and knockabout confrontations escalate into spitting, name-calling, and combustive collisions. Then comes an exciting street chase, a rock fight in a bleak demolition site, and finally, a brawling punchfest cut short only by a piercing police whistle.

As great as it is in the theater, the screen Prologue gains speed, exhilaration, danger, and most of all, a potent sense of place. These kids inhabit a recognizable terrain of dark, crumbling buildings and dingy concrete caverns, of gang graffiti and basketball courts, both ugly and bleakly beautiful in the rushing, buzzing whirl of dancing and maneuvering. The seesawing tension between realism and artifice is established immediately—in the way a Jets procession is shot artily through the filigree of a chain-link fence, in how the dancers move in angular but disruptive patterns, and in the extreme close-ups and heightened music.

Nothing else in the film quite equals this, but later the repositioned "Cool" number, shot in the murky shadows and glaring headlights of a claustrophobic parking garage, comes close. The camera knows how to dance with the dancers here, misses nothing of the kinetic fireworks. And the dancers appear to be coming at us from every direction, weaving and exploding all over the screen. Yet the number is still, like all of Robbins's best work, character-driven: written on the agitated faces of those dancing is their struggle to contain their fear, grief, and blood-lust.

"America" becomes a number for the Shark men as well as the women, and it is utterly exhilarating. Now the biting lyrics and Spanish dance gestures are supplemented with sly boy–girl flirtations and teasing, slapstick mock kicks and punches, with lots of male goofing around. And again, the smoothly edited shots from many perspectives afford a great view of the dance moves, but also a direct engagement with the attractive young people executing them.

These three numbers have been rethought, and reinvigorated, for the screen by Robbins, with cinematographer Daniel L. Fapp and editor Thomas Stanford, who received Oscars for their valuable contributions. But you can feel the absence of Robbins's guiding inventiveness during some of the other musical numbers. Even "The Dance at the Gym," which has a beautiful entrée with flushed colored lighting and shadowy figures, is filmed mostly square-on in long and medium shots and is stiffly interrupted when the camera completely cuts away from the dancing for Tony's arrival at the gym and some dialogue exchanges. The choreography is still some of Robbins's best, performed unstintingly and spiked with Tamblyn's tumbling stunts. But Robbins has spoiled us with the dynamism and freshness of his self-directed production numbers. As for the non-singing dramatic scenes and the ballads, one must be contented with the beauty of the Bernstein–Sondheim score, the eagerness to please and good looks of the lovers (though Wood's accent is truly cringeworthy), and some standout acting by Moreno, particularly in the attempted rape scene in the drugstore (which was wrenching for her to perform, as it had been for Rivera).

Ultimately in *West Side Story,* Wise fulfilled his mission to, as he put it, "make it acceptable for kids to be dancing in the streets." And Robbins demonstrated new and better ways, time-consuming and expensive but rewarding, to turn a stage musical into a film.

When the movie had its October 18, 1961, grand premiere at the huge Rivoli Theatre in Manhattan's Theater District, it was promoted as no less than a major achievement in cinematic history. And if every review didn't concur, the public roared its approval in packed screenings across America and around the world.

Though its imperfections are as obvious today as its attributes, literally millions of *West Side Story* aficionados love the movie exactly as it is. Even those of us who are well aware of the flaws and the dream of what might have been, had Robbins been able to complete the picture himself, can take keen pleasure in the best of what is there, in a movie musical unlike any other.

STAGE TO SCREEN CHANGES

For a Hollywood makeover, the *West Side Story* movie was unusually faithful to the form and essence of the original show's dances, text, and score. Not much was cut (apart from that one major segment, the "Somewhere" ballet), but quite a few things were rearranged, supplemented, and otherwise reworked for the screen.

Some noteworthy differences between the theatrical and screen versions:

1. There is a conventional, pastiche-style overture in the movie; no overture existed in the live show.
2. The Prologue is more than twice as long onscreen, with additional choreography, action, and music.
3. "Cool" is now sung by Ice (a new character who is Riff's successor as Jets leader) rather than Riff. And the number now occurs *after* the rumble instead of before it, so that giving the command to be "coolly cool boy" carries additional intensity in the wake of the slayings of Riff and Bernardo, as frustrations and fears grip the Jets and their girls.
4. The satirical romp "Gee, Officer Krupke," in turn, switches places with "Cool." It is now sung by Riff (instead of Action) *before* the rumble instead of *after* it. The switch pleased Sondheim, who always preferred that order and felt that "kids on the run after watching two murders" would not dally by a fence and "sing a comic song."
5. "America" is moved and occurs between "Maria" and "Tonight" (which are consecutive in the stage score). Men are added to the number, giving it more sexual sizzle, while the more incisive lyrics lend it added satiric bite.
6. "I Feel Pretty" is shifted to *before* the rumble instead of *after,* with Maria celebrating her joy over meeting Tony. But the song's new

position does not have the ironic impact it had in the theater, when the audience knows that the boy she adores has just slaughtered her brother at the rumble.

7. The "Somewhere" ballet fantasia, vocal solo, and choral rendition are not in the film. "Somewhere" is performed as a song duet by Tony and Maria.

8. Velma and Graziella switch romantic partners. Velma is Riff's girl in the stage version, but Ice's gal in the movie. Graziella is Action's squeeze onstage, but Riff's in the film. And the Sharks named Anxious, Nibbles, and Moose onstage are further Latinized with the names Loco, Rocco, and Del Campo on film.

9. Screenwriter Ernest Lehman wrote new lines of dialogue that were inserted here and there to make more explicit what Laurents simply suggested in his leaner libretto for *West Side Story.* (For instance, Ice describes Tony's fighting prowess in a previous rumble with a different gang.)

10. Certain lines of stage dialogue were deemed potentially offensive and "cleaned up" for the movie—though by current standards, they were tame to begin with. "The whole, ever mother lovin street" in "The Jet Song" became "the whole buggin' ever-loving street." Tony and Riff pledge their friendship from "birth to Earth," a poor substitute for "sperm to worm." In a verse of "Gee, Officer Krupke" the line "My father is a bastard / My ma's an S.O.B. / My grandpa's always plastered / My grandma pushes tea" was altered to: "My daddy beats my mommy / My mommy clobbers me / My grandpa is a Commie / My grandma pushes tea."

11. The lyrics to "America" were changed substantially, and the film number is performed by men and women, rather than just Anita and her girlfriends. The opening line that offended Puerto Ricans in the stage version, "Puerto Rico, you ugly island, island of tropical diseases" became "Puerto Rico, my heart's devotion, let it sink back in the ocean," while "The babies crying and the bullets flying" became "And the sunlight streaming and natives teeming."

Instead of facing off with her friend Rosalia, Anita here extols the virtues (rather than the disappointments) of life in America, in a sung debate with Bernardo, who answers with bitter retorts about the limited opportunities and racism experienced by Puerto Ricans in the United States. (Sondheim later explained that these were the lyrics he originally wrote for the song but they were replaced by others in the theatrical version.)

Anita's America now contains "lots of new housing and more space," where you can have a "terrace apartment" and "life can be bright," while you are " free to be anything you choose." But Bernardo sees "lots of doors slamming in our face," and freedom only to "wash dishes and shine shoes." Survival depends on "if you can fight," "get rid of your accent," and "stay on your own side." The coup de grâce: the American dream is only available "if you're all white in America."

MOVIE REVIEWS

The initial film reviews of *West Side Story* reveal nearly as much about movie criticism of the time as about the merits and demerits of the film itself. The raves tended toward gush; the few important pans were far more brutal than the negative and mixed Broadway reviews. Rarely, an astute observer like Stanley Kauffmann would pinpoint the movie's deficiencies while also being willing (and able) to illuminate its strengths.

Overall, the huge chorus of approval drowned out the dissenters. In addition to winning ten Oscars, three Golden Globe awards (including one for best movie musical), and a Directors Guild of America prize for Robbins and Wise, *West Side Story* also received the New York Film Critics Circle Award for best film of 1961.

Excerpts from an assortment of reviews:

> *"'West Side Story' is a beautifully-mounted, impressive, emotion-ridden and violent musical which, in its stark approach to a raging social problem and realism of unfoldment, may set a pattern for future musical presentations. Screen takes on a new dimension in this powerful and sometimes fascinating translation of the Broadway musical to the greater scope of motion pictures. The Robert Wise production, said to cost $6,000,000, should pile up handsome returns, first on a roadshow basis and later in general runs."*

> —WHITNEY WILLIAMS, *Variety* (1961)

"In every respect, the recreation of the Arthur Laurents–Leonard Bernstein musical in the dynamic forms of motion pictures is superbly and appropriately achieved. The drama of New York juvenile gang war, which cried to be released in the freer and less restricted medium of the mobile photograph, is now given range and natural aspect on the large Panavision color screen, and the music and dances that expand it are magnified as true sense-experiences. . . .

"This pulsing persistence of rhythm all the way through the film—in the obviously organized dances, such as the arrogant show-offs of the Jets, that swirl through playgrounds, alleys, school gymnasiums, and parking lots, and in the less conspicuous stagings, such as that of the 'rumble' (battle) of the two kids—gives an overbeat of eloquence to the graphic realism of this film and sweeps it along, with Mr. Bernstein's potent music, to the level of an operatic form."

—BOSLEY CROWTHER, *The New York Times* (1961)

"Because of the quality of the original materials and of the translation, the result is the best film musical ever made. The price of its virtue is our disappointment that it isn't even better. For something more than half the film (as with the play), everything meshes so beautifully . . . that we are led to expect cumulation and a towering conclusion. This does not happen . . .But it is Robbins' vision—of city life expressed in stylized movement that sometimes flowers into dance and song—that lifts this picture high. If a time capsule is about to be buried anywhere this film ought to be included, so that possible future generations can know how an artist of ours made our most congenial theatrical form respond to some of the beauty in our time and to the humanity in some of its ugliness."

—STANLEY KAUFFMANN, *The New Republic* (1961)

"How can so many critics have fallen for this frenzied hokum . . . and with a score so derivative . . . If there is anything great in the American musical tradition—and I think there is—it's in the light satire, the high spirits, the giddy romance, the low comedy, and the unpretentiously stylized dance of men like Fred Astaire and the

younger Gene Kelly. . . . [The West Side Story dancing] is trying so hard to be great it isn't even good. Those impressive, widely admired opening shots of New York from the air overload the story with values and importance—technological and sociological. The Romeo and Juliet story could, of course, be set anywhere, but 'West Side Story' wrings the last drop of spurious importance out of the setting, which dominates the enfeebled love story . . ."

—PAULINE KAEL, anthologized in *I Lost It at the Movies* (1965)

"If director Wise's imagination falters at times, there is always the lilt of Leonard Bernstein's score, and the drive of Jerome Robbins' choreography to sustain the film to its next high point—which is never too far away. The dancing alone is an enthralling experience, whether a frantic mambo or a quiet love duet; and not merely because Robbins is one of our great choreographers in the theatre, but because of the exciting way in which he has reworked his dances for the camera."   —ARTHUR KNIGHT, *The Saturday Review* (1961)

And in retrospect:

"So the dancing is remarkable, and several of the songs have proven themselves by becoming standards, and there are moments of startling power and truth. 'West Side Story' remains a landmark of musical history. But if the drama had been as edgy as the choreography, if the lead performances had matched Moreno's fierce concentration, if the gangs had been more dangerous and less like bad-boy Archies and Jugheads, if the ending had delivered on the pathos and tragedy of the original, there's no telling what might have resulted."

—ROGER EBERT, *Chicago Sun-Times* (2004)

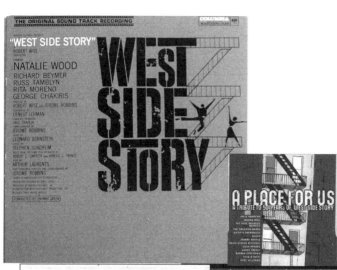

10

THE SWINGINEST THING
WEST SIDE STORY
RECORDINGS

Beginning with the first-rate original cast album for the 1957 Broadway production, *West Side Story* has had an unusually rich, extensive, and various life on disc. This popularity reflects the quality and originality of the score itself, but also the widespread and lasting affection for the show and its compelling story.

In the 1950s and early 1960s, original cast recordings of hit Broadway musicals rode high on the sales charts. Leading music stars in many genres—from Xavier Cugat and Liberace, to Sarah Vaughan and Miles Davis—free-raided the Broadway songbook for good show tunes they might transform into pop hits and future standards.

On the radio, the jukebox, the family hi-fi, at nightclubs—in this pre-Beatles era, show tunes were at least as much a part of the American soundtrack as rock-and-roll. And listening to the original cast recordings of musicals was a widespread national pastime, even if you never attended the live theatrical productions.

The initial Broadway recording of *West Side Story* wasn't as much of a commercial phenomenon as the skyrocketing cast albums for *South Pacific* (number one on the Billboard charts for 69 weeks) or *My Fair Lady* (number one for 15 weeks, on the chart for 480 weeks, five million copies sold in its first decade). But the *West Side Story* disc was snatched up by enough listeners to remain on the charts for 191 weeks (nearly four years), peaking at number 5. More than a million copies of this version were sold. And the compact disc released in the 1990s, has sold in excess of 700,000 copies.

Since *West Side Story* has one of the most recorded scores in Broadway history, you can add to this tally cast recordings (currently in and out of print) of well over a dozen other productions, including the premiere London production recording and foreign versions sung in Japanese, German, Italian, and Swedish. The original cast disc for the 2009 Broadway revival did well in both physical and digital formats and won a Grammy Award.

Like *Porgy and Bess,* the classical range and dramatic breadth of the Bernstein–Sondheim score has also inspired numerous studio sets, featuring prominent Broadway performers and opera stars in the major roles. And in 1961, for a New York Philharmonic gala, Bernstein extracted and rearranged material from his score to create *Symphonic Dances from West Side Story,* a popular orchestral suite. (It includes music from "The Prologue," "Dance at the Gym," "Rumble," "Somewhere," and the Finale.) In 2010 the suite was included on ninety-nine different recordings listed on Amazon, and it is in the repertoire of major U.S. and foreign symphonies—from the Moscow Symphony to the Simon Bolivar Youth Symphony of Venezuela.

But the biggest album seller was, predictably, the musical soundtrack for the *West Side Story* movie. Released in 1961, it also was Grammy-honored. It stayed at number one on the Billboard charts for a record fifty-four weeks, sold robustly afterward, and was ultimately certified multiplatinum (indicating sales of two to 10 million copies).

What must have been gratifying also for Bernstein and Sondheim was the appeal of the *West Side Story* score to musical artists beyond Broadway and the symphony hall. Leading pop singers, jazz combos, rap, R&B and punk bands, salsa artists, brass ensembles, even solo accordion and harmonica virtuosos have transferred the songs successfully into different musical idioms.

True, the score yielded no instant pop hits—no "On the Street Where You Live" (à la *My Fair Lady*) or "Till There Was You" (from *The Music Man*). According to Sondheim, before the movie came out the songs were largely ignored by the pop recording industry. There were some exceptions, including a cover by Rosemary Clooney of "Tonight," and a *West Side Story* medley of seven tunes (including "Gee, Officer Krupke") recorded by Sammy Davis Jr., who knew great material when he heard it. By far the most lucrative early cover was a mawkishly ethereal 1960 recording of "Maria" by Johnny Mathis, which received widespread radio play.

But within a few years, countless well-known singers and instrumental ensembles would record and perform live and on TV the show's indelible ballads "Maria," "Tonight," and "Somewhere."

The score also was enthusiastically embraced by modern jazz artists. Again the timing was good: inventively "cool" jazz was not a specialty niche in the late 1950s, but a commercially viable category. Among the many jazz homages to *West Side Story* were commercially and critically lauded discs by jazz stars Oscar Peterson, Stan Kenton, and André Previn. They and their peers admired the angular rhythms, unorthodox time schemes, Latin accents, and beautiful melodies of *West Side Story* and were eager to reinterpret and record them.

In the 1980s and 1990s, a new multicultural wave of young hip-hop, punk, rap, rock, and soul artists became enamored with the Bernstein–Sondheim tunes via school and community theater productions of the show and videotapes and DVDs of the movie. Covers and parodies of the songs by rock groups, brass bands, salsa orchestras, and others multiplied. A fortieth-anniversary *West Side Story* all-star tribute album issued in 1997 included cuts by a hodgepodge of pop idols, from country thrush Wynonna Judd, to Mexican American singer Selena, to the African American rapper Def Jef.

A full discography for *West Side Story* and its spinoffs would fill many pages. Here is a selective list of some of the best-known, most influential, and most offbeat recordings.

FOUR MAJOR CAST RECORDINGS

1957 Original Broadway Cast. This is generally considered the gold standard. It captures the soulfulness, verve, and freshness of the premiere production and was recorded under the supervision of Sondheim and Bernstein's trusted orchestrators Sid Ramin and Irwin Kostal.

One of the first Broadway show albums to be issued in stereo, the disc was recorded in a long single session (not unusual at the time) at Manhattan's 30th Street Studio, on September 29, 1957, three days after the Broadway premiere.

Months earlier, before *West Side Story* became a Broadway cause célèbre, Bernstein and Sondheim "auditioned" the score for Columbia Records honchos Goddard Lieberson (who had overseen the recordings of *South Pacific, My Fair Lady*, and many other hit musicals) and William Paley (head of CBS, which owned Columbia). The bigwigs seemed unimpressed, and Bernstein recalled it as a bust: "They said no, there's nothing in it anybody could sing, too depressing, too many tritones, too many words in the lyrics, too rangy. 'Ma-ri-a'—nobody could sing notes like that, impossible. They turned it down. . . . There was tremendous animosity to the whole deal."

Seeing *West Side Story* firsthand, during its exciting Washington, D.C., tryout run, helped revise Lieberson's opinion and realize the artistic and commercial potential of a cast album. In a letter to Bernstein quoted by Simeone, Lieberson effusively praised the show's "terrific power—terrific unity," lauded the cast, and enthused, "I've never known anything in musical theater to do me in the way 'West Side Story' did."

So is this initial Columbia recording an accurate facsimile of the score, as performed at the Winter Garden Theatre in 1951? Not precisely. Sondheim told Simeone that Lieberson, to capture "the excitement generated by Jerome Robbins' choreography on stage," sped up the original tempo of some numbers—"The Prologue," and "The Dance at the Gym." He also pared down the latter and excised lines of spoken dialogue (and, in Simeone's view, "some lovely instrumental music") in the "Tonight" balcony number because it was running long. And he reshaped the score's final musical moments, adding a brief choral reprise of "Somewhere."

Though Sondheim found the recording process painful at times (he gingerly reported the details of the session back to an ailing Bernstein), as did the show's exhausted performers, the album was extremely well received in reviews in *Variety* and elsewhere. And overall, Bernstein was pleased with it. Decades later, it's still a vital rendering—heartfelt and at times turbulent and raw, but never sacrificing the music's velocity, lyricism, and bold virtuosity. It also makes you appreciate the rightness of the first cast. Superbly coached by Sondheim and Bernstein, they articulate the words, notes, and phrases with fine clarity. They also convey the emotions with utter conviction—the ecstatic romantic chemistry between Larry Kert's Tony and Carol Lawrence's Maria, the offhand cockiness of Calin's Riff, and the spicy intelligence of Rivera's Anita. Close your eyes while they're singing and you are halfway to being in a theater with them close at hand.

(Note: the album has been reissued with added "bonus tracks," including the Finale and sections of "Somewhere" and "The Dance at the Gym" that were initially not included.)

1961 Movie Soundtrack: There are some who rank this recording from the cinematic *West Side Story* over the Broadway album. It is more comprehensive in some respects: The "Dance at the Gym" number is there in its entirety, and at the original tempo (the film cast had to dance to this prerecorded track). The music for the "Somewhere" ballet, however, was missing because the ballet was left out of the film.

Though the dubbed voices can seem clumsily edited and disconcerting onscreen, on record they are technically strong and capable—if less dramatically expressive than those in the Broadway record. Jim Bryant, as Tony, aces the high notes in "Maria" and "Something's Coming," and Marni Nixon's sparkling soprano affirms why she was the go-to gal to fill in vocals for non-singing female stars. It is curious, though, to hear Russ Tamblyn perform "Gee, Officer Krupke" with panache, then be dubbed by castmate Tucker Smith on "The Jet Song." (Go figure.)

The expanded CD version of the movie album also includes the "intermission" music for the initial two-act film screenings, the overture Bernstein crafted just for the movie, and other extras.

2009 Broadway Revival: There is no recording of the 1980 *West Side Story* revival in New York, so this disc was the first "complete" Broadway cast album since 1957. It was also the first U.S. recording to include the translations of some lyrics into Spanish as mandated by revival director Arthur Laurents, adapted from the English by composer-lyricist Lin-Manuel Miranda, and approved by Stephen Sondheim.

Not long into the revival's run, some of the original English lyrics were restored. But on the disc, the new Spanish lines are scattered throughout the singing parts for the Sharks—most awkwardly when, in the choral "Tonight Quintet" and "I Feel Pretty," the performers are singing in two languages at once.

Though awarded a Grammy, and praised in some quarters, the disc also drew criticism. In *The Sondheim Review,* Michael Portantiere judged it "deeply flawed" and described some cuts as variously "stolid," "sluggish," and "loose."

The somewhat exaggerated New York accents of Matt Cavenaugh's Tony and Cody Green's Riff are distracting. Laurents's decision to have a boy soprano (instead of an adult woman) sing "Somewhere" tips the ballad into more overt sentimentality. And while Sondheim is listed among the recording's arrangers, some of the textures of the orchestration seem diminished. William Ruhlmann suggested, in the online All Music Guide, "Bernstein's music had a jarring angularity the first time around (and many times since); here, it's not so jarring or angular. In fact, it's all smooth and groove-oriented, more about dancing than drama."

On the plus side, the disc boasts a heartfelt, fetching vocal performance by soprano Josefina Scaglione as Maria. And when in his baritone comfort zone, and easing up on his vibrato, Matt Cavenaugh makes an appealingly ardent Tony, rekindling the convincing onstage chemistry he shared with Scaglione.

Leonard Bernstein Conducts West Side Story: Bernstein's only recording as conductor of the full score is another Grammy winner. It was released on CD but also is heard in the fascinating film documentary, *The Making of "West Side Story"*, a production of the British Broadcasting Corporation.

In 1985, as he was toiling with an orchestra of top-shelf New York session players and an A-list lineup of opera stars, the ebullient, emotive, and occasionally cranky maestro is filmed during the studio sessions for the historic recording. While the clock ticks away the expensive minutes, Bernstein prods and pushes the miscast, ill-prepared José Carreras, the famed Spanish tenor singing Tony, to quickly master the score's difficult arrangements and adopt a semi-persuasive American accent. He skirmishes with a recording engineer over the precision and quality of different takes and revels in a lovefest with soprano Kiri Te Kanawa (in her prime, singing Maria) and mezzo Tatiana Troyanos (an earthy Anita). He also marvels at the superb instrumental performances supplied by his hand-picked musicians.

The Deutsche Grammophon compact disc is valuable for preserving the original Bernstein–Ramin–Kostal orchestrations of the score, which sound stunningly good. Vocally, however, the session is a mixed bag—a reminder that opera singers can overpower and bulldoze the nuance out of show tunes, and proof that expecting a Spaniard to pronounce the name Maria without a Spanish accent can be a quixotic endeavor.

The DVD documentary offers something more, too: a rare, close-up account of the difficulties of faithfully transferring great music to disc, and an intimate portrait of the aged Bernstein at work, exulting and kvetching, revisiting and rediscovering one of his crowning achievements.

SELECTED JAZZ *WEST SIDE STORY* RECORDINGS

West Side Story—Oscar Peterson Trio (1962): The masterful pianist and his distinguished compatriots Ray Brown (on bass) and Ed Thigpen (on drums) were in their busy prime as a combo, and had recently issued a hit album of *My Fair Lady* tunes, when they took to the studio in 1962 for this set. The planning was minimal, but some of the results are sublime, particularly in the alternately jittery and lush setting of "Something's Coming," the rollicking version of "The Jet Song," and a heart-rending "Somewhere," with the melody gorgeously bowed on bass by Brown.

West Side Story—Stan Kenton (1961): One of the highest achievements of the esteemed arranger-bandleader's considerable career is this big-band interpretation. Impeccably and intricately orchestrated, for a full complement of brass and horns and a killer rhythm section, the set is dynamic and often unpredictable. A brooding, piano-led "Tonight" and a hot, be-bopping "I Feel Pretty" are among the unexpected highlights.

Buddy Rich and Maynard Ferguson Play Selections from West Side Story (1996): This album compiles previously recorded material by two leading jazz artists, including drummer Rich's *West Side Story* big-band suite (without trumpeter Ferguson), a favorite selection in his live concerts. The recording quality is rather rustic, but much more highly rated are Rich and his band's performances of the suite on film, thought to be destroyed in a fire but later recovered and meticulously remastered for a 2002 DVD, *Buddy Rich and His Band—The Lost "West Side Story" Tapes.* The adventuresome, horn-rich arrangements play around with the pace and bend the melodies. But they are always anchored and fired up by Rich's extraordinary, multidimensional drumming. The tempo varies from a volatile Prologue, to a restrained "Somewhere" with an airing of the melody on solo trombone, to a swinging "Something's Coming."

West Side Story—Earl "Fatha" Hines" (1974): The pioneering piano wonder Hines, one of the earliest jazz keyboard players to branch out from a traditional ragtime/blues formula into improvised solo lines, performs an unaccompanied collage of tunes from the score on this album, along with other numbers. He rips through the Bernstein music with his customary inventiveness, speed, and assurance.

Latin Tribute West Side Story—Nueva Manteca (2004): This internationally known octet is composed of Dutch musicians who specialize in tightly constructed Latin jazz arrangements. The piano, brass, and percussion configuration serves the score well—even though they omit the most Latin-flavored tune, "America" (too obvious?). Highlights of the disc include "Maria," opening with a trumpet fanfare, and a salsafied "Something's Coming" that could send listeners straight to the dance floor.

SOME ROCK AND POP *WEST SIDE STORY* RECORDINGS

The Songs of West Side Story—Various Artists (1996): An "all-star" pop homage to the musical, with a portion of the profits going toward educational music programs (including the Bernstein Education Through the Arts Fund), this release has an oddfellow, cross-genre list of contributors, from country diva Wynonna Judd to rapmaster Def Jef and soul queen Patti LaBelle. The premise for the project, explained executive producer Mike Greene to the *South Florida Sun Sentinel,* was to demonstrate the ongoing relevance of the songs.

"I think the cultural strife within the inner city and the portrayal of gang violence . . . is more poignant today than when Lenny [Bernstein] first created it," Greene suggested. "My belief was that if we used a diverse cast to tell this story—artists from several genres, country, rap, jazz, R&B, pop and rock—we could be consistent in that we'd be using music to bridge cultural differences."

The end product was well received, despite the mishmash of musical styles and inconsistent quality of the interpretations. The cuts range from sappy (Phil Collins's "Somewhere") to campy (Little Richard's whooping "I Feel Pretty"), from stirring ("Somewhere," by Aretha Franklin) to swinging ("Cool," with jazz singer Patti Austin) to disarmingly earnest (Trisha Yearwood's "I Have a Love"). Most impressive is the Tejano (Tex-

Mex) pop star Selena's haunting "A Boy Like That," with its creative overdubbing and brooding, percussive arrangement. Recorded just three weeks before the twenty-three-year-old singer was murdered (by her fan club president), the cut was later rereleased in four different remixes.

Punk Side Story—Schlong (1995): Not for everyone's iPod, but it delivers what it promises: a punk-rock romp through the *West Side Story* score, by a short-lived but semifamous northern California band (named after the Yiddish slang word for a large penis). As Schlong member Gavin MacArthur recalled in the book *Gimme Something Better,* a history of Bay Area punk rock by Jack Boulware and Silke Tudor, the band hatched the idea for the disc, took a couple weeks to learn the songs, then gathered together friends (including a teenage punk princess for the role of Maria) and recorded the whole, deliberately ratty shebang in just three days— "One day for the music, one day for the vocals, and one day to mix it. People got paid in beer," MacArthur noted.

Musically primitive, by intent, this is a strident, squawky, irony-heavy treatment of the show's songs and instrumental numbers, with thrashing guitars and bashing drums interlaced with some bits of piano, acoustic guitar, and French horn. If you can get into their groove, there's something kind of wonderful about a different era of rebel youth fondly but irreverently tackling the show, fearlessly grunging up "Maria" and "I Feel Pretty." (They reportedly did receive a fan letter from Bernstein's daughter Nina, who got what they were up to.)

MacArthur said he thought of the album as a lark, until "people brought up the point that [the musical] was about punks. And it's totally true. They were punks for the time. They did a lot of dancing, punks do a lot of dancing too. It's just a different style of dancing."

Leonard Bernstein's New York—Various Artists—(1996): A delight for Bernstein fans, this outing uses some first-rate actor-singers to perform numbers from *West Side Story,* as well as *On the Town* and *Wonderful Town,* and includes a thrilling version of "Tonight" by leading Broadway players Audra McDonald and Mandy Patinkin, and a breathtaking "One Hand, One Heart" with Broadway's Richard Muenz and opera great Dawn Upshaw.

A Place for Us—Various Artists (2007): All but one of the cuts on this *Tribute to 50 Years of "West Side Story,"* a decent rendition of "Tonight" sung in its original arrangement by Broadway veterans Kristin Chenoweth and Hugh Panaro, were culled from existing recordings. And, not even counting the iconic "Maria" cover by Johnny Mathis, the stuff is mainly schmaltz—a very chipper and British "I Feel Pretty" from Julie Andrews, a cheesy "Tonight" with strings and chorus, crooned by Andy Williams, an echo- and vibrato-laden medley duet by Mathis and Barbra Streisand of "I Have a Love" and "One Hand, One Heart." The disc boasts only two real gems: a more spare, musical, and soulful "One Hand, One Heart" by the vibrant duo of vocalist Patti Cathcart and jazz guitarist Tuck Andress, and an arch, ultrahip "Gee, Officer Krupke" by three smooth-jazz messengers: pianist André Previn, bassist Red Mitchell, and drummer Shelly Manne from their own *West Side Story* tribute album, issued in 1959.

SOME NOTEWORTHY INDIVIDUAL COVERS OF
WEST SIDE STORY MUSIC

"The Jet Song"—Cal Tjader; the Canadian Brass

"Maria"—Sarah Vaughan; Buddy Rich; Maynard Ferguson

"Somewhere"—Barbra Streisand; Aretha Franklin; Tom Waits;
    Dawn Upshaw; the Nice; Dave Brubeck Quartet; Bill Charlap;
    Marilyn Horne

"One Hand, One Heart"—Dawn Upshaw with Richard Muenz;
    Bill Barron; Falla Guitar Quartet

"I Feel Pretty"—Dawn Upshaw; Sarah Vaughan; Marian McPartland;
    Dave Grusin

"Something's Coming"—Mandy Patinkin; Barbra Streisand; Yes;
    Cal Tjader

"Tonight"—Audra McDonald with Mandy Patinkin;
    Dave Brubeck Quartet

"America"—Bill Charlap; Cal Tjader

"Cool"—Marian McPartland; Cal Tjader

West Side Story Suite—Joshua Bell (violin); Katia and
    Marielle Labeque (two pianos)

WEST SIDE STORY (PRODUCTIONS AND EXCERPTS) ON DVD

West Side Story—the 1961 movie, which in the 2003 Special Edition Collector's Set has a bonus disc of the informative documentary film *West Side Memories*. It includes interviews with cast members and creators of the stage and film productions of the musical, along with rare 8mm behind-the-scenes footage shot on location during the filming of the movie.

Other DVDs (listed by wssonstage.com)

Leonard Bernstein: Making of West Side Story

That's Dancing!

The Best of Broadway Musicals from the Ed Sullivan Show

Jerome Robbins: Something to Dance About (documentary)

Dave Grusin Presents West Side Story

Buddy Rich: The Lost West Side Story Tapes

Broadway: The Golden Age

Broadway's Lost Treasures III

Carol Lawrence Bell Telephone Hour, 1960–1967

Gypsy of the Year/WSS Original Cast Reunion 2007
    (online video at broadway.com)

Cher: The Farewell Tour (a surreal twelve-minute musical version
    of the show, with Cher playing all the roles)

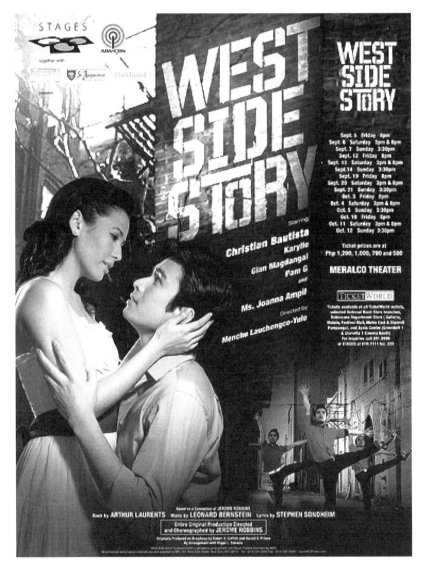

Poster for *West Side Story* at a theater in Manila, The Philippines.

11

HERE COME THE JETS
WEST SIDE STORY
IN PRODUCTION AROUND
THE WORLD

West Side Story is one of the hardiest, most hummable Broadway musicals of all time and one of the most often produced in the United States and internationally. In 2009 alone, about 600 mountings were licensed, to professional and amateur theaters, opera houses, Broadway, touring outfits, and the show's most consistent producing entities: schools and youth centers.

"No matter what country you're in, no matter what language you do it in, it always works," Freddie Gershon, head of Music Theatre International, which licenses all *West Side Story* productions, told NPR.

And yet, despite its resilience, *West Side Story* is also one of the most difficult Broadway musical classics to stage well. To fulfill all demands of the production, be it in a school gymnasium or a community theater or a Broadway show palace, requires performers with superior dance skills, outstanding vocal ability, and solid acting talent, and a strong pit orchestra. The balance is notoriously tricky: since its inception, *West Side Story* has often been evaluated as a lopsided work, largely because it is not often that all the elements of dance, song, story, and instrumental music are equally realized in production.

Any class-A Broadway-level mounting or international tour is expected to recreate the piece with a full cast and orchestra (roughly fifty people), and to resurrect the choreography of Jerome Robbins in some contractually acceptable fashion. But what exactly does the latter mean?

Most prominent English-language revivals have hired someone to do the staging and/or choreography who previously performed in *West Side Story* (or *Jerome Robbins' Broadway*) under Robbins's direction. Or they've deputized someone who was a former associate or direct "descendant" of Robbins, artistically speaking. Gerald Freedman, the assistant director of the initial production, shepherded the 1964 City Center revival in New York. Alan Johnson is one of numerous original cast members who have directed and/or resurrected the choreography for *West Side Story* in high-profile mountings. (Johnson also adapted the Robbins dance moves for the famous 2000 Gap clothing TV ads inspired by *West Side Story,* and he assembled a *West Side Story* dance manual, available to help guide any outfit producing the musical.)

But reviving the Robbins dances is not a clear-cut task, according to Joey McKneely, who performed in the *West Side Story* part of *Jerome Robbins' Broadway* and was one of the choreographer-directors tapped by the master to help keep the work alive. McKneely staged the show in Milan and Paris, and in 2008 directed a well-received European and Mideast touring edition that began its travels at Sadler's Wells Theatre in London. At director Arthur Laurents's request, he also reconstructed the dances for the 2009 Broadway revival. To do so he had to ask himself, "What exactly *is* the original choreography for *West Side Story*?"

"There's 1957, then there's the '61 movie," McKneely told the *New York Times,* "then there's the '80 revival, then there's 'Jerome Robbins' Broadway,' then there's the New York City Ballet [suite]. So O.K., and [Robbins] did all of those versions."

In addition to using Johnson's manual, McKneely prepared for his revivals by watching an archival videotape of the Robbins-directed 1980 *West Side Story* at Broadway's Minskoff Theatre. And since the chronically dissatisfied Robbins kept tinkering with the moves, McKneely has felt emboldened to put his own stamp on them—mainly through small shifts of emphasis, nuance, and attitude.

Like Robbins did, McKneely teaches the numbers body to body—by dancing and modeling the choreography "full-out" himself for the performers. And he believes that when casting revivals, youth is even more of a critical factor in the twenty-first century than it was in 1957. "When you're in your early 20s, you still have your hormones flaring, you're still partying out at night, you're getting into trouble," he observed. "The closer you to get to that age group, the more in touch in a really natural way they are to those emotions, so you believe them."

One advantage *West Side Story* productions have today, over the original show, is how dance, as an art form, has changed. The strict boundaries between classical ballet, modern dance, and show dancing that persisted in the 1950s have blurred and softened. Dancers often develop additional skills by studying gymnastics and martial arts. In McKneely's view, the technical bar is continually being raised—choreographers can expect kicks to be higher, leaps wider, isolations more pronounced from their Broadway talent pool. And the last few decades of new dance-oriented musicals, with their highly demanding choreography by the likes of Twyla Tharp, have created a demand for superbly agile, classically *and* jazz-trained Broadway "gypsies"—who also can act.

PUTTING IT TOGETHER

Most *West Side Story* productions do not have the resources, the requirements, or the mandate to try to replicate the original show (or the movie). Stock, amateur, and regional theater mountings are licensed to have as few as five players in the pit, and they generally use fresh choreography. But what choreographer taking up the task has not, at the very least, watched the film? And been inspired by it? And wouldn't be driven to borrow many of Robbins's moves? Since most patrons will also have seen the Robbins choreography done to perfection on celluloid, expectations of a live version can be sky-high—and easily let down.

Most veteran theater critics can recall productions where the Tonys strained and failed to hit the high notes in "Maria" and "Something's Coming," where the dance numbers looked elementary and wimpy compared to the film versions, where the pared-down pit bands struggled valiantly but sloppily through the score.

And yet there have been many instances when, in the right talented hands, more was achieved with less. And *West Side Story* can be a terrific showcase and proving ground for extraordinary talent. In a suburb of Seattle, for instance, a 2001 production at the Village Theatre, a professional mid-sized venue, used a smaller pit orchestra and less-taxing choreography than a Broadway rendition. But the show was absorbing nonetheless. And it cast a spotlight on Cheyenne Jackson (who played Tony) and Benjamin Schrader (Riff), two gifted young locals who went on to Broadway careers.

The universal resonance of the movie, and the saga of verboten romance between members of rival tribes, has helped to make *West Side Story* a hot property abroad—in English-language stagings, and often in foreign-language editions. It's been a popular title, for instance, in the Philippines, in Austria and Germany, and in Hungary (in two different translations). A young, largely black cast in Port Elizabeth, South Africa, performed the show, and companies in Brazil and Portugal have presented hit renditions in Portuguese.

One of the more intriguing foreign productions is in the repertoire of the famed Japanese all-female musical-theater troupe the Takarazuka Revue. First mounted in 1968, their Japanese-language adaptation of *West Side Story* faithfully preserves the Robbins choreography. But the male roles, including Tony, Bernardo, and Riff, are enacted by highly skilled women performers (known as *otokoyaku*) who play it "straight," using lowered voices and masculine physicality to impersonate the gang members. Though the gambit may seem odd or even ludicrous by American standards, cross-gender casting has a long and illustrious history in Japan, where the revered Kabuki theatrical tradition still uses men (known as the *onnagata*) in lead female roles. The Takarazuka, founded in 1914, is a major attraction with theaters in Osaka and Tokyo. It boasts a fifty-thousand-member fan club and maintains high production standards for its musicals, glitzy song-and-dance revues, and dramatic adaptations of such literary classics as *Gone with the Wind*. And *West Side Story* is one of the most successful pieces in the company's repertoire.

But the majority of *West Side Story* airings each year are the scores, sometimes hundreds, of school productions. And the lion's share take place in high schools—as evidenced by the multitude of amateur videos of excerpts posted on YouTube, Facebook, and other video-sharing Internet sites.

Some obvious factors make the show so enticing for teachers and their adolescent charges. One is student familiarity with the material, due to the ongoing popularity of the movie and the frequent pop cultural references to it. Another: the piece conveys a story *about* teenagers, with a predominance of roles *for* teens—plenty of them. And the number of Jets and Sharks can always be expanded.

Gershon says the high school outings can be a revelation, because "when you see a 17-year old girl play Maria, that's far more believable than a 28-year old girl trying to pretend she's a 17-year old girl." And despite how much has changed about American adolescence since 1957, in essential ways, *plus ça change, plus c'est la même chose.* The risky romance, the playground bullying and clashing, the peer pressure, the scapegoating of "the other" (especially foreign newcomers), the intense and inchoate feelings that can erupt into fatal violence: these are things many American youths throughout the country are on intimate terms with—or at least can vividly imagine. Schools and educational theater troupes often use the social ills the story evokes to create meaningful writing projects and class and post-show student discussions that bring the subject matter into the present.

Patricia M. Gleeson, head of Boston Children's Theatre and director of its 2007 teen production of *West Side Story,* seized such opportunities. "Every day in Boston, just as in New York City 50 years ago, young people find themselves in a world filled with violence—on the news, on the street, in school, and even at home," she commented in a publicity release for the show. "Boston Children's Theatre chose to produce 'West Side Story' as a way for young people not only to take part in a wonderful musical theatre experience, but also to learn about themselves and their peers, and to participate in discussions about possible roots and remedies to the violence of today."

Since the 1990s, *West Side Story* has periodically been tweaked to reflect different youth populations than the original did. There have been numerous productions blending deaf and hearing-impaired actors, including a fascinating 2000 outing jointly produced by MacMurray College and Illinois School for the Deaf, chronicled in the book *Deaf Side Story* by Mark Rigney.

In 2008, at a high school in Plantation, Florida, teacher Jason Zembuch decided to involve interested hearing and impaired kids on the campus in a bilingual version of the show. The Sharks, including Maria, communicated in American Sign Language but had their songs vocalized by hearing actors. And the students playing the Jets signed as they spoke and sang. A video snippet on YouTube captured the show's touching and novel balcony scene, in which Tony and Maria embrace during "Tonight" by caressing each other's hands as they sign.

"What's inherent in the script is that we have a clash of two cultures," Zembuch told ABC News. "The original production is a clash between the Puerto Ricans and the Americans. In this production, we have a clash of not only the Puerto Ricans and the Americans but also the deaf and the hearing."

Inevitably, there have also been hip-hop adaptations of *West Side Story*. One staged in 2008 at the Pioneer Arts Center in Easthampton, Massachusetts, had break dancers in the cast, and youths of Puerto Rican, Nigerian, Haitian, and other ancestry—some completely new to theater.

Students at SAR High School, a yeshiva (Jewish religious school) in the Bronx, brought another perspective to their school version of *West Side Story*. NPR reported that both Sharks and Jets wore yarmulkes (religious skullcaps), and because of Orthodox Jewish laws there was no touching allowed between boys and girls during dance numbers.

A teacher involved, Kenny Birnbaum, said the musical was still meaningful when homogenously cast, because the students "have to deal with the real issues that the play raises: How do we treat other people of different religions and ethnic groups and races? And sometimes when you're in an insular community . . . it really challenges us and really pushes us to think outside the box. And that's part of why this play is so important."

SOMEWHERE, IN JAIL

West Side Story can also be a revelatory experience when presented in criminal institutions, especially when inmates incarcerated for gang-related crimes are the actors. At New York's Sing Sing Correctional Facility in 2007, outside actors were brought in by the jail's Rehabilitation Through the Arts program to portray the Sharks, opposite prisoners who played the Jets.

Inmate John Whitfield, a convicted murderer who switched real-life roles to play Officer Krupke, told the *New York Times,* "Theater has a magical way of bringing out the humanity in people." Another performer, convicted armed robber and ex–gang member Clarence "Divine Eye" Maclin, also touted the experience.

In an NPR interview Maclin explained, "This particular play really brought the guys together, because of the [gang] issue . . . The original play was Latinos against white guys. Here, we don't really have a large population of white people in our production company, but it was more Latinos [against] blacks. And these are issues that we really deal with, in the yard here, in the mess hall here, all throughout the jail system, we really deal with these issues: Latinos and blacks, now how to co-exist?"

Britain's Pimlico Opera has staged *West Side Story* (and other musicals) in prisons in Ireland and England, including in a 2009 production at HMP Wandsworth in London, Britain's largest prison. That show also mingled inmates with professional singer-actors.

London Observer columnist Fiona Maddocks was moved by the performance she took in at Wandsworth. "As Bernstein's tale of gang warfare, violence and murder was enacted at our very feet, the audience sat transfixed by this highly charged union of life and art . . . not yards away and just out of reach . . . were wives, girlfriends, parents." One woman, a mother of a prisoner, told Maddocks that seeing her jailed son act in the show was the first time she'd felt proud of him.

And Seumas Milne of London's *Guardian* newspaper wrote of the Wandsworth show, "When the Jets and the Sharks clashed, the street brawl seemed a good deal more authentic than a run-of-the-mill theatrical stage fight—as did the lines 'We ain't no delinquents, we're misunderstood, deep down inside us there is good.' And the fact that Officer Krupke was played by the only prison officer in the show . . . almost rubbed out the dividing line between art and real life altogether."

One can only imagine the intensity of the moment when the leading Welsh opera star Bryn Terfel dropped in on a Wandsworth rehearsal and lent his magnificent baritone to the chorus. Observers said he was "blown away" as he sang along with the inmates on a chorus of "Somewhere," which voices the yearning for "a new way of living" and "a way of forgiving."

The creators of *West Side Story* may not have devised it as a rehabilitation or educational tool. But John Mauceri, a conductor, chancellor of the North Carolina School for the Arts, and close former musical associate of Bernstein, believes the show "not only changed the way we view the possibilities of what a musical could do, it actually changed the world. But if you talk to Lenny or to Steve Sondheim or Arthur Laurents or Jerome Robbins, they would tell you, 'We were just trying to write a show.' That's the beautiful part of it. They weren't trying to make history. They were just trying to tell a story that needed to be told."

NOTABLE PRODUCTIONS

1957–59—World premiere in New York City at the Winter Garden Theatre and the Broadway Theatre. Original cast, with Larry Kert as Tony, Carol Lawrence as Maria, Chita Rivera as Anita. (732 performances.)

1958–61—Premiere London run at Her Majesty's Theatre in London with George Chakiris as Riff, Marlys Watters as Maria, Don McKay as Tony, and Chita Rivera encoring her New York stint as Anita. (1,039 performances.)

April–December 1960—Return New York engagement with original cast, Winter Garden Theatre and Alvin Theatre. (249 performances.)

April–May 1964—Limited New York City Center revival with Don McKay as Tony, Julia Migenes as Maria. Directed by Gerald Freedman, with Robbins choreography reproduced by original cast member Tom Abbott. (31 performances.)

1968—Lincoln Center revival in New York starring Barbara Luna as Maria and Kurt Peterson as Tony. Robbins production recreated by original cast member Lee Becker Theodore, who initiated the role of Anybodys. (89 performances.)

1974—Tokyo production, first Japanese-language version.

February–November 1980—Broadway revival of Robbins staging at the Minskoff Theatre, starring Jossie DeGuzman as Maria, Ken Marshall as Tony, and Debbie Allen as Anita. "Co-directed" by original *West Side Story* co-director Gerald Freedman, with choreography reproduced by Lee Theodore and Tom Abbott; Peter Gennaro credited as co-choreographer. (333 performances.)

1984—London revival with Robbins direction and choreography recreated by Tom Abbott.

1995—U.S. national tour with Scott Carollo as Tony and Marcy Harriell as Maria. Directed and choreographed by Alan Johnson, with Robbins and Laurents as "creative advisors."

2000—Hong Kong production, first in Cantonese.

2003—Bregenz Festival production in Austria, staged on a pier on Lake Constance by Francesca Zambello.

2007—Fiftieth-Anniversary World Tour with Robbins direction-choreography reconstructed by Joey McKneely.

2007–Sanctioned fiftieth-anniversary American revivals–at the Fulton Opera House in Lancaster, Pennsylvania (in conjunction with the Lancaster Symphony Orchestra), and at the 5th Avenue Theatre in Seattle.

2008–The Philippines, first production in Tagalog.

2008–Lisbon, adapted in Portuguese as *West Side Story–Amor Sem Barreiras.*

2009–1–Broadway revival at the Palace Theatre, directed by Arthur Laurents, with some lyrics and dialogue translated into Spanish by Lin-Manuel Miranda. With Matt Cavenaugh as Tony, Josefina Scaglione as Maria, Karen Olivo as Anita. (748 performances.)

2010–Australian tour directed by Jerry McKneely.

ONE DEGREE FROM JEROME ROBBINS

As Alan Johnson noted in *Dancing with Demons,* many veterans of the original production of *West Side Story* have "gone on to become writers, directors, producers, teachers, choreographers. I call it the University of "West Side Story." When you do a production that can teach you about the theater–the definitive kind of lessons of what's required of you onstage at every moment, it's incredible."

Here are some of the associates of Jerome Robbins (cast members and assistants in various productions of *West Side Story,* the *West Side Story Suite,* and *Jerome Robbins' Broadway*) who went on to direct and/or choreograph *West Side Story* productions (in a list compiled by wssonstage.com):

Gerald Freedman, Tom Abbott, Tony Mordente, Lee Becker Theodore, Alan Johnson, Joshua Bergasse, Lenny Dale, Ben Vargas, Robert Arditti, Jay Norman, Richard Caceres, Jeffrey Dunn, Mary Lynn Suseck, Pamela Khoury, Kevin Backstrom, and Joey McKneely.

2009 BROADWAY REVIVAL

The first twenty-first-century Broadway production of *West Side Story* was not simply a reconstruction of the original staging. Arthur Laurents, at age ninety still sharp and fit, was the director. And he had some scores to settle with the show.

In his book *Mainly on Directing,* Laurents critiqued recent revivals of the musical he found inadequate and stale, and described how he came to the conclusion that "what was most needed for any new production was a fresh, original look at the show. What that was, I had no idea."

The idea he latched on to ultimately came from Tom Hatcher, Laurents's longtime life partner, after Hatcher attended a Bogotà, Colombia, production of *West Side Story* performed in Spanish. He reported to Laurents that because it was in their native language, the Sharks were seen more as the heroes and the Jets more as villains. "That sent mind and blood racing," Laurents recounted. "'If we could equalize the gangs here,' I said, 'both would be the villains they are.' 'Why not have the Sharks speak Spanish?'Tom asked. And there it was—the reasons for a new production."

With Stephen Sondheim's blessing, Laurents selected lyrics and dialogue that he and Lin-Manuel Miranda, the dynamic young director-composer of the hit Latino musical *In the Heights,* then adapted into Spanish.

The only stipulations Sondheim made about the Spanish lyrics were that the original imagery and rhyming structure remain—because, Miranda reported to the *Washington Post,* the ears of "an English-speaking person familiar with the music . . . will expect it to rhyme at these places." Miranda had directed the show in high school, and his Puerto Rican father was a big *West Side Story* fan also. After accepting the assignment, Miranda "holed up in my parents' house, and used my dad as a human thesaurus."

"I learned a ton of Spanish in terms of wrestling this thing into couplets and syllables, and working with my dad gave me a whole new appreciation of the complexity of writing lyrics," said Miranda in an interview with this book's author. "It was a really fun bonding event for us."

What he and Laurents eventually arrived at was not a rote translation, but one that they felt gave the Sharks more cultural authenticity and dramatic sizzle. Lyrics were changed into Spanish in every song sung by the Sharks and their women, but the amount of Spanish and its impact was greater in some numbers than in others.

Anita's angry "A Boy Like That," in Spanish, was still answered by Maria with the original English lyrics of "I Have a Love." Laurents explained to London's *Guardian* newspaper, "You have to ask, where is the emotional point? Anita went back to Spanish when her [Puerto Rican] lover was killed, and Maria goes to English. To put it crudely, love is a universal language."

In the "Tonight Quintet," the Sharks sing their parts in Spanish in counterpoint to the English lyrics of the Jets, and Maria and Tony also sing in English. In "I Feel Pretty," the lyrics were changed entirely into Spanish. And at the finale, the dying Tony sings a shaky bit of "Somewhere" in Spanish to Maria—providing more evidence of his deep bond with her, according to Laurents.

Through his direction and the textual changes, Laurents also wanted to remedy what he had long felt was an overly benign image of the gang kids. He lamented that the Jet members too often came off as "likeable tough little thugs" and noted that "kids in gangs today are angry, vicious and violent, heedless killers, but they were in the fifties, too. They haven't changed, the theatre has. Somehow they would have to be played as what they are." That meant a Prologue with rougher pranks, and an edgier, nastier posture for the gangbangers in general.

Laurents also felt the story was sometimes overshadowed and should be brought to the fore and strengthened through a greater emphasis on realism. To that end, he made many small but meaningful changes in the original staging. One of the most striking: instead of having the Jets and Sharks come together at the finale to carry the slain Tony off, the show closes with Maria weeping over the body, comforted only by another Jet.

"The show has to be realistic," Laurents told the *Los Angeles Times*. "What cop in his right mind would let kids carry a body away from a crime scene?" (By that level of logic, however, what police department wouldn't put Doc's under heavy surveillance, to prevent further bloodshed?)

Laurents brought in Joey McKneely to conjure the original *West Side Story* choreography in a more freehanded manner than usual (which made for a much-altered "Somewhere" ballet). And he chose set, costume, and lighting designers who would refresh the look of the piece. With some engaging young talent aboard led by Matt Cavenaugh as Tony, Josefina Scaglione as Maria, and Cody Green as Riff, the show began its Washington, D.C., tryout run in December 2008 at the National Theatre (where *West Side Story* had its world debut fifty-one years prior). Reviews for the run were mostly positive, while pointing out some perceived weaknesses.

Heartening for Laurents were the affirmative reactions of many Latino patrons, like those interviewed by the *Washington Post* who lauded his "rebalancing" of the show. With the addition of the Spanish (and more Hispanic cast members), they felt the Sharks were presented more sympathetically than in other stage productions and in the movie.

"I thought [the Spanish speaking] made it more authentic and probably less offensive and less comical, for somebody who might find it offensive," said Mercedes Lemp, director of the D.C. Office on Latino Affairs. And in his *Washington Post* review, Peter Marks declared, "No matter how you conjugate them, it seems, the giddy verbs of 'I Feel Pretty' (or rather 'Siento Hermosa') ring out with verve."

When the revival moved on to New York's Palace Theatre for an official opening on March 19, 2009, it was welcomed warmly by most drama critics, with special praise heaped on Scaglione. The production received a great deal of national attention and TV play (with the cast performing live excerpts on such shows as *Dancing with the Stars* and *Good Morning America*). It garnered four Tony Award nominations, including one for best musical revival of the season, a prize that went to *Hair* instead. (The only Tony win was for Karen Olivo's performance as Anita.) The original cast album received a Grammy. And by the time this *West Side Story* closed on January 2, 2011, it had racked up 748 performances, recouped its $14 million investment, and launched what had every sign of becoming a lengthy and lucrative national tour.

Yet Laurents's mission to make the Jets more menacing and "real" was not entirely successful. Few critics were buying the Jets as stone-cold sociopaths, or the 1957 equivalents of modern gangsta ruffians who'd murder another kid for his athletic shoes or cell phone. Charles McNulty of the *Los Angeles Times* found Cavenaugh "about as tough as a lanky J. Crew model." And the opening sentence of Ben Brantley's *New York Times* review read, "Even when they're flashing switchblades and kicking people in the ribs, the teenage hoodlums who maraud through Arthur Laurents's startlingly sweet new revival of 'West Side Story' seem like really nice kids."

The insertions of Spanish proved more problematic as the run progressed. There were complaints by patrons, non-Spanish speakers, who found the language switch confusing or annoying or just incomprehensible. During one random 2009 matinee packed with school kids, the crowd went dead during the Spanish passages—presumably because there were not a great many speakers of the language in attendance. If you couldn't comprehend what they were uttering, including their wisecracks and endearments, the Sharks could seem *more* remote and "exotic" than in the all-English version.

(A translation of lyrics was in the program, but who goes to Broadway to peer at tiny print in darkness?)

Realizing the difficulty, five months into the New York run Laurents and the producers decided to switch some of the Spanish back to English. "Audiences were getting the general idea of 'A Boy Like That,' but they weren't getting hammered by it," Mr. Laurents acknowledged to the *New York Times*. "The sheer power of 'A boy like that who'd kill your brother' has no real equivalent, and for people who don't understand Spanish, the impact was diluted."

Miranda was philosophical about the reversals. "I went in knowing this was an experiment at the outset. It's one thing to have bilingual musical numbers in my show 'In the Heights.' It's new. But it's another thing to mess with a classic. It had been so long since 'West Side Story' had been on Broadway, people didn't want to see a 'take' on it. They wanted to see '*West Side Story.*'"

For all its attempts at greater authenticity, the production wound up underscoring the intrinsically imaginative, mythic nature of the show—and its limitations as docudrama. But it sure must have pleased its surviving creators that, unlike the wanly received 1980 encore of *West Side Story* on Broadway, this revival demonstrated the show's ongoing theatrical viability. Praising the "consummate craftsmanship" of the piece, and Laurents's stewardship, critic David Rooney in *Variety* surmised what many other scribes expressed—that "the 1957 show remains both a brilliant evocation of its period and a timeless tragedy of disharmony and hate."

The Sharks, led on Broadway by Kenneth LeRoy as Bernardo (second from the right), endure taunts and bigotry in *West Side Story*. Courtesy of Photofest.

12

STICK TO YOUR OWN KIND
BIGOTRY AND
WEST SIDE STORY

Spic!, lyin' spic!"
　　"Polack!"
　　"Tin-horn immigrant scum!"

The demeaning epithets fly in *West Side Story*—racial and ethnic slurs like those heard and hurled on Manhattan streets in 1957, but new to Broadway musicals.

West Side Story was initially considered discomfitingly raw, even shocking in its overt expressions (verbal and physical) of bitter bigotry among New York City ethnic groups. The insults the second-generation European American Jets spew at their Puerto Rican peers sounded especially savage and cruel. And the primary representative of the adult establishment, Schrank, came on like an equal-opportunity bigot playing both sides off the middle, addressing his constituents as "half breed" and "gold teeth" and "trash," and mocking the Jets' alcoholic and prostitute parents ("How's your old man's d.t.'s, A-Rab?" "How's the action on your mother's mattress, Action?") while continually implying the inherent "racial" inferiority of the Sharks. "I've got the badge," he sneers at Bernardo, "and you've got the skin."

Anxieties about race and ethnicity run like a deep fault line throughout the American experiment. In ways blunt and subtle, obvious and opaque, the frictions between racial and ethnic groups have been fragmenting, tormenting, and fascinating our polyglot culture for more than two centuries.

Before mainstream radio, TV, and film began to confront the cross-cultural strains and inequities in our society with candor, the American theater at least suggested they existed. In some instances, the song-and-dance pleasures of musicals (and the populist, multi-ethnic shows of variety and vaudeville) acknowledged, even celebrated our growing diversity as a nation. Some of the early architects of the Broadway musical, most of them first- or second-generation Jews with European roots, were motivated to address the sting of xenophobia and ethnic bigotry. Stephen Whitfield suggested in a *Jewish Daily Forward* essay that their interest in the subject likely stemmed from their own knowledge of anti-Semitism and minority status.

Wrote Whitfield, "The dream that ancient rivalries might be overcome for the sake of love is a topic that long fascinated Jewish dramatists and librettists, who have given it a kick no doubt heightened by their own membership in a minority long stigmatized in the Diaspora." Charles Kaiser's book *The Gay Metropolis* quotes Laurents as saying the shared fact of being Jewish was the thing that most informed the *West Side Story* collaborators' "passion against prejudice, our theatrical vision, our aspiration."

Between the two world wars, Broadway musicals gradually moved a step or two away from recycling the most offensive virulently comedic and villainous stereotypes of the "other" (Asians, Latinos, African Americans). And some writers and composers more attuned to America's cultural diversity crafted shows that touched on intolerance.

Yet while it had important predecessors in this vein, *West Side Story* took a giant leap forward in exploring prejudice, assimilation, and xenophobia as its central themes—not as sociological abstractions, as historical (as in *Show Boat*) or distant and foreign (in *South Pacific*) conditions, but as pressing contemporary problems being played out within a few short blocks of the Winter Garden Theatre—and by extension, in other major American cities.

Offstage, American racial and ethnic bigotry was being exposed and protested in the 1950s with new intensity. After all, the country had just been at war with a fascist, genocidal nation that had murdered millions of Jews and members of other minority groups to further an alleged Caucasian "Master Race." And when blacks, Jews, Japanese Americans,

Latinos, and other minorities returned from serving the United States in World War II, still to be treated as inferior citizens in their home nation, the lid blew off and the issue of civil rights rose to the top of the national agenda.

But the progress over the decade was touch-and-go. In 1957, the year of the *West Side Story* premiere, the first federal Civil Rights Act was passed to finally guarantee in law that all U.S. citizens had the right to vote—despite a round-the-clock filibuster by "Dixiecrat" U.S. senator Strom Thurmond of South Carolina. On the other hand, Operation Wetback was under way, a government effort that located and deported over one million undocumented U.S. residents of Mexican descent, often without formal hearings. And on September 25, 1957, the day before the *West Side Story* opening, President Dwight D. Eisenhower had to send federal troops to Little Rock, Arkansas, to protect nine African American youths trying to integrate an all-white high school— after Governor Orval Faubus had called up state National Guard units to block them from entering the building.

The sympathies of the *West Side Story* team were solidly pro–civil rights. Laurents had written about anti-Semitism in his early play *Home of the Brave,* later reworked into a film about racism against African American soldiers, and he would continually address different kinds of prejudice in his work. The refusal of Laurents and his collaborators to soften the element of bigotry in the musical, or resolve the schisms between Puerto Rican and white gang members with feel-good socio-platitudes, was courageous for the time. It repelled some potential *West Side Story* investors who considered the subject too controversial for a Broadway tuner. And it also kept away some showgoers with uninformed, preconceived negative opinions of Puerto Ricans.

West Side Story was not only unorthodox in its portrayal of cross-cultural prejudice and strife. It also was unusual at the time for its rather jaundiced critique (in the song "America" and elsewhere) of the sacrosanct notion that the United States was a shining beacon of liberty, where prosperity and freedom were automatically showered upon the "huddled masses" of every race, creed, and color who migrated to the country from other lands.

THE LATINO BROADWAY BREAKTHROUGH

West Side Story was also the first mainstream musical that aimed to depict American characters of Latin heritage authentically and empathetically. Hispanic featured roles in previous Broadway (and Hollywood movie) musicals had been mostly stereotypes of sweaty bandidos or dashing Zorro types, smarmy male Latin lovers (malevolent, or just ludicrous), and fiery, va-va-voom women singer-dancers and maracas-wielding bandleaders, with exaggerated accents.

Before she became a fruit-hatted icon in Busby Berkeley movie musicals, effervescent Brazilian-Portuguese star Carmen Miranda broke through on Broadway in 1939 singing and samba-ing in the musical revue *Streets of Paris*. The Cuban-born future *I Love Lucy* TV star Desi Arnaz had a somewhat less clichéd showcase for his talents in *Too Many Girls,* a Broadway musical comedy with a collegiate setting and a Rodgers and Hart score. Some Latinos also snagged chorus roles, or all-purpose foreign parts. (Chita Rivera played a French prostitute, Fifi, in the failed 1955 musical *Seventh Heaven* and was a French dancer in *Can-Can*).

Before *West Side Story,* however, no Broadway musical had focused on Puerto Rican culture and characters or centered on a cross-cultural romance between white and Hispanic youths. The show was also the first to costar a Puerto Rican actress (Chita Rivera) in a Puerto Rican role, and the first to concern itself with La Migración, an influx of tens of thousands of Puerto Rican U.S. citizens to New York City in search of better lives. According to census figures, in the 1950s more than 45,000 Puerto Ricans immigrated to New York City each year. By 1960, Puerto Ricans accounted for 9.3 percent of the city's overall population but were densely settled in East Harlem, between 116th and 145th streets, north of Central Park.

Though *West Side Story* deserves commendation for being one of the first mainstream musicals to dramatize this incoming wave, being "first" has its drawbacks and limitations. Despite the sympathies and the noble intentions of its creators, *West Side Story* became something of a lightning rod in the Latino-American community—thanks to its high visibility and great popularity, particularly on film.

Leading Latino entertainers speak of their great affection for the show, and how it inspired them. Nuyorican pop singer Jennifer Lopez was eager to pose as Anita in a 2009 photo homage to *West Side Story* in *Vanity Fair.* Rivera, Rita Moreno, Karen Olivo, and other Latinas who have appeared in the show and movie tend to praise it as an important outlet for Hispanic talent.

On the other hand, a love–hate relationship with *West Side Story* was brewing in the Latino community before the show even landed on Broadway. It's since been decried in some quarters as a font of negative myths and stereotypes—charges elaborated in academic and political circles, and in periodic derogatory references to the show in the Puerto Rico and U.S. media.

For instance, a 1999 story in the *Puerto Rico Herald,* about how Puerto Rican team members helped lead the New York Yankees to a World Series victory, contained this sharp slap: "'In a few months, [the ball players] have done much to undo the decades of damage done by 'West Side Story,' said local Sen. Kenneth McClintock, referring to the U.S. musical that portrayed Puerto Ricans as street gangsters."

A decade later, when Judge Sonia Sotomayor became the first Puerto Rican to ascend to the U.S. Supreme Court, a woman interviewed on a San Juan street told the *New York Times* that Sotomayor's appointment would help "remove the stigma of 'West Side Story.'"

A 2009 *Washington Post* article centered on the strong feelings, negative and ambivalent, Hispanics have about the show. *In the Heights* creator Lin-Manuel Miranda called it "our greatest blessing and our greatest curse." A woman who saw the movie as a youth living in Puerto Rico recalled it was "her first exposure to what Puerto Ricans were going through when they moved to New York" and spoke of the pride her community took in Rita Moreno's performance.

Another native Puerto Rican described the musical "as exciting in many ways and worrisome in some ways, because it gives a monochromatic view of what Puerto Ricans are in the United States."

Yesterday's groundbreaking message art can become today's punching bag, as progress outpaces earlier protest and minority groups gain the platforms to speak for themselves rather than through white surrogates. Famous cases include Harriet Beecher Stowe's abolitionist novel *Uncle Tom's Cabin* and Mark Twain's fierce protest yarn *Huckleberry Finn,* both lauded as daring exposés of the horrors of slavery but decades later attacked and censured as racist depictions of African Americans by myopic white authors.

Such cycles of celebration and rejection are probably inevitable, even a measure of social progress. But ultimately the representations that transcend such criticism and attempts at censure do so because of their continuing artistic potency and entertainment value.

Miranda, whose family background is Puerto Rican, believes that "the Bernstein music is immortal, it's going to outlive all of us. No one would even have a chance to criticize 'West Side Story' if it wasn't any good. It's a mixed blessing because it's a masterpiece."

Nor was *West Side Story* designed to provide positive cultural role models or definitively portray the behavior and values of either poor European American whites or migrant Puerto Ricans. As *The New Republic* film critic Stanley Kauffmann so insightfully observed, "As a sociological study, it is of no use, in fact, it is somewhat facile. What it does is to utilize certain conditions artistically—a vastly different process . . . [Much] of the work, dance and song and cinematic skill fuse into a contemporary theatrical poem."

Puerto Rican civil rights lawyer Cesar Perales told the *Washington Post,* "While I understand that subsequent generations of Puerto Ricans took umbrage at what they thought was a stereotyping of Puerto Ricans, I don't think Bernstein and the others behind that show were disparaging of Latinos but wanted to talk about the complexity involved in a migration."

But whenever artists convincingly portray the reality of racial or ethnic prejudice and injustice, they run the risk being accused of it themselves in something of a catch-22. And criticisms of *West Side Story* as an inaccurate, insensitive hotbed of Latino caricatures are unsurprising and cannot be just waved away. Given that *West Side Story* was not just the *first* popular drama to focus on Puerto Ricans but, for the vast majority of those who see it, the show/film is the *only* representation of this ethnic group they've seen, the images it conjures have extra weight.

West Side Story is a phenomenon of international reach. "The movie is all over the world, and for many people it's their only exposure to even the *term* Puerto Rican," Miranda pointed out. "They might not even know that Puerto Rico is an island in the Caribbean. So when your only image is that of a knife-wielding guy in a pompadour with dark makeup, that's hard. The show is a major export of our image, and we didn't really have a hand in it."

The success of contemporary music and acting stars of Puerto Rican heritage like Jennifer Lopez, Marc Anthony, Ricky Martin, Jimmy Smits, and others have given the public a more multifaceted, demystified view of their culture.

PROTESTS AND POLEMICS

The first significant Puerto Rican protest was raised against *West Side Story* just before the Washington, D.C., tryout production opened. The lyrics of the showstopper number "America" were circulated, and though the song was intended as a colorful display of Latin flair and an ironic debate on the virtues and deficiencies of life in the United States versus Puerto Rico, one lyric rankled: "Puerto Rico, you ugly island / Island of tropical diseases."

"We got a letter complaining about the one line," remembered Bernstein. "It wasn't just the line they objected to. We were insulting not only Puerto Rico but the Puerto Ricans and all the immigrants." Sondheim was not about to bow to censorship, especially when the song was satirical. He refused to change the wording, even under the threat of pickets appearing at Washington, D.C.'s National Theatre. No protestors showed up. And after opening on Broadway, the show got a thumbs-up from no less than the distinguished Puerto Rican resident commissioner Antonio Fernos Isern, who told the press the production expressed a genuine understanding of his people and their culture.

In the film of *West Side Story,* the lyrics for "America" were replaced with an earlier version of them by Sondheim that gives a more caustic critique of the treatment of Puerto Ricans on U.S. soil. As Anita champions the "American way," Bernardo retorts with the shortcomings of a country where liberty means freedom to "wash dishes and shine shoes" and a glad hand to Puerto Ricans turns into a face slap or a kick in the butt. It is, in fact, highly sympathetic to such immigrant struggles.

However, the case against "America" did not die there. It was most fulsomely revived in the 1990s, in an attack on the musical by Alberto Sandoval-Sanchez, an author and professor of Spanish at Mt. Holyoke College, in his book *José, Can You See?: Latinos on and off Broadway* and in some of his other works of cultural criticism.

In Sandoval-Sanchez's "alternative, provocative and ex-centric reading" of *West Side Story,* he slams "America" by oddly branding it "a patriotic and propagandistic" song that champions the virtues of the United States. In attempting to discern an ideology in a non-ideological show, he likens the song to "God Bless America" and Neil Diamond's flag-waving pop anthem about immigration, "America." The Diamond ode to the "melting pot," he points out, was used as a theme song for Ronald Reagan's 1980 presidential campaign.

Sandoval-Sanchez wrote that he understood "the power and vitality of the musical, not just as pure entertainment, but as an iconic ideological articulation" of identity among Puerto Rican and other Latino immigrants to the United States.

But his deconstructive analysis of *West Side Story* validates the most negative possible interpretations of the show's meaning and its creators' motives. The Puerto Rican characters, he charged, "are only defined in their criminal potentiality, as carrying weapons that the Jets will have to face." The plot "establishes the impossibility of an interracial marriage. Romantic melodrama is a strategy of power to hide and soften the racist discourse." Most of the Anglo-Americans are "blond, strong, dynamic and healthy," while the Puerto Ricans are "black haired, dark skinned and skinny," which "installs the spectator within readymade, stereotypical models of race and socio-cultural behavior."

Though one of the most vociferous Latino critics of *West Side Story,* Sandoval-Sanchez is far from alone in faulting its portrayal of Puerto Ricans. Hunter College and New York University professor of Puerto Rican studies Juan Flores told the *New York Sun* that the musical had damaged the image of Puerto Ricans. It cast them "in a stereotyped role of gangs and youth violence which often hounds oppressed groups in society." He also pointed out, as have others, that the heart of the New York Puerto Rican community in the 1950s was the Upper East Side, not the West Side. And he underscored that residents of Puerto Rico are full-fledged American citizens who vote in federal elections and are protected under the U.S. Constitution. (A point actually made also by Sondheim, in the line "Nobody knows / Puerto Rico's in America," in "America.")

In her probing essay "Feeling Pretty: 'West Side Story' and Puerto Rican Identity Discourses," writer-filmmaker Frances Negrón-Muntaner, a faculty member of the Center for the Study of Ethnicity and Race at Columbia University, termed the musical "nothing short of a Puerto Rican 'Birth of a Nation': a blatant, seminal . . . valorized, aestheticized eruption into American consciousness."

She identified other problems *West Side Story* poses for its Puerto Rican critics: (1) the racial assumptions in the dark makeup lathered on the Sharks in the film. (Puerto Ricans have a range of complexions, from very light, to black for those of African ancestry); (2) the casting of non-Latinos as Sharks; (3) the Madonna/whore dichotomy between the virginal Maria and sexpot Anita, which plays into what writer Judith Ortiz Cofer has described as a "one dimensional view" of Latina women as "Hot Tamales" and sexy firebrands. (Cofer recalled as a girl "hearing about the harassment that Puerto Rican women endured in factories where the 'boss men' talked to them as if sexual innuendo was all they understood and, worse, often gave the choice of submitting to advances or being fired.")

Negrón-Muntaner also found objectionable the switching of ethnic groups in the story from "white" Jews and Catholics to Anglos and Puerto Ricans—a move she charges was mere opportunism, exacerbated by the artists' ignorance of the Latino culture they were appropriating. But she does concede that *West Side Story* was useful, in that it offered "U.S. Puerto Ricans a world stage on which to negotiate their ethno-national identity."

Arthur Laurents was sensitive to the charges that the film, with which he had little to do, was especially guilty of negatively stereotyping the Puerto Rican figures. And he wanted to alter this perception in his 2009 revival production on Broadway. "I thought it would be terrific if we could equalize the two gangs somehow," Laurents told the *New York Times*. In an attempt to prevent cultural inaccuracies, he hired only Latino actors to play the Sharks (and thanks to a more inclusive entertainment industry, the Latino talent pool had substantially widened). And converting a significant amount of the text and lyrics into Spanish (as adapted from the English version by Miranda) was another strategy to put the two ethnic groups, and two gangs, in better balance.

Though critical opinion was mixed on the language changes, and some of the Spanish lines were eventually turned back into English to make them more accessible to a predominately white audience, Laurents's gestures did not go unappreciated, including by those he was working with on the revival. In the *Washington Post,* the show's Anita, Karen Olivo (who is part Puerto Rican) commented, "There are Spanish-speaking people who will come to this show and they won't be on the outside any longer; they'll finally have the inside track."

But sometimes, critics of the show have endorsed the sticky contention that simply by portraying negative behavior and attitudes, a dramatic work is promoting and endorsing them. And *West Side Story,* like *Romeo and Juliet,* does not traffic in detailed realism but in heightened romanticism, which often paints characters in wide strokes.

In a 2008 story in the Hispanic-oriented magazine *AARP Viva,* by Elizabeth Llorente, National Institute for Latino Policy president Angelo Falcon admitted he welcomed the movie of *West Side Story* when it came out, but "after the civil rights movement and the Puerto Rican empowerment movement . . . we viewed it in retrospect and thought, 'Oh my God, it makes us look like we're all in a gang.'"

Conversely, Reuben Torres, a West Side New York native of Colombian ancestry, commented that the musical got the situation he grew up in during the 1950s right. "It showed the truth—there was gangs, there was danger. I remember that in my school, a lot of kids were proud, actually, that they made a movie about the West Side, about their area"—even if it wasn't an entirely flattering portrait.

The debate on the merits and demerits of the show resurfaces in the public sphere periodically. In 1999, in the mostly Anglo, largely academic community of Amherst, Massachusetts, teenager Camille Sola launched a successful petition drive to stop a planned production of *West Side Story* at her high school, on the grounds the show was racially insensitive. The school's principal agreed that the show be "postponed" as a way of honoring those concerns and said his action was not "censorship, but sensitivity." Semantics aside, the situation sparked a spirited debate in the school and the wider community over whether dropping the musical was the correct way to show sensitivity. In the end, the high school did not present *West Side Story.*

But two years later, when Boston's Tufts University was set to present their own student version of the show, Tufts Latino Center director Ruben Salinas Stern was critical of *West Side Story* but thought it should be staged and seen.

"Despite its many redeeming qualities, the film . . . reinforces the image of Puerto Ricans as violent gang members, criminals and welfare recipients," he wrote in the *Tufts Daily.* "It also promotes the image of Puerto Rican women as subservient to the men. Do I advocate cancelling the play at Tufts? Absolutely not! In fact, I want every Tufts student to see it, think about it and discuss it."

THE WORLD IS MORE THAN AN ADDRESS

Though the specific milieu and locale of *West Side Story* are important, the show's larger themes have long resonated in other cultures, fractured by other social rifts. What society does not experience some measure of cross-ethnic enmity and violence? And stark divisions between groups, be they ethnic, racial, religious, cultural, economic? And if romances between young people from different backgrounds are fine and dandy in some enlightened places, taboos on such matches still exist in just as many locales.

The *Romeo and Juliet/West Side Story* myth continues to be relevant, provocative, and theatrically viable. And if a piece of musical entertainment isn't about to resolve inequities, it can perhaps invest them with more passion and immediacy than most documentary films or research studies do—particularly for young people.

West Side Story has frequently been presented in communities and countries scarred by deep internal divisions—including Bosnia, Ireland, Israel, Korea, and South Africa. And it has inspired such adaptations as *West Bank Story,* an Oscar-honored musical short film about a cross-cultural romance in Israel, which is both an uproarious comedy and a sincere attempt to imagine an alternative to the bloody, ongoing polarization of Jews and Arabs in the region.

Back in the United States, in a 1998 article in the Lexington, Kentucky, *Herald-Leader,* Lexington Shakespeare Festival artistic director Trish Clark told Dag Ryen that the show's theme of young people destroyed by mutual intolerance often had a powerful effect on adolescents in the audience. "We all absorb attitudes about inter-ethnic dating," Clark said. "You just don't fall in love with somebody not of your own race . . . [Kids] do label, they do judge, they do tend to become cliquish."

An unusually personal and candid response to the way bigotry is dramatized in *West Side Story* appeared in iMagazine, an online literary journal produced by the Baruch College/CUNY Writing Center. Siddiq Mohamed, a Muslim American student, wrote an essay about seeing the movie for the first time and finding that it provoked in him "many conflicting emotions; it was not only a compelling work of art, but a production that left me with many more questions than answers."

Mohamed noted that the movie brought to his mind some "unexpected and long forgotten memories from my elementary and middle school" years in Howard Beach, Queens, a historically Italian American community at the time. Because of his Guyanese background, Mohamed was the "victim of many minor racial incidents." The gym dance scene in particular reminded him of "the underlying tension" between ethnic groups that was "always present at my school, but rarely spoken about in the presence of adults."

The song "America" paralleled Mohamed's "own fears and conflictions [*sic*] about the role of immigrants in the United States." He believed Puerto Ricans were caricatured in the number and in other scenes but was "left conflicted" over whether to "adore this movie" or despise its "use of stereotypes."

"Regardless, with all its innovations and drawbacks, 'West Side Story' still deserved to be revisited; for its account of a modern day tragedy was still posed as a timeless work of art," he concluded.

The "timelessness" of *West Side Story* is both a great virtue of the musical and a sad commentary on how many Americans are still subjected to and divided by bigotry. It is an indication of how far the nation still has to go, in making the United States a "somewhere" that honors the differences of its increasingly diverse citizenry—especially its young.

BIGOTRY ON BROADWAY

West Side Story was certainly not the first Broadway musical to depict and comment on racial or ethnic prejudice and divisions. In fact, popular musicals began reflecting such social ills well before movies and TV dramas did.

It is no accident that the artists who first avidly tackled racial/ethnic concerns are some of the finest and most esteemed composers and writers to grace Broadway. And that most of them were from ethnic minority groups—Jews like Richard Rodgers, Kurt Weill, and George and Ira Gershwin, and such African Americans as Langston Hughes—whose own people had been on the receiving end of bigotry and xenophobia.

Here are some of the landmark Broadway musicals to meaningfully address these concerns before *West Side Story:*

Show Boat (1927). This Florenz Ziegfeld–produced show is often cited as Broadway's first true "book musical." An affectionate homage to the popular American entertainment genres that preceded it (minstrelsy, vaudeville, variety, operettas), the Oscar Hammerstein II–Jerome Kern work was far ahead of the curve in integrating music, dance, drama, and comedy within a comic/romantic plot—in this case, a panoramic American tale (based on an Edna Ferber novel) about several generations of performers working on a Mississippi River show boat.

It also introduced a still-topical subplot about the racial travails of Julie, a light-skinned black woman married to a Caucasian man at a time when interracial unions were generally reviled and, in many states, illegal. (Between 1918 and 1943, thirty out of forty-eight states had antimiscegenation laws on the books and enforced them.)

In this representation of the "tragic Mulatto" archetype (also explored in such later movies as *Imitation of Life* and *Pinky*), Julie endures persecution and great unhappiness because of her true racial heritage. And she loses her husband and her job on the riverboat when she tries but fails to pass for white.

The musical also handily, permanently dashed the false image of the "happy darky" slave in American musical theater, thanks to "Ol' Man River"—a haunting lament by dock black workers, who "sweat and strain" as they lift barges and tote bails while "de white folks play," and an indifferent, American river Jordan that "just keeps rolling along."

As Thousands Cheer (1933). This Broadway revue, typical for the era in its varied menu of songs and sketches, satirical and serious, is not formally adventurous. Written by Moss Hart, with a score by Irving Berlin, the show was bold nonetheless in introducing "Supper Time," a searing ballad about a lynching (an execution by hanging, without trial, usually racially motivated). It was a timely number, as southern lynchings of African Americans were drawing more attention in the North in the 1930s, sparking (unsuccessful) attempts to pass federal antilynching laws.

If the lyrics do not refer directly to the gruesome practice, the emotionally wrenching context of the song implies as much. It is sung by a poor black mother (movingly played by the superb Ethel Waters), whose husband has just been murdered. She must soon serve supper to her children and sings out her maternal anguish: "How can I remind them to pray at their humble board? / How can I be thankful when they start to thank the Lord?"

Porgy and Bess (1935). Though not primarily focused on racial relations, the Gershwin classic was an early, serious attempt to dramatize an impoverished black community in the Deep South in an opera-theater format. The fable of the crippled Porgy, his fallen-woman paramour Bess, and other residents of the Charleston, South Carolina, enclave of Catfish Row was based on the characters in white South Carolina native DuBose Heyward's hit play *Porgy*.

Heyward's libretto is in some respects hackneyed and cliché-driven. What was new and radical for the time, apart from composer George Gershwin's incorporation of authentic African American musical idioms, along with Western classical music, was the elevation of the indigenous subject matter as valid material for grand opera. (It also provided a showcase for gifted black opera singers, who found few opportunities in major opera companies.)

Explained Gershwin, in a 1935 *New York Times* essay, "I have adapted my method to utilize the drama, the humor, the superstition, the religious fervor, the dancing and the irrepressible high spirits of the [African American] race. If doing this, I have created a new form, which combines opera with theater, this new form has come quite naturally out of the material."

In its debut this vanguard work was caught in the crossfire between music critics arguing about whether it was a bona fide opera, and white segregationists who wouldn't allow the show (or the movie later based on it) to be seen in the South. Some African American critics chimed in to complain that the portrayals of blacks were insulting and branded Porgy an "Uncle Tom." But *Porgy and Bess* and its splendid score have endured, and in 2010 it was announced that a new adaptation for Broadway was in the works. In praising its resilience, musical scholar James Stander suggested that along with "the ironies and contradictions and even the stereotypes, 'Porgy' carries with it universal themes of community and belonging."

Finian's Rainbow (1947). Though not a sober-minded or hard-hitting indictment of prejudice, in its own goofy and whimsical fashion the Yip Harburg–Burton Lane–Fred Saidy musical furthered the cause of unmasking racial hypocrisy. Not only was it a racially well-integrated show, with prominent roles for black cast members as well as whites, it also skewered the character of a bigoted, greedy southern white U.S. senator by having a leprechaun's daughter magically transform him into a black sharecropper—and make him endure what as a white man he'd been dishing out.

The show incited some controversy at the time for such satirical gambits. In ensuing years it, too, was accused of racial stereotyping, but a 2009 Broadway revival restored the musical's reputation as a frisky and slyly subversive romp.

Lost in the Stars (1949). Based on Alan Paton's famed novel *Cry, the Beloved Country,* composer Kurt Weill's final Broadway musical was, as critic Edward Seckerson put it in a review of a London revival, a "deeply compassionate drama of division and reconciliation in apartheid South Africa." It contained some glorious music by Weill and a story, adapted by playwright Maxwell Anderson, with some obvious parallels between South African racism and the American strain.

A portrait of the tragic toll poverty and discrimination can exact—on two African fathers, one black and the other white, united in the loss of their sons—the show was faulted by critics of the premiere for its talky, ill-shapen book and the incongruity of its operatic elements. Though still challenging to produce, it has since been rediscovered and revived in well-received, high-profile opera productions.

Jerome Robbins practices the "Cool" number with members of the London cast of *West Side Story*, including George Chakiris as Riff. Courtesy of The New York Public Library for the Performing Arts, ©Billy Rose Theatre Division.

13

GOLD-MEDAL KID WITH THE HEAVYWEIGHT CROWN
THE RISE OF THE DANCER-CHOREOGRAPHER

Jerome Robbins's multipronged achievement in *West Side Story* was not his triumph alone. It was shaped in part by his artistic mentors, and shared by the choreographer-directors to follow him in an ongoing Broadway continuum of craft, artistry, and invention.

Robbins led by example in making credible and bankable a new kind of Broadway auteur—a showmaker with substantial theatrical skills, who was also grounded in movement and physicality. This auteur role evolved over time and in stages, and with great assistance from Robbins's forbears and teachers, including George Balanchine, George Abbott, and Agnes de Mille.

And ever since Robbins obliterated the conventional musical-theater job divisions in *West Side Story,* many other first-rate, double-threat talents followed in his footsteps to choreograph and stage groundbreaking musicals. Based on the Robbins example, producers have invested their faith and small fortunes in such projects, and today the director-choreographer model Robbins championed is firmly established and dominant on the Great White Way.

A thread runs from *West Side Story* through such later auteur musicals as *Chicago* and *A Chorus Line* and *The Producers* and *Fela!* After Robbins, producers believed that hit musical-theater productions could be molded from scratch by a multitalented dynamo responsible for the original premise, the theatrical style, and both the dramatic and musical staging of the work.

These roles are compatible, declared Graciela Daniele, one of the inheritors of the Robbins tradition, in Lawrence Thelen's *The Show Makers:* She emphasized, "I am a director-choreographer. I can't ever forget the choreographic. Even when I do a straight play. I don't mean that by dancing—doing steps—but the idea of the structure of something, of working with music, or dealing even with the text as music, and thinking in those terms."

Susan Stroman, one of Robbins's most successful artistic offspring, believes there's a natural synthesis of her dance and theater sides. She told *Dance Magazine*'s Sylviane Gold, "As a theater choreographer, you are choreographing for characters. You are a storyteller, servicing and supporting the lyrics and the plot. You are immersed in the scene work, because it should never look like the show stops or starts when a scene begins or a song begins."

And Jerry Mitchell, a former dancer and protégé of both Bennett and Robbins who has grown into the auteur role, recalled that "Robbins told me to never waste a second. Audiences today don't like to sit still very long—you need to keep the story moving . . . Choreographers know about transitions. We know how to keep a story in motion."

Virtually all thoroughbred choreographer-directors start out as dancers. And like Robbins, they bring the physical rigor, focus, and discipline of the ballet barre with them into the Times Square rehearsal room. A focus on movement and music as primary storytelling tools has also pushed the prototypical "book musical" into more open formats, allowing for increasingly fluid theatricality in Oscar Hammerstein's vision for musicals of "continuous action."

TU-TU FANTASIES AND KICKLINE CHORUSES

How did choreographers evolve from hired-hand dance fabricators to theatrical masterminds? It took time. In the late nineteenth century, and a good chunk of the twentieth, dance on Broadway was a matter of corps de ballet or lines of chorus girls coyly revealing as much female flesh as the times allowed, twirling or kicking or time-step tapping in unison.

Elaborate fairytale nineteenth-century spectacles aped the operatic tradition, with classically trained ballerinas (including, briefly, a very young Isadora Duncan) in toe shoes and tutus, pirouetting like jewelry-box princesses. In variety halls and vaudeville houses of the Gay Nineties and on, dancers in line formation gradually flashed more leg, and their steps began to reflect the popular social and cabaret dances of the time, from the can-can to the Charleston.

Early Broadway also drew heavily on African American dances appropriated from minstrel shows, like the cakewalk, tap-dancing, and the buck-and-wing—often performed by white and "colored" performers made to "black up."

In the Teens and Twenties, the tide turned to opulent Broadway revues such as the *Ziegfeld Follies,* with faux-dance numbers in which throngs of comely chorines paraded in fancy gowns and headdresses. And through the 1930s, musical comedies by the likes of the Gershwins and Cole Porter typically began and ended with interchangeable, peppy choruses of dancers and tap novelties.

In the 1940s, the growing narrative sophistication of such Rodgers–Hammerstein shows as *Oklahoma!* and *Carousel* gave forward-thinking choreographers the chance to do more. At last, they could tell stories and convey character through movement, making dance part of the story and not merely an accessory to it.

Given the tightly-knit "family" web of musical Broadway, and the master–apprentice relationship that persists in every facet of dance theater, it is not surprising that the baton has been passed from artist to artist in this field.

ROBBINS'S FORERUNNERS

Agnes de Mille was a pioneer choreographer in this regard, and her work in the early Rodgers and Hammerstein hits *Oklahoma!* and *Carousel* was a revelation. For these Broadway shows, she created extended fantasy/dream ballet sequences in which young female characters acted out in movement their repressed romantic fears and desires.

Ballet-trained herself, de Mille, like Robbins, was interested in using serious dancing in popular arenas to explore American themes—starting with her successful piece for the Ballet Russe de Monte Carlo, the Old West–flavored *Rodeo*, with music by Aaron Copland.

Robbins worked with her in a comic piece she choreographed in 1941 for Ballet Theatre (later called American Ballet Theatre), *Three Virgins and a Devil,* which de Mille also performed in. Later she cheered on his own aspirations as choreographer. The night his ballet *Fancy Free* premiered, de Mille recalled rushing backstage to compliment Robbins. "I told him he was safe and need never be frightened again, because with such humor and tenderness, with such a grasp of form, he could do whatever he intended to."

De Mille realized her own ambition to become a Broadway director-choreographer just once, by staging the Rodgers and Hammerstein show *Allegro*—an offbeat fable that was one of the team's least commercially successful efforts. Hammerstein hoped to redo the piece later, but the opportunity never arose.

George Balanchine was another pathfinder who mentored Robbins. The lionized Russian-born choreographer, widely admired for distilling the formalism of European ballet into modern American dance, also bridged the gap between Broadway and the ballet world.

In addition to leading his own esteemed company, New York City Ballet, Balanchine eschewed "highbrow" snobbery by crafting dance numbers for Hollywood movies and Broadway book musicals, revues, and operettas, including Irving Berlin's *Louisiana Purchase* and Rodgers and Hart's *The Boys from Syracuse* and *On Your Toes* (which boasted Balanchine's most famous theatrical ballet, *Slaughter on 10th Avenue,* recreated in the film *Words and Music*).

Jack Cole was often tagged as the first theatrical jazz-dance choreographer, Cole made his biggest splash on film, by creating the sultry moves for Marilyn Monroe in *Gentlemen Prefer Blondes* and Rita Hayworth in *Gilda.* A stage dancer who started out with the esteemed modern dance troupe the Denishawn Dance Company (run by Ruth St. Denis and Ted Shawn), he began choreographing on Broadway in the 1940s, distinguishing himself with a terrific array of showstopper dances for *Kiss Me, Kate,* elaborate quasi-Asian numbers for *Kismet,* and the comedic choreography for *A Funny Thing Happened on the Way to the Forum.*

Cole was reported to be as much of a martinet in the rehearsal hall as Robbins. But the sophisticated, stylish routines he developed to jazz rhythms and cadences, and the emotional expressiveness he demanded, inspired not just Robbins but also Bob Fosse and other top theater choreographers and, among other star performers, Gwen Verdon. Though he directed some shows, Cole was ready to roll before the role was ready for him. As critic-biographer Glenn Loney observed in *Dance Magazine,* he "seldom had major artistic control; instead, he tailored his contribution to the demands of others."

ROBBINS'S CONTEMPORARIES

Michael Kidd made his first huge splash by starring in Eugene Loring's celebrated *Billy the Kid* ballet, to Aaron Copland's music. He went on to choreograph athletic, high-energy numbers for such top Broadway attractions as *Finian's Rainbow,* but Kidd, too, thought like a director and blossomed when given the chance to handle the complete staging of the memorable music and dance numbers in *Guys and Dolls* and *Can-Can,* for which he won choreography Tony Awards. He went on to direct and devise dances for many more shows—including *Li'l Abner,* a hit on Broadway when *West Side Story* appeared, and his film choreography can be seen in the classic Fred Astaire flick *The Band Wagon* and the boisterous *Seven Brides for Seven Brothers* (co-starring Russ Tamblyn). With a philosophy similar to Robbins's, Kidd stated that he wanted dance to express "human behavior and people's manners, stylized into musical rhythmic forms . . . I always use real-life gestures, and most of my dancing is based on real life."

Bob Fosse was a standout jazz show dancer, molded by Jack Cole into a featured performer in *Kiss Me, Kate,* when Robbins urged that he be hired to help him choreograph *The Pajama Game* (which Robbins was also directing). At one point producer George Abbott wanted to cut Fosse's "Steam Heat" number. Robbins objected, and the slinky, impish dance became a Fosse signature piece. As Fosse's own star rose with his choreography and direction for *Cabaret* (directed by Harold Prince on Broadway, Fosse on film), *Chicago, Sweet Charity,* and other triumphant shows, Robbins and Fosse maintained their collegial mutual respect. For decades, the two shared a good luck charm: a pair of gold cufflinks they passed back and forth to each other on the opening nights of their shows.

Gower Champion began as a dancer, but not in ballet or on Broadway. He came up through nightclubs and films (including *Show Boat*), executing elegant ballroom-style duets with his partner and wife Marge Champion, waltzing along on the tail end of the Fred-and-Ginger craze.

Champion broke into theatrical choreography, and his first Broadway choreography gig, *Lend an Ear,* brought him a Tony Award. As movie musicals and TV variety shows dwindled, Champion gravitated back to Broadway in the 1960s, to choreograph and direct such hits as *Bye Bye Birdie, Hello, Dolly!,* and his boffo finale, *42nd Street.* Unlike Robbins's oeuvre, Champion's theatrical work often had a retro bent, drawing on past showbiz dance styles, and his specialty was lighthearted romantic fare. But it took a strong guiding hand to make those shows glide so smoothly between story, song, and dance. Even in the biggest razzle-dazzle numbers, Champion made it all look effortless.

SOME ROBBINS HEIRS

Michael Bennett got his first break as a teenage dancer in a Robbins-directed European production of *West Side Story,* and so the next-wave genius learned at the feet of a master. According to Bennett biographer Kevin Kelly, "What Michael Bennett perceived early in Robbins' work was totality, all the sums of a given piece adding to a unified whole."

Bennett was a fearless maverick, too, and if he cut his teeth as a Broadway choreographer doing strong work in fairly conventional shows (*A Joyful Noise, Promises, Promises*), he came into his own in fresher musicals—first as the co-director and choreographer of the Stephen Sondheim–James Goldman show *Follies,* with its cinematic blurring of the present and pasts of a group of former showgirls; and later as the instigator of the highly original, smashingly successful *A Chorus Line,* which pushed Robbins's Method acting-directing techniques further in a new kind of musical based on the experiences of actual "gypsy" show dancers.

Bennett caused another splash with his glitzy, also innovative soul-music tuner *Dreamgirls.* His death at forty-four from AIDS robbed Broadway of more dazzling work from one of its brightest musical-theater stars of the 1970s and 1980s.

Tommy Tune was several years older than his mentor Bennett, but a later bloomer as a director. As choreographer, Bennett hired the imposing 6'6" Texan to dance in *A Joyful Noise* and showcased Tune's talents in featured dance spots in the musical *Seesaw* (based on the romantic drama *Two for the Seesaw*), for which both men won Tony Awards.

While Robbins and Bennett strove to merge dancing with narrative and characterization, Tune as a director-choreographer took the Gower Champion tack of revisiting chorus lines, tapping sprees, and dapper Fred Astaire and Ginger Rogers coupling in shows like *My One and Only,* but with his own brand of witty panache. He also put his own spin on the Western Americana that so entranced de Mille and Kidd, in the revue-style *The Will Rogers Follies* and lusty brothel bash *The Best Little Whorehouse in Texas.* Tune had a long string of hits in the 1980s and early 1990s and was the personal recipient of nine Tony Awards.

Susan Stroman fell in love with dance musicals when she saw Tommy Tune in a touring production of *Seesaw.* She became a "gypsy" dancer in Fosse's *Chicago* and other shows, and then an in-demand choreographer acclaimed for the captivating eclecticism of her work in topline revivals of *Oklahoma!*, *Show Boat,* and *The Music Man* (which she also directed), along the way winning her first Tony Award for her effervescent dances in a new Gershwin-scored musical *Crazy for You,* directed by her husband Mike Ockrent.

After Ockrent's untimely death, she funneled her growing artistic authority and well-honed savvy with both novelty and narrative numbers into directing as well as choreographing new shows, including the critically hailed *Contact,* an anthology of three appealing story dances; and two Mel Brooks musicals, the smash hit *The Producers* and the less successful *Young Frankenstein.* In 2010, she brought to Broadway an unlikely but well-received musical based on a famous case of racial injustice, *The Scottsboro Boys.* Stroman has won multiple Tonys and became the first woman honored with Tonys for directing and choreographing the same production (*The Producers*).

Twyla Tharp has a similar background to Robbins, in the sense that her roots are deeply planted in modern dance and ballet. And among her Broadway peers, Tharp is a latecomer to the director-choreographer role. Also like Robbins, her friend and onetime collaborator (on the ballet *Brahms/Handel,*) she developed a style integrating common gesture and natural movement with the vigorous precision of classical dance. Tharp was at the forefront of the so-called postmodern dance revolution of the 1970s and 1980s.

Tharp's love of popular music and culture from her own youth led her to choreograph the movie version of the rock tuner *Hair*; a dance homage to the Beach Boys, *Little Deuce Coupe*; and later to her first Broadway auteur gig, crafting a stage version of *Singin' in the Rain*. Nearly two decades later, she returned to choreograph and stage the more successful *Movin' Out!*, a bookless musical with a coming-of-age antiwar story communicated through virtuosic dances and the songs of pop songsmith Billy Joel.

That dance "jukebox" format was employed again in Tharp's *The Times They Are A-Changin'*, a box-office bomb set to Bob Dylan's music. In 2010, Tharp expanded her successful American Ballet Theatre suite *Nine Sinatra Songs*, into a well-received Broadway tribute to Frank Sinatra's music, *Come Fly Away*.

THE CHOREOGRAPHER-DIRECTOR BROADWAY REIGN: ALIVE AND KICKING? THE NEXT PHASE?

Fifty years after Robbins paved the way with *West Side Story*, the ranks of choreographer-directors commandeering musicals on Broadway have steadily expanded. In addition to Stroman and Tharp, those ranks include Patricia Birch, Graciela Daniele, Kathleen Marshall, Jerry Mitchell (a protégé of Robbins and Bennett, who says, "I owe everything in my work to Michael and Jerry"); Rob Ashford, Walter Bobbie, and Bill T. Jones.

For a time, in the 1980s and 1990s, it looked like their services would no longer be the most required or preferred for Broadway musicals. At the time, the imported "pop operas" of Andrew Lloyd Webber and others ruled, mesmerizing audiences with dazzling spectacle and wall-to-wall music but very little in the way of dance. It was almost as if Broadway had turned the clock back to the era of semimythic operettas and fairytale tableau-extravaganzas—but with a pop-rock beat.

What brought back the choreographers to run the show? Primarily the next crazes after the pop opera fervor cooled: revivals of great American musicals with generous amounts of dance (i.e., *The Music Man, Chicago*), and nostalgic "jukebox" or retro-themed musicals that referenced and reworked social-dance crazes of the past.

But as costs for Broadway tuners grow ever more daunting, and the tourist-heavy audiences become increasingly risk-averse (many prone to return visits to long-running megahits like *The Phantom of the Opera* and *Wicked*), it's a risky time for the damn-the-torpedoes daring that characterized Robbins's work on *West Side Story.*

West Side Story returned to Broadway in 2009 as a show likely to draw in audiences and reward investors. But as Sylviane Gold pondered in 2007, who "is working on a Broadway musical with a tragic story, a profound theme, social issues, serious music, and complicated dancing? Where are the producers who would hire 40 performers and 30 musicians to put it on?"

Today, in an entertainment universe of so many different kinds of competing media and so much megacorporate showbiz hype and so many economic imperatives, it could be all that much harder for new genius, big visions, and creative gumption to slip through. Yet somehow, it always does.

The original cast of the Broadway production of Rent. ©Joan Marcus. Courtesy of Photofest.

14

WE GOT TROUBLES OF OUR OWN
BROADWAY'S YOUTH MUSICALS

West Side Story was a show created by and aimed at cosmopolitan adult theater aficionados. But it was also a Broadway musical, one of the first, that was about post–World War II youths and conveyed from their vantage point.

By the mid-1950s, Hollywood had uncovered a highly lucrative new market for movies about teenagers, but Broadway was behind that curve. Film studios could quickly churn out and circulate cheapie teen flicks (and the occasional prestige teen drama like Rebel Without a Cause). But Broadway premieres (especially musicals) took a great deal more time, care, and, in many cases, financial backing to mount. And it was harder for young writers and composers to break in, or for mavericks to boldly reflect the youth culture without significant compromise.

Content was, given the difficulties West Side Story encountered in raising money, a pivotal issue. Broadway began to slowly make room for serious dramas about wayward adolescents (i.e., Blackboard Jungle, Take a Giant Step). And young people in love had always been a constant staple of musical theater. But young lovers conjured by grownup writers and composers tended to be: (1) either childlike teens, or adults in their twenties; (2) in a different historical or cultural context than modern urban America; and/or (3) wholesome "squares" rather than hostile rebels.

Suddenly, in West Side Story, young hooligans were carpet-bombing the stage of the Winter Garden Theatre with their angst, hostility, and ugly feuds, their fiery dancing and rebellious attitudes.

Since then, the Broadway musical stage has periodically been injected with a needed infusion of youth hormones. Each popular show in this vein has redefined the genre somewhat, and since the late 1960s the most popular have usually sung and danced to a rock or pop music beat and focused on misfits and renegades.

Most lauded youth-focused shows have not strayed very far from the mythic template of young love and death charted in *Romeo and Juliet* and several centuries later in *West Side Story*. They include:

Hair (1968), the first hit rock musical, centers on a floating commune of Aquarius Age 1960s hippies who are protesting a war in Vietnam and who, after a lot of irreverent commentary on their America and a joyous (and sometimes disrobed) bacchanal of songs (written by Gerome Ragni and James Rado), and tribal-style dance, lose their collective innocence and one of their own to the war.

Rent (1996), created by Jonathan Larson and based loosely on Puccini's *La Bohème,* is a later rock epic about another band of young rebels. They are artists and musicians, merry but more jaded, living in the late 1980s in romantic semi-squalor on the Lower East Side of New York and losing one of their own to the modern plague of AIDS.

Spring Awakening (2006) is equipped with Duncan Sheik's more eclectic but folk-rock-centered score and travels back in teen-time to provincial nineteenth-century Germany. Based on Frank Wedekind's controversial play of that era, the loose knot of confused and repressed German teens portrayed here lose *more* than *one* of their own—this time to suicide, and a botched, primitive abortion—in a reminder of how lethal the oppression of youthful bodies and spirits can be.

American Idiot (2010) is a raw, in-your-face, and anguished expansion of a chart-topping concept album by the American punk band Green Day. Though none of the alienated suburban teens in this largely danced and sung, visually blaring mosh pit of a show has to perish in the loose storyline, they endure trials by fire through combat service in a war, drug addiction, and aimless passivity in a culture stunted by consumerism and media bombardment.

Though there are stark differences between the gritty gang clashes of Jets and Sharks, and the twenty-first-century existential confusions of *American Idiot*, and among the other rebel-youth musicals in between, there are also similarities in the shows' visceral appeal, riveting theatrics, and expression of the torments of disenchanted youth in an American dream-turned-nightmare. And each show ends with a sliver of silver-lining hope for understanding, acceptance, a better world—enough to "let the sunshine in," as the *Hair* anthem goes.

In their own ways, in their au courant music and dance vocabularies, each of these Broadway works cries out some version of Action's impassioned plea to Doc in *West Side Story*. "When you was my age; when my old man was my age; when my brother was my age!" Action rails. "*You was never my age, none of you!* And the sooner you creeps get hip to that, the sooner you'll dig us."

The opening dance number in *West Bank Story*.

15

SUNS AND MOONS ALL OVER THE PLACE
WEST SIDE STORY IN POPULAR CULTURE

Wether in boom or bust mode, Broadway musical theater has been a part of the pop-cultural conversation since the early twentieth century. And no American musical speaks louder, or is more tightly entwined in the fabric of the Zeitgeist, than *West Side Story.*

Over generations and across the cultures and decades since its debut, *West Side Story* has been subject to countless adaptations, homages, and parodies and a long stream of references—in other Broadway shows, in television programs, in films, in pop music, on the Internet. It has been a continuing object of reverence or (quite often in the twenty-first century) affectionate/barbed satire. And it is now as prone to caricature as it is to canonization.

The main reason for its ubiquity, as a totem or camp target, is that *West Side Story* is packed to the gills with unique and vivid musical and dramatic iconography. A certain dance move, or pose, a line from a song or a few bars of music, even the characters' names (Tony and Maria, Bernardo and Anita), can be shorthand for the entire show. And as an emblem of doomed love, youth violence, and dance-till-you-drop dramaturgy, it is ever-present.

Thanks to the hardiness and ubiquity of the movie, and the stage musical's deep inroads into the high school and college curriculum, allusions to *West Side Story* keep popping up. And as the mass media formats have multiplied, so have allusions to the show.

 Both direct and subliminal references to *West Side Story* (in a line, a song title, a scrap of dialogue, a musical phrase, a posture or gesture) seem to be everywhere you look. And the show's influence on the work of contemporary stage, pop music, film, and TV artists is immeasurable.

A selection of nods to *West Side Story* in American and global popular culture over several decades:

ON FILM

West Bank Story (2006). A zany musical comedy set in Israel, about two competing falafel stands in the West Bank (the Kosher King and the Hummus Hut), and the problematic romance between an Israeli soldier and the daughter of the Palestinian owners of one of the stands. Winner of the 2007 Oscar for best live-action short, it parallels *West Side Story* with a similar plot (but a happier ending), an ingenious original score, big finger-snapping dance numbers, and pointed but hopeful satire of Mideast tensions. (Note: the film was actually the creation of an American Jew, not Mideast Arabs and Jews.)

Anchorman: The Legend of Ron Burgundy (2004). Includes a spoofy rumble between two rival TV news teams, by a highway, to music suggestive of the Bernstein score. (The star of the movie, Will Ferrell, is a big fan of the musical and has also participated in other well-known pop parodies of it.)

The Gendarme in New York (1965). A French movie comedy filmed on location in Manhattan soon after the celluloid *West Side Story* came out, lampoons the Jets-versus-Sharks hostilities, with a rumble on a basketball court pitting middle-aged French cops against New York hoodlums.

The Young Girls of Rochefort (1967). Directed by Jacques Demy and Agnes Varda, this is an elaborate French tribute to classic movie musicals, including *West Side Story*. This third film in a trilogy sports a jazzy score, opens with overhead shots of Paris, has young people playing basketball to music, and features choreography that relishes Robbins-like leaps and turns. The film also prominently features *West Side Story* stage alums George Chakiris and Grover Dale.

Okkadu (2003). A well-received Indian film that opens with two rival groups of intense-looking young men meeting in a dusty town square, snapping their fingers to music, then engaging in a stylized chase scene. Though the plot diverges from *West Side Story* later, this number is a clever takeoff on "The Prologue." (Note: This is a Telugu language film, a product of the "Tollywood" film industry catering to India's Telugu ethnic community.)

Analyze That (2002). Robert DeNiro stars as a mobster who tries to avoid prison by proving he's crazy. The proof? He sometimes bursts into vocal renditions of "I Feel Pretty," "Tonight," and "Maria." DeNiro approached the assignment with his usual Method acting seriousness and worked hard with a singing coach on the numbers.

Anger Management (2003). In this Hollywood comedy, Adam Sandler portrays a man mistakenly sentenced to an anger-management program, and Jack Nicholson plays his obnoxiously aggressive instructor. In one scene, Nicholson forces Sandler to stop his car in traffic and defuse anxiety by singing "I Feel Pretty."

Josh (2000). A Bollywood movie musical from India inspired by *West Side Story,* transfers the essential storyline of warring gangs and forbidden love to the coastal region of Goa, in southwest India.

Bring It On: In It to Win It (2007). The fourth in a series of fizzy "Bring It On" teen comedy flicks, pits the West Coast Sharks high school cheerleading team against the East Coast Jets team, with numerous plot points reminiscent of *West Side Story.*

ON TELEVISION

The 2009 MTV Video Music Awards was promoted with a very slick, extensive filmed homage to the "Tonight Quintet," shot in numerous picturesque urban settings (including the New York subway) and featuring pop stars Cobra Starship, Katy Perry, Ne-Yo, Taylor Swift and comic Russell Brand singing new adaptations of Stephen Sondheim's lyrics set to Bernstein's music.

David Letterman Show. In addition to presenting actual numbers from Broadway revivals of *West Side Story,* the program hosted a memorable comedy bit by Will Farrell, who performed a spoofy, one-man mini-version of the show, culminating in a rendition of a humorously reworded "Maria."

Flight of the Conchords, an HBO comedy series, aired a mock "Cool" number, a dance with bystanders on a New York City street joining in.

Sesame Street, the long-running public TV children's program, frequently appropriated *West Side Story* songs for educational comedy skits performed by the Muppets puppet troupe. Examples: "Veg Side Story," "Inside / Outside Story," "There's a Grouchy Place."

Saturday Night Live aired several *West Side Story* takeoffs. In one, Robert Downey Jr., Will Ferrell, and others are gang toughs who keep breaking into song, to the disdain of their cohorts. In another skit, the song "I Feel Pretty" is performed by actress Madeline Kahn, in horror-film mode, in the guise of the Bride of Frankenstein. In a third, Molly Shannon is a klutzy parochial schoolgirl who so longs to play Maria in a student version of *West Side Story,* she destroys the show with her antics as prop mistress.

In Living Color, a multiracial 1980s skit comedy program, aired a sketch about racial tension in Crown Heights, Brooklyn, with a mock commercial for "Crown Side Story."

House of Buggin', another sketch series, presented a pan-Latino *West Side Story* lampoon sans racial tension, featuring actor John Leguizamo as the benign head of a Sharks-like gang, rumbling with a rival crew led by fellow Latino spoofer Luis Guzman.

Scrubs, a medical comedy-drama series, broadcast an elaborately choreographed homage to the musical with singing doctors and surgeons as rival gangs holding a danced rumble in hospital hallways.

Ugly Betty, a comedic series about an unglamorous young Latina New Yorker who works in the fashion industry, presented a season finale with direct allusions to *West Side Story,* in which the songs "Something's Coming" and "Somewhere" are woven into the storyline.

The Daily Show, a news-parody broadcast starring Jon Stewart, spoofed the 2010 British Petroleum disaster in the Gulf of Mexico with a bit about a "West Side Story Oil Spill Parody Songbook," with a brief rendition of "I Feel Gritty" to the tune of "I Feel Pretty."

Hamish Macbeth, a BBC TV program made in Scotland and starring Robert Carlyle, aired an episode about the lead character taking part in an amateur production of *West Side Story.*

Animaniacs, the Steven Spielberg–produced animated series of the 1990s, parodied the musical in "West Side Pigeons," a song-studded episode about two rival groups of birds and a cross-species feathered romance that begins at a "dance."

ON THE INTERNET

The advent of the Internet has brought a flood of related online postings—clips from the *West Side Story* movie, renditions of the songs by singers famous and obscure, a smorgasbord of scenes from amateur, professional, and student productions of the musical, related TV bits, and homemade-for-the-Web amateur video lampoons.

Since sites like YouTube exist as open forums, where anyone with a video camera (or a cell phone) can shoot and post nearly anything, the many "original" video riffs on *West Side Story* range from the creative and entertaining, to the ludicrous and gross. They bear such titles as "West Upper Side Story," "West Chula Story," "Weird Side Story," "Harbor Side Story," "Midwest Side Story"—many of them the work of adolescent fans with, it appears, a lot of spare time on their hands.

There are also dozens of *West Side Story* "mashups" on YouTube and similar sites, which are pastiches of related and unrelated video clips (including some with zombie and werewolf themes) set to excerpts of the movie score. And there are collages of visual clips from the movie set to contemporary pop songs.

Web Site Story is a humorous, five-minute, online conflation of the show set to Bernstein's melodies. It lampoons youth obsession with the Internet as much as it pokes fun at *West Side Story.* Here Tony is a computer nerd who sings, "When you're on the net on the net you will stay / 'Cause the whole Google Earth is just one click away." Maria meets him on the social networking tool Twitter, and there's a rooftop number based on "America" refashioned as eHarmony (a popular Web dating service). And the "Tonight" duet on the fire escape becomes "Evite" (named for the online invitation service) with Tony and Maria crooning to each other, "Now I can't wait / To read about me later on your blog." Produced by the Web-based troupe College Humor, the video went viral quickly on YouTube and by 2010 had been "clicked" nearly a million times.

MISCELLANEOUS

"West Side Story" Ads for the Gap. The hip clothing manufacturer hired original *West Side Story* performer Alan Johnson to adapt Jerome Robbins's choreography and staging for a trio of television ads promoting its line of khaki pants. The best-known commercial, which aired during the Tony Awards broadcast in 2000, was a truncated but fairly faithful version of the "Cool" number—albeit with the dancers in pastel and white Gap pants and T-shirts. The other ads paid tribute to "America" and the "Mambo" section of "The Dance at the Gym."

Vanity Fair created a lavish magazine homage to *West Side Story,* with photos by Mark Seliger, which had singer Jennifer Lopez and a group of up-and-coming young Hollywood actors recreating in detail famous images from the film.

Skating to "West Side Story." Figure skating is essentially dancing on ice, and Bernstein's score is filled with superior and beloved dance music. Medleys from the score and individual tunes have often been used for their routines by high-level competitive and professional skaters, including Olympic champs Ilia Kulik, Sasha Cohen, Katarina Witt, and the teams of Duchesnay and Duchesnay, and Belbin and Agosto.

Flash Mob West Side Story videos. Flash mob performances occur in public, with advance notice given mainly through Twitter and other social media. Examples include the Cork, Ireland, cast of *West Side Story* performing dance numbers from the show in a shopping district, and the Dutch Radio Orchestra performing the Mambo movement of "Dance at the Gym" in a train station in The Hague. (Both were posted on YouTube in 2010.)

WEST SIDE STORY ON TV WITH BROADWAY CASTS (COMPILED BY THE SONDHEIM REVIEW)

Look Up and Live. On this religious talk show, Robbins chatted about juvenile delinquency in relation to *West Side Story,* and there were musical performances by Mickey Calin ("The Jet Song" and "Cool"), Larry Kert ("Something's Coming"), and Carol Lawrence and Kert ("Tonight"). (February 23, 1958).

The Ed Sullivan Show. The Broadway company, with Hank Brunjes as Riff, performed "Cool" (September 14, 1958). Lawrence and Kert performed the balcony scene and "Tonight" (November 2, 1958).

Award Telecasts. Debbie Allen, Anita in the 1980 Broadway revival of the musical, and company performed "America" for the 1980 Tonys ceremony. The cast of *Jerome Robbins' Broadway* performed "The Dance at the Gym" for the 1989 Tonys broadcast. The cast of the Broadway revival appeared in a pastiche of excerpts from *West Side Story* on the 2009 Tony telecast and in a PBS eightieth-birthday concert tribute to Stephen Sondheim.

MICHAEL JACKSON AND *WEST SIDE STORY*

One of the most influential and internationally successful entertainers of the 1980s and 1990s, Michael "The King of Pop" Jackson was very open about his admiration of and fascination with *West Side Story.*

Original Broadway and film cast member David Winters recalled that Jackson told him, when they first met in 2001, that he "knew" Winters, because "I watch you almost every week, you know . . . 'West Side Story,' and he snapped his fingers and did a little step and smiled. I understood."

"It's my favorite film, David, or should I say A-Rab," declared the pop singer, "and I have loads of questions I'd like to ask you about it, if that's all right." According to Winters, every time the two met after that they talked about *'West Side Story'* and "I know secretly he would have loved to have been in it."

That was never to be, but many have spotted similarities of choreography and theatrical sensibility in two hit Jackson music and dance videos, which helped to define that emerging genre.

The first was the elaborately staged "Beat It." To a hard-driving song critiquing macho teen violence, Jackson plays a Tony-like former gang member who goes from slouching around in a diner to breaking up a gang fight with switchblades in a parking garage. (Some of the performers were actually members of LA's notorious Crips and Bloods gangs.)

Despite the parallels in the storyline, the gritty ambience, and the exuberant choreography by Michael Peters (featuring the tight spins, hip thrusts, and high kicks that would become signature moves for Jackson), "Beat It" director Bob Giraldi insisted the video was inspired by his own youth in New Jersey, not by *West Side Story*. But given Jackson's passion for the musical, and the realities of growing up in a rough section of Jersey, it's hard to deny some influence. (Not to mention the echo of the line "Beat it!" which was hurled by Schrank at Bernardo and the Jets.)

The video for the Jackson tune "Bad," on the other hand, was in part a conscious homage to *West Side Story,* according to co-choreographer Jeffrey Daniel. Here Jackson, decked out in black leather and chains, is the unapologetically nasty leader of a gang that's wreaking dance havoc in a subway station.

Toward the end of the number, the dancing gets more frenzied and athletic and clearly quotes the Robbins choreography–leaps and falls out of "Cool," running and leapfrogging à la "The Prologue," and a backflip similar to some of Russ Tamblyn's moves for Riff in the movie.

Jackson avidly studied and borrowed the styles of other works and specific entertainers he admired. And there's little doubt that this Lost Boy identified deeply with *West Side Story* and absorbed some of its genius into his own.

Jerome Robbins and Robert Wise overseeing the filming of a scene in *West Side Story*. Courtesy of Photofest.

APPENDIX

WEST SIDE STORY ORIGINAL BROADWAY PRODUCTION CREDITS

Run Dates:

Winter Garden Theatre, (9/26/1957–2/28/1959)
Broadway Theatre, (3/2/1959–5/10/1959)
Winter Garden Theatre, (5/11/1959–6/27/1959)
 Total Performances: 732

Produced by Robert E. Griffith and Harold S. Prince; produced by
    arrangement with Roger L. Stevens
Book by Arthur Laurents; conceived by Jerome Robbins; music by
    Leonard Bernstein; lyrics by Stephen Sondheim; musical director
    Max Goberman; music orchestrated by Leonard Bernstein; co-
    orchestrators Sid Ramin and Irwin Kostal
Directed by Jerome Robbins; choreographed by Jerome Robbins*; co-
    choreographer Peter Gennaro
Scenic design by Oliver Smith*; costume design by Irene Sharaff; lighting
    design by Jean Rosenthal; sound design by Sound Associates, Inc.

* Received Tony Awards (out of seven nominations)

Opening Night Cast:

Mickey Calin	Riff
Larry Kert	Tony
Carol Lawrence	Maria
Ken Le Roy	Bernardo
Chita Rivera	Anita
Art Smith	Doc
Lee Becker	Anybodys
Grover Dale	Snowboy
Arch Johnson	Schrank
Tony Mordente	A-Rab
Eddie Roll	Action
David Winters	Baby John

Tommy Abbott	Gee-Tar
William Bramley	Krupke
Hank Brunjes	Diesel
Erne Castaldo	Toro
Martin Charnin	Big Deal
Marilyn Cooper	Rosalia
Wilma Curley	Graziella
Carole D'Andrea	Velma
Al De Sio	Luis
Marilyn D'Honau	Clarice
Gene Gavin	Anxious
Frank Green	Mouth Piece
Reri Grist	Consuela
Carmen Gutierrez	Teresita
John Harkins	Glad Hand
Lowell Harris	Tiger
Ronnie Lee	Nibbles
George Marcy	Pepe
Jack Murray	Moose
Jay Norman	Juano
Julie Oser	Pauline
Liane Plane	Marguerita
Nanette Rosen	Minnie
Lynn Ross	Estella
Jamie Sanchez	Chino
Noel Schwartz	Indio
Elizabeth Taylor	Francisca

WEST SIDE STORY FILM CREDITS (ABRIDGED)

Directed by Robert Wise and Jerome Robbins*
Music by Leonard Bernstein and Stephen Sondheim*
Choreography by Jerome Robbins
Screenplay by Ernest Lehman (based on the book of the stage show by
    Arthur Laurents)
Produced by Robert Wise, Saul Chaplin, and Walter Mirisch
Cinematography by Daniel L. Fapp*
Edited by Thomas Stanford*
Production design by Boris Leven, set decoration by Victor A. Gangelin*
Costume design by Irene Sharaff*
Music conducted and supervised by Johnny Green*
Sound design by Fred Hynes and Gordon Sawyer*
* Received Academy Awards (out of 11 nominations)

Cast:

Natalie Wood	Maria
Richard Beymer	Tony
Russ Tamblyn	Riff
Rita Moreno	Anita*
George Chakiris	Bernardo *
Simon Oakland	Schrank
Ned Glass	Doc
William Bramley	Officer Krupke
John Astin	Glad Hand/Social Worker
Tucker Smith	Ice
Tony Mordente	Action
Eliot Feld	Baby John
David Winters	A-Rab
Harvey Hohnecker	Mouthpiece
Tommy Abbott	Gee-Tar
Susan Oakes	Anybodys
Gina Trikonis	Graziella
Carole D'Andrea	Velma
Jose DeVega	Chino

Rita Moreno shakes a leg in the film version of "Dance at the Gym". Courtesy of Photofest.

NOTES

CHAPTER 1

"overwriting, purpleness": Merle Secrest, *Stephen Sondheim,* 117.

"we were influenced by the movies": Deborah Jowitt, *Jerome Robbins: His Life, His Theatre, His Dance,* 280.

"he has sat through it": Alberto Manguel, "How I Learned to See from a Blind Master," *Times of London,* August 15, 2006.

"theatrical truth, theatrical time": *Dramatists Guild Landmark Symposium: West Side Story* (Autumn 1985).

CHAPTER 2

"I didn't like the idea we had to separate ourselves": *Something to Dance About* (documentary film), 2009.

"making a musical that tells a tragic story": Amanda Vaill, *Somewhere: The Life of Jerome Robbins,* 251.

"There was this wonderful, mutual exchange": *Dramatists Guild Landmark Symposium: West Side Story* (Autumn 1985).

"We all had real respect": *Dramatists Guild Landmark Symposium: West Side Story* (Autumn 1985).

"If you want to be polite": *Dramatists Guild Landmark Symposium: West Side Story* (Autumn 1985).

"Jerry's performance experience": Robert Lewis, *Slings & Arrows,* 185.

"seems very passive": Nigel Simeone, *Leonard Bernstein: West Side Story,* 17.

"very good and very harsh": Mel Gussow, "'West Side Story': The Beginnings of Something Great," *New York Times,* October 21, 1990.

"'East Side Story' would settle": Arthur Laurents, *Original Story By,* 330.

"I want to make one thing clear": Vaill, *Somewhere,* 251.

"You'll never write it": Greg Lawrence, *Dance with Demons: The Life of Jerome Robbins,* 232.

"We didn't bury it": Gussow, "'West Side Story': The Beginnings of Something Great."

"the intimidation of Shakespeare": Vaill, *Somewhere,* 256.

"Steve had always regarded himself": Craig Zadan, *Sondheim & Co.,* 12.

"I've never been poor": Zadan, *Sondheim & Co.,* 14.

"We [would work] on the show wherever": *Dramatists Guild Landmark Symposium: West Side Story* (Autumn 1985).

"Without any consciousness of it": *Dramatists Guild Landmark Symposium: West Side Story* (Autumn 1985).

"thin somehow" : Keith Garibean, *The Making of West Side Story,* 42.

"I said, Cheryl": Laurents, *Original Story By,* 328.

"We thought at this point": Jonathan Cott, *Back to a Shadow in the Night,* 193.

"Now I had heard the entire score": Horatia Harrod, "50 Years of West Side Story," *The Telegraph,* July 20, 2008.

"All the kids on Broadway": Harrod, "50 Years of West Side Story."

"people like Lena Horne": Harrod, "50 Years of West Side Story."

"they hate it": Carol Lawrence, "The Real Backstage Story," 2.

"I'd suggest that the House": Vaill, *Somewhere,* 193.

"It'll be years": Vaill, *Somewhere,* 219.

"Maybe I can't": Jowitt, *Jerome Robbins,* 499.

CHAPTER 3

"We could make poetry": *Dramatists Guild Landmark Symposium: West Side Story* (Autumn 1985).

"providing the briefest of lead-ins": Arthur Laurents, *Mainly on Directing,* 145.

"Gang tears wildly": "*West Side Story,* Birth of a Classic," Library of Congress online exhibit.

"You are way off track with Anita": Jowitt, *Jerome Robbins,* 270.

"if you keep each scene down": Jowitt, *Jerome Robbins,* 271.

"Even before I began actually writing": Laurents, *Mainly on Directing,* 145.

"yearnings are strong and shared": Simeone, *Leonard Bernstein*, 41.

"mystic coolness": Roger Faris Thompson, *Flash of the Spirit*, 12.

CHAPTER 4

"Give me a show to do": Lawrence Thelen, *The Show Makers*, 194.

"an awful man": *Something to Dance About.*

"to do our best": *Something to Dance About.*

"He had style": Frank Rich, "Journal—Shall We Dance?," *New York Times*, August 1, 1998.

"making it believable": *Remembering Jerome Robbins*, New York City Ballet tribute videos on www.youtube.com.

"I happened to turn": *Dramatists Guild Landmark Symposium: West Side Story* (Autumn 1985).

"far beyond myself": *Something to Dance About.*

"hardest show to cast": Cott, *Back to a Shadow in the Night*, 193.

"[The] characters had to be able to": Cott, *Back to a Shadow in the Night*, 193.

"generally they lacked the kinetic": "Murray Schumach, Talent Dragnet," *New York Times*, September 22, 1957.

"Lenny leaned over": Zadan, *Sondheim & Co.*, 18.

"was two Jets shy. . . . I got into my tightest, et al.": author interview with Martin Charnin, 2010.

"was one of the most gang-infested": Harrod, *50 Years of West Side Story.*

"a full page": Teri Roberts, "*West Side Story:* We Were All Very Young," *Sondheim Review* 9, no. 3 (Winter 2003).

"we broke a lot of": Harrod, *50 Years of West Side Story.*

"None of us knew": Tom Abbott interview, www.wssonstage.com, 1984.

"People always ask": Roberts, "*West Side Story:* We Were All Very Young."

"Rehearsals were a very painful": Maya Delinsky, "The Dance Master: The Legacy of Jerome Robbins," *Humanities* 25, no. 5 (September/October 2004).

"Jerry not only attacked you": Lawrence, *Dance with Demons*, 252.

"Every dancer in the cast": Melissa Berry, *Review: Jerry Robbins,* www.buzzinefilm.com, June 9, 2009.

"Even when he yelled at me": Lawrence, *Dance with Demons,* 253.

"When you worked with Jerry": Peter Boal, interview with the author, 2010.

"Hit him in the head": Lawrence, *The Back Stage Story,* 44.

"I thought it was pretentious": *Dramatists Guild Landmark Symposium: West Side Story* (Autumn 1985).

"Jerry loved it": Harrod, *50 Years of West Side Story.*

"the other Jets": Lawrence, *Dance with Demons,* 251.

"crazy and wonderful": Jowitt, *Jerome Robbins,* 275.

"We human, civilized": Lawrence, *The Backstage Story,* 43.

"If I had known": Roberts, "West Side Story," *Sondheim Review.*

"belong to me": Jowitt, *Jerome Robbins,* 274.

"stole from Peter Gennaro": Harrod, *50 Years of West Side Story.*

"Jerry got his hands": Lawrence, *Dance with Demons,* 251.

"All Peter's work": Laurents, *Original Story By,* 357.

"polarized between stunning and scabby": Laurents, *Original Story By,* 360.

"muted indigo": Irene Sharaff, *Broadway and Hollywood: Costumes Designed by Irene Sharaff,* 100.

"forty subtly different": Harold Prince, *Contradictions,* 36.

CHAPTER 5

"violently opinionated": Zadan, *Sondheim & Co.,* 23.

"Steve and I worked together": Zadan, *Sondheim & Co.,* 21.

"To tell a compelling story": Sondheim, *Finishing the Hat: Collected Lyrics (1954-1981) with Attendant Comments, Principles, Heresies, Grudges, Whines, and Anecdotes,* 29.

"Lenny's endless complaint": Charles Simeone, *Leonard Bernstein: West Side Story,* 77.

"He never lost his temper": Lawrence, *The Backstage Story,* 46.

"If he'd had time": Humphrey Burton, *Leonard Bernstein,* 270.

"what Lenny did was fairly unheard of": *Zadan, Sondheim & Co.,* 25.

"'West Side Story' means more to me": Burton, *Leonard Bernstein,* 277.

"millions of lyrics to insanely fast music": Burton, *Leonard Bernstein,* 269.

"some strength at the beginning of the show": Simeone, *Leonard Bernstein,* 62.

"a breathless pre-echo of 'Maria'": Simeone, *Leonard Bernstein,* 96.

"have character and flavor": Meryl Secrest, *Stephen Sondheim,* 116.

"came across the room and kissed me": Sondheim, *Finishing the Hat,* 37.

"as the score developed": Sondheim, *Finishing the Hat,* 40.

"language problem": Sondheim, *Finishing the Hat,* 40.

"as with Wagner's 'Tristan und Isolde'": Geoffrey Block, *Enchanted Evenings,* 298.

"fired up . . . by a dance rhythm": Sondheim, *Finishing the Hat,* 41.

"rooted in real character conflict": Sondheim, *Finishing the Hat,* 42.

"gloriously flamboyant big band": Simeone, *Leonard Bernstein,* 102.

"a little too simply": Sondheim, *Finishing the Hat,* 44.

"It's the fulcrum of the show": Jeff Lunden and Scott Simon, National Public Radio (NPR), September 26, 2007.

"Tony would never agree to rumble": Sondheim, *Finishing the Hat,* 47.

"My collaborators would have": Sondheim, *Finishing the Hat,* 48.

"find yourself wanting to say": William Burton, *Conversations About Bernstein,* 180.

"Lenny came up with": Sondheim, *Finishing the Hat,* 50.

"Perhaps that was the most important thing": Sondheim, *Finishing the Hat,* 52.

"I can't tell you how many times": Simeone, *Leonard Bernstein,* 77.

"Maria is alone": Burton, *Conversations About Bernstein,* 171.

CHAPTER 6

"They generally emerge": Edwin Denby, *Dance Writings,* 282.

"Once you work with Jerry Robbins": Rose Eichenbaum, "Grover Dale Re-defining Success," *Dance Magazine* (January 2002).

"The emotions I felt": Joey McKneeley, "My Twenty Year Rumble with 'West Side Story,'" www.broadway.com, February 24, 2009.

"When I do [Robbins's choreography] right": Julie Bloom, "Rekindling Robbins, a Step at a Time," *New York Times,* March 4, 2009.

"They do dances I've never seen": Jowitt, *Jerome Robbins,* 275

"It's an entire history": Michael Kantor and Laurence Mason, *Broadway: The American Musical,* 265.

"By the time you notice": Jowitt, *Jerome Robbins,* 279.

"The boys are too kempt" : Kenneth Tynan, *Curtains,* 281.

"in which groups form": Elizabeth Wells, "*West Side Story* and the Hispanic," in *Echo* 2., no. 1 (Spring 2000).

"the most difficult choreography": Harrod, *50 Years of West Side Story.*

"one of the great musical episodes": Burton, *Conversations About Bernstein,* 108.

"No one else": Laurents, *Original Story By,* 348.

"Here, you feel": Alan Ulrich, "Robbins' Nest," www.voiceofdance.com, March 7, 2008.

"one of the true highlights": "Dancers and the Dance: Remembering the Dream Ballet," www.wssonstage.com.

"This is what the ballet means": "Dancers and the Dance," www.wssonstage.com.

"a new 'Sleeping Beauty'": Vaill, *Somewhere,* 522.

CHAPTER 7

"melodrama than tragedy": Garebian, *The Making of West Side Story,* 80.

"Neither is Romeo": Simeone, *Leonard Bernstein,* 42.

"lovesick for Rosalind": Laurents, *Original Story By,* 348.

"because the play no longer": Laurents, *Original Story By,* 349.

"it's prejudice": Laurents, *Original Story By,* 349.

"we had a death scene": *Dramatists Guild Landmark Symposium: West Side Story* (Autumn 1985).

"sickening sense of shock": Robert Wallace, "Crime in the U.S.,"

Life Magazine (September 9, 1957), 48.

"Just 20 blocks from my office": original 1961 *West Side Story* lobby brochure, reissued with the 2007 DVD, *West Side Story (Special Editions Collector Set).*

"They feel they have to band : " original 1961 *West Side Story* lobby brochure.

"the rumble that": Marilyn Hunt, "Robbins Speaks!," *Dance Magazine* (September 1997).

"in recent months": Thomas Doherty, *Teenagers and Teen Pics,* 31.

"flout indecency" : Jeffrey Goldstein, *Why We Watch,* 120.

"Marlon Brando": Donald Spoto, "The Lost Boy," *Los Angeles Magazine,* April 1996.

CHAPTER 8

"Our investors": Zadan, *Sondheim & Co.,* 29.

 "broke up with somebody": Susan Goodman–Pauline Kael Interview, *Modern Maturity* (April 1998).

"In the movie gangs became": Laurents, *Original Story By,* 332.

"Some of it's wonderful": Jowitt, *Jerome Robbins,* 292.

"was a believable and touching": Jowitt, *Jerome Robbins,* 284.

"the greatest experience": Garebian, *The Making of West Side Story,* 143.

"extremely hot and painful": *West Side Memories* (movie).

"feet were bleeding": Pam Grady, "Hey, Mr. Tamblyn Man," www.filmstew.com, December 8, 2005.

"I remember she was aloof": Richard Knight, *Windy City Times,* November 14, 2007.

"They didn't let Jerry go": Lunden and Simon, NPR, September 26, 2007.

"too dancey": Vaill, *Somewhere,* 329.

"didn't give technical advice": Lambert, *Natalie Wood,* 170.

"To make it acceptable": "Conversation with Robert Wise," Institute of International Studies, UC Berkeley, 1998.

"a group of kids who are running": Simeone, *Leonard Bernstein,* 71.

CHAPTER 9

"They said no": *Dramatists Guild Landmark Symposium: West Side Story* (Autumn 1985).

CHAPTER 10

"No matter what": Lunden and Simon, NPR, September 26, 2007.

"have to deal with": Lunden and Simon, NPR, September 26, 2007.

"This particular play": Lunden and Simon, NPR, September 26, 2007.

CHAPTER 11

"gone on to become": Lawrence, *Dance with Demons,* 260.

"Kids in gangs": Laurents, *Mainly on Directing,* 157.

CHAPTER 12

"It wasn't just the line": *Dramatists Guild Landmark Symposium: West Side Story* (Autumn 1985).

"the ironies and contradictions": James Standifer, "The Complicated Life of Porgy and Bess," *Humanities* 18, no. 6 (November/December 1997).

"hearing about the harassment": Judith Ortiz Cofer. "The Myth of the Latin Woman: I Just Met a Girl Named Maria," in *The Latin Deli: Prose and Poetry,* 150.

"with many conflicting emotions": Siddiq Mohamed, "West Side Story," imagazine, Baruch College/State University of New York, February 2, 2010, http://blsciblogs.baruch.cuny.edu.

CHAPTER 13

"as a theater director": Sylviane Gold, "Movers & Shapers," *Dance Magazine* (May 2009).

"Robbins told me to never": Gold, "Movers & Shapers."

"I told him he was safe": Agnes deMille, *And Promenade Home,* 178.

"seldom had artistic control": Anna Kisselgoff, "Recalling an Innovator of Film Choreography," *New York Times,* February 7, 1994.

"human behavior": Patricia Elliot Tobias, "Michael Kidd, Choreographer, Is Dead," *New York Times,* December 24, 2007 "what Michael Bennett perceived": Kevin Kelly, *One Singular Sensation: The Michael Bennett Story*, 38.

George Chakiris as Bernardo faces off against Russ Tamblyn's Riff in the movie "Rumble". Courtesy of Photofest.

BIBLIOGRAPHY

BOOKS

Bernstein, Burton, and Barbara Haws. Leonard Bernstein: *An American Original*. New York: Harper, 2008.

Bernstein, Leonard. *Findings*. New York: Anchor, 1993.

Block, Geoffrey. *Enchanted Evenings: The Broadway Musical from "Show Boat" to Sondheim and Lloyd Webber*. 2nd ed. Oxford: Oxford University Press, 2009.

Burton, Humphrey. *Leonard Bernstein*. New York: Anchor, 1995.

Citron, Stephen. *Stephen Sondheim and Andrew Lloyd Webber: The New Musical*. The Great Songwriters series. Oxford: Oxford University Press, 2001.

Cofer, Judith Ortiz. *The Latin Deli: Telling the Lives of Barrio Women*. New York: Norton, 1995.

Conrad, Christine. *Jerome Robbins: That Broadway Man*. London: Booth-Clibborn, 2000.

Cott, Jonathan. *Back to a Shadow in the Night: Music, Writings, and Interviews, 1968–2001*. New York: Hal Leonard, 2003.

Dash, Irene G. *Shakespeare and the American Musical*. Bloomington: Indiana University Press, 2010.

De Mille, Agnes. *And Promenade Home*. New York: Little, Brown, 1953.

Denby, Edwin. *Dance Writings*. New York: Knopf, 1986.

Burton, William Westbrook. *Conversations about Bernstein*. Bridgewater, N.J.: Replica, 2001.

Doherty, Thomas. *Teenagers and Teenpics: The Juvenilization of American Movies in the 1950s*. Philadelphia: Temple University Press. 2002

Flinn, Denny Martin. *The Great American Book Musical: A Manifesto, a Monograph, a Manual*. New York: Limelight, 2008.

Garebian, Keith. *The Making of "West Side Story"*, Oakville, Ontario, Canada: Mosaic Press, 2001

Goldstein, Jeffrey. *Why We Watch: The Attractions of Violent Entertainment*. Oxford: Oxford University Press, 1998.

Gottfried, Martin. *Stephen Sondheim.* New York: Henry N. Abrams, 2001.

Hine, Thomas. *The Rise and Fall of the American Teenager.* New York: Harper Perennial, 2000.

Jones, John Bush. *Our Musicals, Ourselves: A Social History of the American Musical.* Waltham, Mass.: Brandeis University Press, 2003.

Jowitt, Deborah. *Jerome Robbins: His Life, His Theater, His Dance.* New York: Simon and Schuster, 2004.

Kantor, Michael, and Laurence Maslon. *Broadway: The American Musical.* New York: Bulfinch Hachette. 2004.

Kael, Pauline. *I Lost It at the Movies: Film Writings, 1954–1965.* London: Marian Boyars, 1994.

Kelly, Kevin. *One Singular Sensation: The Michael Bennett Story.* New York: Doubleday, 1990.

Lambert, Gavin. *Natalie Wood.* New York: Back Stage Books, 2005.

Laurents, Arthur. *On Direction: "Gypsy", "West Side Story", and Other Musicals.* New York: Knopf, 2009.

Laurents, Arthur. *Original Story By.* New York: Knopf, 2000.

Lawrence, Carol, and Phyllis Hobe. *The Backstage Story.* New York: McGraw-Hill, 1990.

Lawrence, Greg. *Dance with Demons: The Life of Jerome Robbins.* New York: Berkley Trade/Penguin, 2002.

Lewis, Robert. *Slings & Arrows: Theatre in My Life.* New York: Applause, 2000.

Long, Robert Emmett. *Broadway, the Golden Years: Jerome Robbins and the Great Choreographer-Directors, 1940 to the Present.* London: Continuum Press, 2001.

Miller, Scott. *From "Assassins" to "West Side Story": The Director's Guide to Musical Theatre.* Portsmouth, N.H.: Heinemann Drama, 1996.

Mirisch, Walter. *I Thought We Were Making Movies, Not History.* Madison: University of Wisconsin Press, 2008.

Morrden, Ethan. *Coming Up Roses: The Broadway Musical in the 1950s.* New York: Oxford University Press, USA, 2000.

Monush, Barry. *"West Side Story": Music on Film.* New York: Limelight, 2010.

Nixon, Marni, with Stephen Cole. *I Could Have Sung All Night: My Story.* New York: Billboard Books, 2007.

Prince, Harold. *Contradictions: Notes on Twenty-six Years in the Theatre.* New York: Dodd-Mead, 1974.

Rosenthal, Jean, and Lael Wertenbaker. *Magic of Light: The Craft and Career of Jean Rosenthal, Pioneer in Lighting for the Modern Stage.* New York: Little, Brown, 1992.

Sandoval-Sanchez, Alberto. *José, Can You See: Latinos on and off Broadway.* Madison: University of Wisconsin Press, 1999.

Secrest, Meryle. *Stephen Sondheim: A Life.* New York: Delta, 1999.

Seldes, Barry. *Leonard Bernstein: The Political Life of an American Musician.* Berkeley.: University of California Press, 2009.

Shakespeare, William, and Arthur Laurents. Romeo and Juliet *and* West Side Story. New York: Laurel Leaf Books, 1965.

Sharaff, Irene. *Broadway and Hollywood: Costumes Designed by Irene Sharaff.* New York: Van Nostrand Reinhold, 1976.

Simeone, Nigel. *Leonard Bernstein: "West Side Story".* Landmarks in Music since 1950 series. Surrey, England: Ashgate, 2009.

Sondheim, Stephen. *Finishing the Hat: Collected Lyrics (1954–1981) with Attendant Comments, Principles, Heresies, Grudges, Whines, and Anecdotes.* New York: Knopf, 2010.

Thelen, Lawrence. *The Show Makers: Great Directors of the American Musical Theatre.* Oxford, England: Routledge, 2002.

Thompson, Roger Faris. *Flash of the Spirit: African & Afro-American Art & Philosophy.* New York: Vintage, 1984.

Tynan, Kenneth. *Curtains: Selections from the Drama Criticism and Related Writings.* New York: Atheneum, 1961.

Vaill, Amanda. *Somewhere: The Life of Jerome Robbins.* New York: Broadway, 2008.

Williams, Mary E., ed. *Readings on "West Side Story".* San Diego, Calif.: Greenhaven Press, 2001.

Zadan, Craig. *Sondheim & Company.* Cambridge, Mass.: Da Capo Press, 1994.

PERIODICALS AND WEBSITES (OFTEN CONSULTED / QUOTED)

Dance Magazine.
Dramatists Quarterly
The New York Times.
The Sondheim Review
The Telegraph (London)

www.jeromerobbins.org
www.leonardbernstein.com
www.loc.gov (Library of Congress)
www.npr.org
www.sondheimguide.com
www.westsidestory.com
www.wssonstage.com

INDEX